THE GOOD HEART

The Good Heart

A Buddhist Perspective
on the Teachings of Jesus

HIS HOLINESS THE
Dalai Lama

Introduction and Christian Context by
Laurence Freeman, OSB

Translated from the Tibetan and Annotated by
Geshe Thupten Jinpa

Edited and with a Preface by
Robert Kiely

Wisdom

Wisdom Publications
199 Elm Street
Somerville, Massachusetts 02144 USA
wisdomexperience.org

First Edition 1996 • Paperback Edition 1998

Library of Congress Cataloging-in-Publication Data
Names: Bstan-'dzin-rgya-mtsho, Dalai Lama XIV, 1935– | Kiely, Robert.
Title: The good heart : a Buddhist perspective on the teachings of Jesus /
    His Holiness the Dalai Lama ; introduction and Christian context by
    Laurence Freeman, OSB ; translated from the Tibetan and annotated by Geshe
    Thupten Jinpa ; edited and with a preface by Robert Kiely.
Description: 3 [edition]. | Somerville : Wisdom Publications, 2016. |
    Includes bibliographical references and index.
Identifiers: LCCN 2015029150 | ISBN 1614293252 (pbk. : alk. paper)
Subjects: LCSH: Jesus Christ—Buddhist interpretations. | Jesus
    Christ—Teachings. | Christianity and other religions—Buddhism. |
    Buddhism—Relations—Christianity.
Classification: LCC BT304.914 .B78 2016 | DDC 232.9—dc23
LC record available at http://lccn.loc.gov/2015029150

ISBN 978-1-61429-325-5   ebook ISBN 978-0-86171-952-5

25 24 23 22
5 4 3 2

Cover design by Philip Pascuzzo. Cover photo by Jeremy Russell.
Interior design by Gopa & Ted2, Inc. Set in Diacritical Garamond Premier Pro 11/14 pt.

Printed in the United States of America.

Please visit fscus.org.

Contents

A Note to the Reader

THIS BOOK EXPLORES the Gospels with the Dalai Lama and the participants of the 1994 John Main Seminar. In addition to capturing the proceedings of the Seminar, this book has been augmented with additional contextual material on the Christian and Buddhist traditions to enhance its use as a tool for future interreligious dialogues.

The main body of *The Good Heart* is organized around individual passages from the Gospel upon which the Dalai Lama is commenting. Each chapter begins with His Holiness's reading of and comments on a particular Gospel passage. The Gospel passages used in *The Good Heart* are based on the New English Bible (University of Oxford Press, 1970), which was John Main's preferred version.

Robert Kiely's preface evokes the mood and atmosphere of the Seminar itself. Laurence Freeman's introduction provides an overview of interreligious dialogue in general, and Christian-Buddhist dialogue in particular.

Occasionally in the body of the text, a narrator's voice briefly appears to set the scene. This is Robert Kiely, highlighting some of the experiences of the Seminar as they occurred. These narrative interludes are set apart in italic type in order to help the reader distinguish them from the actual dialogue. The end of some chapters include the Seminar discussion periods, during which panelists shared insights and queries with the Dalai Lama. In these sections, the speakers are identified.

In the back portion of *The Good Heart*, there is additional information to assist and broaden the understanding of the two spiritual traditions. Father Laurence Freeman has written the section entitled "The Christian Context," in which he offers a Christian interpretation of the Gospel passages commented upon by the Dalai Lama. He also provides a glossary of Christian terms mentioned in the dialogue.

Geshe Thupten Jinpa, the Dalai Lama's interpreter, has written the section entitled "The Buddhist Context" in order to provide a general understanding of central Buddhist concepts to readers unfamiliar with Buddhism. Thupten Jinpa also compiled a glossary of Buddhist terms.

Throughout *The Good Heart*, but especially in the back section, both Tibetan and Sanskrit terms from Buddhism are used. For the most part, Sanskrit terms have been rendered in their appropriate scholarly form, with the exception of individuals' names, which have been written with ease of pronunciation in mind. Tibetan terms have been spelled in phonetics also for ease of pronunciation. Appropriate scholarly spellings of all names and terms can be found in the Buddhist glossary.

For those unfamiliar with the way that Sanskrit words are rendered into English, the chart below offers an easy way to approximate the pronunciation of the Sanskrit terms in this book. For more precise instructions, please see Michael Coulson's *Teach Yourself Sanskrit*. In all cases, remember that straightforward explanations for many terms are provided in the glossary.

APPROXIMATE ENGLISH EQUIVALENTS OF SANSKRIT SOUNDS

Sanskrit	English	Sanskrit	English
a	'b*u*t'	*ā*	'f*a*ther'
i	'f*i*t'	*ı̄*	's*ee*'
u	'wh*o*'	*ū*	'b*oo*'
ṛ and *r̄*	'c*r*ust'	*ḷ* and *l̄*	's*l*ip'
ṃ	'*m*om'	*ṅ*	'ri*ng*'
c and *ch*	'*ch*ain'	*ñ*	'Bu*ny*an'
ṭ, ṭh, t, and *th*	't*o*p'	*ḍ*	'*d*o'
ṇ	'*n*o'	*ś* and *ṣ*	'*sh*e'

And last, we have also included brief biographies of the participants: the Dalai Lama, Father Laurence, Geshe Thupten Jinpa, Robert Kiely, and the individual panelists who participated in this momentous interreligious dialogue.

PREFACE

O NE OF THE reassuring things about Tenzin Gyatso, His Holiness the Fourteenth Dalai Lama, is that, except when he is meditating, he does not seem capable of sitting still. As he spoke before an audience of three hundred and fifty Christians and a sprinkling of Buddhists in the auditorium of Middlesex University, London, in mid-September of 1994, his face and body were a testament to the Buddhist doctrine of perpetual flux. He not only punctuated his remarks with strong-handed gestures, coy smiles, dancing eyebrows, and guffaws, he seemed constantly to be folding or flinging about the loose ends of his maroon habit, seizing the limbs of panelists sitting on stage with him, waving to friends in the audience, and flipping through the program while his translator dispatched a lengthy remark.

The occasion—it would not be an exaggeration to say, the historic occasion—of the Dalai Lama's appearance in London in the autumn of 1994 was the John Main Seminar. This yearly Seminar is sponsored by the World Community for Christian Meditation[1] in memory of John Main, the Irish Benedictine monk who taught meditation in the tradition of John Cassian and the Desert Fathers and founded centers of Christian meditation throughout the world. Each year hundreds of Christian meditators, from virtually every continent and many denominations, gather to hear a series of talks on ethics, spirituality, scripture, interfaith dialogue, and prayer. In the recent past, speakers have included Charles Taylor, a Canadian philosopher; Bede Griffiths, an English Benedictine author and founder of an ashram in India; and Jean Vanier, the originator of L'Arche, Christian lay communities that are dedicated to living with the disabled.[2]

The invitation to the Dalai Lama to comment for the first time publicly on the Gospels came from Dom Laurence Freeman, OSB, an Oxford graduate in literature and a monk of the Olivetan Benedictine priory in Cockfosters, London. Laurence Freeman has been the most active and influential teacher in the Community since Main's death in 1982.

The Dalai Lama was given in advance eight passages from the Christian

Scriptures—including the Sermon on the Mount and the Beatitudes (Matthew 5), the parable of the mustard seed and the Kingdom of God (Mark 4), the Transfiguration (Luke 9), and the Resurrection (John 20). He was invited to comment on these texts in any way he saw fit. And he was told that his audience was Christian (Roman Catholic, Anglican, and Protestant),[3] mostly English-speaking though from all continents, and that virtually all of them practiced silent meditation daily in their own lives.

Because the Dalai Lama was a head of state as well as a religious leader, many present, while looking forward to his remarks, wondered whether His Holiness would be able to break through the inevitable barriers of press, cameras, and attendants, and truly communicate what was on his mind and in his heart.

The answer came swiftly and with breathtaking ease. Early each morning before breakfast, before anything else on the packed schedule of the conference, he entered the darkened hall with his monks and, with the assembled Christians, he sat perfectly still and meditated for half an hour. In the silence, broken only by a rustle or a cough, anxiety fell away, and a bond of trust and openness for what was to come took its place. Then, at last, he bowed his shaved head over the text and, tracing the script with his finger like a rabbi, read, "How blest are those of a gentle spirit . . . . How blest are those whose hearts are pure . . . . How blest are those who have suffered persecution for the cause of right." And as he read, it was impossible not to be moved, almost stunned, by the power of these familiar words re-cadenced and re-keyed by a Tibetan voice and a Buddhist sensibility.

Conscious of the devastation of the Tibetan culture and people by China and of the Dalai Lama's own suffering as a refugee and exile, the audience could not help hearing a poignant resonance in the reading. But striking as the political moment was, something else carried the significance of the three-day meeting deeper even than history. There was little doubt in the minds of those present that they had come to hear a spiritual teacher and that what they were experiencing was a profoundly religious event that encompassed history but was not circumscribed by it.

The actual framework of the Seminar was flexible and simple enough to provide an informal atmosphere to the proceedings. It began with meditation, then proceeded to a reading of the Scripture passages in English by His Holiness, commentary, panel discussions, closing chants and prayers, breaks for meals, and back again for meditation and more of the same. But such a description does not really convey an accurate or full sense of the mood or atmosphere at these proceedings. During the readings and commentaries, the Dalai Lama was seated behind a low table, with a person seated on either side of him. On the left sat Laurence Freeman in his Olivetan Benedictine white habit taking notes, nodding agreement, smiling, and looking quizzical—in short, unconsciously acting as a mirror of the audience at large. On the right sat Geshe Thupten Jinpa, the young, slightly built Tibetan Buddhist monk in crimson robes who was acting as interpreter. Serene, collected, focused, and incredibly proficient, he translated His Holiness's Tibetan almost simultaneously into fluent English. His own modesty and grace, attentive to the master but never servile, was a constant reminder and example to the audience of near-perfect concentration and selfless dignity.

Because of this arrangement, and perhaps also because of the Dalai Lama's way of being and expressing himself, an apparent monologue was really a dialogue and, more often, a three-way conversation. Neither Dom Laurence nor Jinpa interrupted the discourse, but they were incorporated into it spontaneously as His Holiness excitedly moved in one direction or another, seeking a reaction, correcting a phrase, raising a questioning eyebrow, and releasing tension with a laugh. During the panel discussions, when two members of the audience were invited to sit on the platform and raise questions, the neat format tended to melt down into interconnecting streams of thought, language, accent, age, gender, temperament, and religious persuasion. Yet there was never confusion. The Dalai Lama, as a Buddhist teacher and exile, is at home with change, and he has the ability to calm Western nerves afloat in unfamiliar and shifting currents. Like all great teachers, he also has a talent for seizing and salvaging a good idea that is drifting unobserved beneath the surface.

It has been said that the Dalai Lama is a simple man. Though this may be meant as a compliment, it is difficult to dissociate such a label from a Western tendency to condescend to the religions and cultures of the East, treating them as exotic but philosophically primitive traditions. Insofar as he is earthy, direct, warm, and *simpatico,* the Dalai Lama may be called "simple"; but in every other sense, he is a subtle, quick, complex, and extraordinarily intelligent and learned man. He brings three qualities to a spiritual discourse—traits so rare in some contemporary Christian circles as to have elicited gasps of relieved gratitude from the audience. These qualities are gentleness, clarity, and laughter. If there is something Benedictine about him, there is a Franciscan side as well, and a touch of the Jesuit.[4]

From the outset, he gently and quietly reassured his listeners that the last thing he had come to do was "sow seeds of doubt" among Christians about their own faith. Again and again, he counseled people to deepen their understanding and appreciation of their own traditions, pointing out that human sensibilities and cultures are too varied to justify a single "way" to the Truth. He gently, but firmly and repeatedly, resisted suggestions that Buddhism and Christianity are different languages for the same essential beliefs. With regard to ethics and the emphasis on compassion, brother-hood, and forgiveness, he acknowledged similarities. But inasmuch as Bud-dhism does not recognize a Creator God or a personal Savior, he cautioned against people calling themselves "Buddhist-Christians," just as one should not try "to put a yak's head on a sheep's body."

In the course of long sessions, reading and commenting on theologically complex texts and responding to challenging questions from panelists, the Dalai Lama never lost his astonishing mental clarity. At one point, he described Mahayana Buddhist meditative practices as disciplines to keep our consciousness alert and focused rather than "scattered" or "sunken" in torpor. One of the forms of respect he paid to his audience was to give it his attention. It is rare for a public figure, even a religious one, not to have "prepackaged" remarks at hand. There are, most likely, occasions when the Dalai Lama is no exception. But it became evident that his moment-by-moment engagement with the Gospels and the people in his presence had a constancy and intensity of mind and heart of which few people are capable. When asked what adherents of different faiths *could* do together without mixing up yaks and sheep, he recommended scholarship, meditation, and pilgrimages. And then he told of going to Lourdes and finding there such an aura of the sacred that he bowed down and prayed to "all holy beings" for the sustenance of its healing powers. At moments like this, one could hear the audience catch a collective breath, perhaps of pleasure and surprise at an expression of reverence at once so pure and yet so uncompromising of the Buddhist tradition from which it came.

In his reflections on the Transfiguration, he offered a learned discourse on Buddhist views of miracles and supernatural emanations. Without a hint of dogmatism or sentimental piety, he evoked an ancient tradition that has long accommodated a highly rational system of self-discipline and psychology with accounts of experiences beyond the usual limits of reason and nature. He modestly disclaimed having had such experiences himself, but did not see that as a cause to doubt their authenticity. Somehow, listening to him made all the centuries of Christian quarreling over miracles and the possible explanations for them seem foolish.

His reading of the meeting between Mary Magdalene and Jesus in Saint John's account of the Resurrection brought many to tears. It would be hard to say exactly why. Some said later that it was as if they were hearing the words for the first time, as though their tenderness and mystery and beauty had been taken for granted and were brought to life again, like a gift from an unexpected courier.

When faced with a philosophical or religious paradox or the inexpressible, Westerners tend to grow solemn. Buddhists undoubtedly have a rich array of reactions, and one that enlivened the spirit of the conference was laughter. The Dalai Lama likes to crack jokes about monks, yaks, reincarnation, and visions, but often a gesture, expression, or pause in the flow of discussion—a moment of potential awkwardness—sets him off into infectious gales of laughter. Toward the end of the Seminar, when nearly everyone was beginning to feel the fatigue of so much concentrated emotion, his superb interpreter, Jinpa, the young monk who had maintained superhuman composure day after day, burst into uncontrollable body-shaking laughter while trying to translate an anecdote told by His Holiness. In answer to the observation that some people say they do not meditate because they are too busy, His Holiness told the story of a monk who keeps promising his pupil that he will take him on a picnic but is always too busy to do so. One day they see a procession carrying a corpse. "Where is he going?" the monk asks his pupil. The punch line, delayed for at least five minutes until the translator, the audience, and the Fourteenth Dalai Lama could control themselves, was, "On a picnic."

For many Christians, attending ecumenical conferences, like going to church, is "no picnic." But, of course, feasting and celebration are as much a part of the symbolism and reality of Christianity as they are of all religions. Hearing the Dalai Lama comment on the Gospels was definitely a feast. What impressed and surprised everyone was how much the "outsider" touched them. The exile, the person with no authority over Christians except that which was given by the Spirit, was able to show people of every faith the riches of their own banquet.

Robert Kiely
Cambridge, Massachusetts

INTRODUCTION

I N SEPTEMBER OF 1994, in London, His Holiness the Dalai Lama led the John Main Seminar, an annual international spiritual event held in honor of the Benedictine monk John Main, whom Father Bede Griffiths once called the most important spiritual guide in the church today.

The Dalai Lama and Dom John Main met on only two occasions. The first took place in 1980 at the Catholic cathedral in Montreal, Quebec, where Dom John had been asked to welcome the Dalai Lama as a fellow monk at the opening of a large interfaith evening. During the preparations for the evening, I remember how strongly Father John argued for the inclusion of a substantial period of silent meditation. Religious leaders were present, from archbishops to Native American medicine men, making speeches of goodwill and reciting beautiful prayers. There were choirs, chants, and in the cathedral itself all the visual beauties of Christian art and culture. The organizers were frightened at the suggestion of a twenty-minute period of silence in the middle of such a large and public ceremony. Father John insisted, and Father John got his way.

After the ceremony, the Dalai Lama sought out the Benedictine monk who had welcomed him and remarked how impressed he was with the unusual experience of meditation in a Christian church. Standing beside them, I could sense the affinity between the two men. While they may have been speaking rather superficial words, I felt they were also exploring a deeper, silent level of dialogue. Father John then invited the Dalai Lama to visit our small, recently started Benedictine community that was dedicated to the practice and teaching of meditation in the Christian tradition. We resided in a small suburban house at that time, and an extended lay community lived in apartments around us. It was a new kind of Christian urban monasticism that derived its life and vision from the rediscovery of meditation in the Christian spiritual tradition.

I remember wondering what the Dalai Lama would make of it, coming as he might with images of medieval European monasteries in his mind.

When his hovering secretary intervened, after hearing Father John's invitation, to say that regrettably His Holiness's schedule was too full and there was no free time for him to accept, I was not surprised. But then the Dalai Lama turned to his secretary and said, in a tone that lost none of its gentleness but had gained new force, that he *would* accept and they would have to make time. The Dalai Lama insisted, and the Dalai Lama got his way. He and Father John exchanged a look, smiled, and separated.

The following Sunday, a few hours after we had been swept through by the Royal Canadian Mounted Police, the Dalai Lama's cortege of limousines pulled up outside the Benedictine community's house. His Holiness joined us for the midday meditation in our small meditation room and then for lunch with the Community. We ate as usual in silence. After lunch there was conversation, and then Father John and the Dalai Lama withdrew for a private conversation. At the end of the visit we presented him with a copy of the *Rule of Saint Benedict*, and he gave Father John the traditional Tibetan white silk cloth of respect.[5] The Dalai Lama drove away. Father John went back to his work of founding the Christian Meditation Community, and they never met again after that fall afternoon in 1980.

A great deal happened between this meeting and our invitation to His Holiness in 1993 to lead the John Main Seminar. Father John had died in 1982 at the age of fifty-six. The Meditation Community was barely founded at his death, but his teaching on Christian meditation had begun to percolate throughout the Church. It continued to expand in the following years and to nourish the deepening of the spiritual life of many Christians. Twenty-five centers had formed, and over a thousand small weekly meditation groups that sustained people's individual practice had spread through more than a hundred countries. The International Center of the World Community for Christian Meditation, which had been founded during the 1991 Seminar in New Harmony, Indiana, led by the Benedictine monk and pioneer in interfaith dialogue, Bede Griffiths, had been opened in London. Previous Seminars had been led by the Sanskrit scholar Isabelle Glover; the philosopher Charles Taylor; the literary critic Robert Kiely; the psychologist and Sister of Saint Joseph, Eileen O'Hea; the scholar John Todd; the founder of L'Arche, Jean Vanier; and the Jesuit scholar and theologian William Johnston.[6]

To my surprise and delight I received a quick personal response from the Dalai Lama. He remembered his meeting with John Main thirteen years before, was pleased by the growth of his community worldwide, and would be happy and honored to lead the latest Seminar. The brief meeting of the two monks long before had brought us to a wonderful opportunity. The question was, how were we going to grasp it?

We had invited His Holiness to lead the Seminar, the first non-Christian to do so, for a number of reasons. His meeting with Dom John Main, although brief, had been highly significant. It had illuminated the importance of developing the necessary dialogue between the two religions at the deeper level that is made possible and widely accessible through meditation. Something is touched in sharing deep silence together that words can point to but never quite express. His Holiness, as an individual, has also become one of the most loved and accessible spiritual teachers in the world today. Tibet's agony, which he carries constantly with him, has elevated him to a global spiritual role in which the universal religious values of peace, justice, tolerance, and nonviolence find a joyful and yet profoundly serious embodiment. This was evident the moment His Holiness read aloud the Beatitudes at the first session of the Seminar. Everyone felt they were more than words in his case; they were insights he had personally experienced.

In searching for a way to grasp this opportunity, the answer seemed clear: by letting it go. It seemed to me that this was an unprecedented opportunity. A Seminar in which the Dalai Lama would spend three days with a group of spiritually committed Christian meditators and their equally committed non-Christian friends was too unique to use as just another interfaith discussion group. I had already informed His Holiness that our Seminars included times of meditation as well as times of vocal dialogue. We would have three periods of meditation together each day, and these periods would not be squeezed in; they would be central to the whole event. Naturally, he had no problem with that. The problem now was not that we would be silent but determining a topic of discussion.

We considered the usual kind of philosophical and religious themes for such a Buddhist-Christian event and felt they did not do justice to the uniqueness of the opportunity. Then we decided to really let it go. We would make a gift to His Holiness of that which is most precious, holy, and profound for us as Christians: we would ask him to comment on the Christian Gospels. He accepted without hesitation, remarking only that, of course, he knew little about the Gospels. His comment struck me as a most impressive sign of his self-confidence, and of his humility.

Two or three years earlier he had stunned his audiences in London by his learned and scholarly presentations of Buddhist philosophy. Any academic would have been proud of this achievement. Now he was willing to come before a Christian audience, albeit a sympathetic and contemplative one, and talk about what, *he* said smilingly, he knew very little about. Once he had accepted this idea, the Seminar became an event of great anticipation. It was a gamble, a risk of faith on both sides. We had no doubt that the time of meditation and presence together would be worthwhile in its own right. Anyone who has spent any time with the Dalai Lama knows that his presence bestows peace, depth, and joy. But, even with the Dalai Lama, there was no guarantee that the Seminar would succeed as a dialogue.

Instead, the 1994 John Main Seminar, *The Good Heart,* succeeded in a way no one could have anticipated. And I would like to reflect now on the success of this historic event. The Dalai Lama's commentary on the Christian Gospels constitutes the heart of this book, and the implications of these words reach far forward into the continuing dialogue in the coming millennium between the religious traditions of the human family. This book suggests the importance of this dialogue for the future of the world and offers a much-needed strategy to meet the challenge of creating world peace and universal cooperation in the decades ahead: it offers a *model of dialogue.*

Presence

In a way, the John Main Seminar originated many years before in the special way that the Dalai Lama and Dom John Main were present to each other during their meetings. The Dalai Lama has also spoken about this factor of presence in the description of his meetings with Thomas Merton.[7] It was this same chemistry of presence that ensured the meaningful dialogue at the 1994 John Main Seminar. (Afterward the Dalai Lama remarked that he had learned more about Christianity during the Seminar than at any other time since his conversations with Merton thirty years before.)

Presence is one of the most important lessons *The Good Heart* has to teach us—Buddhists, Christians, and the followers of all faiths—if we are to learn a better way to respond to the contemporary challenge to dialogue. As this presence in dialogue is nonverbal and nonconceptual, it might sound vague or platitudinous; but it is nonetheless a hard fact. It is difficult to describe, but it is the first thing we experience in dialogue. *How* are we perceived by each other? The success of the verbal dialogue depends upon and builds directly upon this foundation of mutual presence. Words cannot achieve a successful dialogue if presence is not there. And without this insight, words can go wildly wrong.

In his opening remarks, the Dalai Lama spoke about the importance of all the different forms of dialogue being practiced today between religions. He affirmed the importance of scholarly dialogue. But he also said that he felt the most important and—to use a characteristic term for a Buddhist— the most effective dialogue was not intellectual exchange, but a conversation between sincere practitioners from the position of their own faiths, a conversation that arises from a sharing of their respective practices.

This idea is common to Christian and Buddhist thinkers. In the early Christian monastic tradition, the Fathers spoke warmly about the importance of *praktike*, the knowledge born from experience rather than conceptual knowledge. Cardinal Newman[8] spoke of the danger of living your faith simply from a position of "notional assent," lacking experiential, personal verification. John Main's insistence that it was necessary for Christians to recover the contemplative dimension of their faith was based on the assertion that we must "verify the truths of our faith in our own experience." What is new about this idea in the context of *The Good Heart* is that the concept is applied to dialogue between different faiths, and not just to the deepening of the discovery of one's own traditional religious beliefs.

This is very challenging and, to many sincere practitioners, also disturbing. It suggests that there exists a universal, underlying level of common truth that can be accessed through different faiths. When people of different faiths are in experiential dialogue with one another, the truth can be experienced through their willing suspension of exclusivity toward one another. If this is true, then does it follow that each particular faith is no more (no less?) than a particular door into the great audience chamber of Truth? As we will see shortly, the Dalai Lama addresses this challenge very subtly and directly.

It is important here simply to note the relevance of presence for this kind of new and indeed pioneering dialogue. This presence is human, ordinary, affectionate, friendly, and trusting. All four hundred people felt this the instant His Holiness walked into the hall at the opening of the Seminar. This quality of presence should not be underestimated when we think about modern interreligious and intercultural dialogue. It should certainly not be dismissed as an emotional element subordinate to the realm of pure ideas. If, as the Dalai Lama believes, the proof and authentication of all religion is the realization of a good heart, a human being's innate qualities of compassion and tolerance, the same standard can be applied to dialogue, which has today become an important work and activity of all religions.

In the past, religious action could be viewed more narrowly in terms of the celebration or exploration of one's own beliefs or rituals. Today an additional element has entered human religious activity, as we enter with empathy and reverence into the beliefs and rituals of other faiths without adopting them as our own. The fruit and authentication of this new activity, largely unknown to earlier generations of humanity or even regarded by them as disloyal and blasphemous, is the same as that of all religions: compassion and tolerance. Dialogue should not only make us feel better about others but also make us more conscious of ourselves and more true to our own essential goodness. Dialogue makes us better people.

We cannot achieve this in the abstract. Dialogue demands not just clarity of ideas and a certain degree of knowledge about one's position and the position of other people; it demands a personal involvement. The objectivity, detachment, and intellectual organization needed for dialogue are not ends in themselves—any more than efficiency or the profit motive should be ends in themselves for any business or social group. The intellectual discipline required for dialogue allows the natural tendency toward egotism to be filtered or contained. This releases the individuals involved in dialogue to find the deeper levels of their own consciousness where dialogue opens onto a common window of truth through an experience altogether beyond the conceptualizing mind.

Friendship

The Dalai Lama's openness to presence was crucial for the success of the Seminar. His self-confidence and ease, despite the risk he was taking, set others at their ease and gave us all confidence that we had nothing to lose except our fears. It became, too, the basis of a friendship that was also the bedrock of fruitful dialogue. Dialogue will certainly reduce our fears and suspicions of one another. It will make us better friends, even with people we regard as enemies or threats. Yet friendship, or at least the readiness to be real friends, is also a precondition for good dialogue. To be friends is to trust and to be vulnerable. It involves running the risk of sharing something precious and then, perhaps, of being disappointed that this precious gift is not being valued or has been treated badly. As the days of the Seminar passed, the intensity of human friendship among all the participants grew. It radiated, so people remarked, from the Dalai Lama and his Christian interlocutors, who sensed that the risk they had taken in coming together was entirely justified—and was even becoming highly enjoyable in itself.

Friendship occupies a central place in Christian thought and tradition. The Christian ideal of friendship is built upon a long classical Western tradition that did not understand friendship, as we often do today, as a diluted form of intimacy. Cicero or Saint Augustine would not have understood modern journalists who say that a couple are "just friends" as if the only really interesting relationship is that which progresses "further" than friendship. For them and for many of their preceding and succeeding generations, friendship was the goal of all the formative experiences of human relationships. Education in the widest sense was a preparation for the achievement of friendship that allowed one to share the deepest and truest part of oneself with another.

Saint Aelred of Rievaulx, a thirteenth-century Yorkshire monk, wrote a treatise called *Spiritual Friendship*. This work focused on the Christian understanding of this classical ideal of friendship and was based on Cicero's great work *On Friendship*. Aelred speaks of the disciplined preparation and mutual testing that precedes the full flowering of friendship, when the ineffable sweetness of trust and confidence, intimacy and openness, between the friends flows out through the friendship to the world around them. Significantly, he says that such friendship cannot be based on anything less than the essential goodness of each friend. There cannot be friendship based on exploitative desire or hatred of others because these negative qualities betray human nature. Partners in crime do not make good friends. Friendship is the perfection of human nature. "A truly loyal friend," says Saint Aelred, "sees nothing in his friend but his heart."[9] This leads Aelred to describe without embarrassment particular instances of personal friendship in his own life, as well as the joy he feels as he walks around his cloister knowing that there is none there whom he does not love and none whom he does not feel loved by. For Aelred, the perfection of human friendship is an epiphany of the real presence of Christ. Christ, he says, makes the *third* between us. In this Christian vision, all true friendship will "begin in Christ, continue in Christ and be perfected in Christ."[10] It is a beautiful and profound understanding of the humanity of the Risen Jesus.

Christ does not, in this view of human nature, represent an obstacle or intellectual barrier separating us from others. He is not some *thing* we speak about and dissect. He is the unobtrusive presence in which we become really present to one another. He can be named, or he can remain unnamed; in either case his reality is neither increased nor diminished. Theologically, too, the idea of friendship is also central to Christian faith. Speaking to his disciples at the Last Supper, Jesus declared himself to be their friend: "I call you servants no longer. A servant does not know what his master is about. I call you friends because I have made known to you everything I have learned from my Father."[11] The Holy Spirit, which flows into the realm of human consciousness from the glorified Body of Jesus, is also described in the images of friendship. She is an advocate, someone *on our side*, to remind us of that which we have forgotten, to repair the ravages of our mindlessness. Modern feminist theology has recognized the centrality of the symbol of friendship in Christian faith and rescued it to serve as a foundational metaphor of the human relationship to the divine.

What is so powerful about this ideal of friendship is the way it can reconcile the absolute and the personal. You can disagree about the choice of carpet color and remain friends. A Buddhist can be friends with a Christian without either trying to convert the other. In friendship differences can be respected and even enjoyed. In relationships lacking friendship, differences can zoom out of proportion and become ethnic, religious, or ideological divisions. We demonize the threatening *other*, project our shadow upon them, and find conflict. Friendship is the supreme expression of compassion and tolerance with a respect for the primacy of truth over all subjective tendencies. But friendship reminds us that the objectivity of truth does not reject the subjective. It integrates the particular and the universal, achieving the *coincidentia oppositorum*, the reconciliation of opposites. Nicholas of Cusa, a fifteenth-century cardinal, statesman, mathematician, and mystic, said that God is found "beyond the coincidence of contradictories."

There is a simple test to determine whether one's pursuit of truth has lost contact with this touchstone of friendship. When we hear on the news that a Catholic person has been shot in Belfast, or an Israeli soldier has died on the West Bank, or so many Chinese baby girls have disappeared from an orphanage, or so many Tibetans have been killed—are we hearing a news item about individual people, or about ethnic or religious groups? Do we perceive the murdered Israeli soldier or Palestinian demonstrator as a Jew or an Arab, or as a human being who happens also to be a Jew or an Arab? How do the figures strike us—as individual tragedies or as statistics that are being used as political weapons?

In the course of the Dalai Lama's comments at the John Main Seminar, as in all his spiritual teaching, His Holiness did not use the occasion to speak of the Chinese occupation of Tibet. However deeply he must carry the crucifixion of Tibet in his heart, his personal grief does not intrude on others. Nevertheless, all the participants of the Seminar gave their unreserved support to the Dalai Lama's cause for Tibet, and they did so all the more freely because he joined them in personal friendship. He does not turn friendship into political expediency. I suspect this is one of the qualities that makes him such a refreshing politician and exemplary spiritual leader. It is because he has such a powerful gift of friendship that the Dalai Lama is so beloved and respected around the world. This gift of friendship may also be the key to his great gift for dialogue and his respect for differences while seeking unity. In this perspective, the warmth of human friendship does not water down the concentration of pure Truth. Truth is not merely the right ideas well expressed. Truth without the human warmth of friendship is a pale shadow of reality.

Model of Dialogue

The success of dialogue is especially dependent upon the spirit of friendship as we converse with one another in so many particular dialects. Even within our mother tongue, we may find that dialects and accents seem strange at first but learn to understand and respect them. These widely spoken dialects of the common language of truth are today learning to communicate. The Good Heart Seminar was a model of dialogue as mutual listening.

Shortly after the Seminar, the dialogue taking place between Christianity and Buddhism suffered a setback. This arose from the controversy sparked by the general remarks on Buddhism of His Holiness Pope John Paul II in his best-selling book *Crossing the Threshold of Hope*. These remarks expressed a view of Buddhism that was vehemently contested by many Buddhist monks and teachers. Feelings ran high. Sri Lankan Buddhist leaders boycotted the Pope's visit to their country. Thich Nhat Hanh expressed his own feelings in his book *Living Buddha, Living Christ*.[12] Friendship seemed to stumble everywhere. The Vatican issued statements saying that the Pope did not mean to dismiss Buddhism as a life-denying philosophy.

It looked as if the Pope, representing a long tradition of Christianity, was caricaturing and dismissing Buddhism without attempting to understand it. Buddhists tried to be compassionate, but many could not avoid the opportunity to lump all (or most) Christians together and caricature *them* as intolerant, arrogant, and exclusivist. The feelings of some Western Buddhists toward their own Christian upbringing were plainly aroused as well. This is what happens to dialogue when friendship breaks down. Until goodwill, trust, and friendship have been restored there is little point in trying to discuss the meanings of the terms in question—such as nirvana, void, and enlightenment. Maybe *The Good Heart* can contribute a little to this restoration.

Caricature is always based on the exclusion of qualifying detail in favor of one easily identifiable feature. Religions do this to each other just as cartoonists do. For many Christians, Buddhism is caricatured as a religion that believes in rational moral behavior motivated not by love of a personal God or fear of punishment but by the desire to achieve a better rebirth in an apparently endless series of reincarnations. This is achieved, so the summary goes, by denying the world and one's own feelings. The immensely subtle and highly intricate philosophical arguments on these and all other elements of Buddhism are ignored by such a caricature. And this view certainly glosses over the central place of compassion in Buddhism.

Behind the caricatures, Buddhism is, philosophically, one of the greatest achievements of the human mind. Yet despite a general body of agreed principles, such as the Four Noble Truths, Buddhist philosophy, particularly Tibetan Buddhism, falls into many schools and complex dialogues between the schools; thus it represents one of the highest achievements of the diversity of human opinion. The Dalai Lama is one of the most accomplished of modern philosophers in many of these Buddhist schools. And, as his book *The World of Tibetan Buddhism* (Wisdom Publications, 1995) illustrates, he has the gift not only of understanding but of lucid exposition. On several occasions during the Seminar he stated that his comments represent a particular Buddhist view, but he also pointed out that there are other Buddhist perspectives to take into account—some of them quite complex and opposed to his own position. Among other ways in which *The Good Heart* will help dialogue, it draws attention—with simplicity—to the many different traditions within every religious tradition.

Christianity certainly has no fewer internal dialects of belief. Any religion that can contain a movement like Opus Dei and a minister like the Reverend Ian Paisley will never risk uniformity.[13] Even more, however, *The Good Heart* should remind Buddhists of something many Christians have now discovered—that "the Church" is a very general term. It can mean many things: a cold building on a wet Sunday morning; a global religion; a mystical tradition; a spiritual body extended backward and forward in history from the birth of Jesus; or the cultural group I was born into, brought up in, and now have mixed feelings about. Perhaps one cannot entirely separate institutional and spiritual Christianity, any more than one can separate form and content, or body and mind; but it is important to preserve the distinction. There are many examples in history of Christians who have remained outside the institutional church but who knew with the full force of their being that they belonged to the Church.

Who, therefore, really "speaks for" Christianity? Who "speaks for" Buddhism?

And given this diversity, how does *The Good Heart* suggest a model for the resumption and redirectioning of the Buddhist-Christian dialogue? And indeed, this model is applicable for dialogue in general: between Catholics and Protestants, Mahayanists and Theravadans, Republicans and Democrats, men and women, and people of every ethnicity and culture in the world.

Modest Ambitions

Above all, we must have modest ambitions as we set forth in this dialogue. In *The Good Heart*, the Dalai Lama does not try or pretend to give a complete or exhaustive commentary on the Gospels, Jesus' teaching and life, or the deeper truths of Christian faith such as the Resurrection and the Holy Spirit. The Dalai Lama's approach is exploratory rather than definitive, and he expands this method to his dialogue with the Christian panelists. It is in *seeking* truth that we find enlightenment, not in declaring it. Just as Saint Benedict says that the monk is one who "truly seeks God." And in the process of seeking, something is always found. "Seek and you will find; knock and the door will be opened."[14] Reading the Scriptures with a good heart takes us beyond the bleakness of today's deconstructionist pessimism about meaning. There *is* something to be found, but it is only found in the *seeking*. Saint Gregory of Nyssa put it this way: "To seek God is to find him; to find God is to seek him."

One of the earliest Christian thinkers, Saint Irenaeus,[15] said that God can never be known as an object, or as a reality outside ourselves. We can know God only through our participation in God's own self-knowledge. These early theologians were writing their thoughts about God and the mystery of Christ from the mystical experience of the inclusivity—or non-duality—of God.[16] The first theologians were, and today the best ones still are, expressing their experience of prayer, not just of thought. Dialogue in such a context and among such people becomes fluent, fluid, and dynamic. Truth is sensed as something that emerges as we enter a clearing where the obscuring clouds of ignorance, prejudice, and fear have, at least momentarily, been lifted. The Greek word for truth, *aletheia*, means precisely that, a "clearing." This is something that can only be done step by step, moment by moment. It means staying in touch with the delicate balance that friendship requires, above all the balance between speaking and listening. Great schemes to translate Buddhism into the Christian dialect and vice versa lack the modest ambitions with which the Good Heart Seminar began and ended. Dialogue has little to do with translation. But a good translator, such as we had in Geshe Thupten Jinpa, helps to remind the partners in dialogue that they are not trying to write a dictionary.

Another aspect of modesty in regard to the Dalai Lama's approach was his saying that he knew little about Christian Scriptures or theology, but that he was eager to learn. He hoped he would give no offense, and he certainly did not want to shake the faith of the Christians taking part in the Seminar. It is not easy to admit a lack of knowledge because it makes us seem vulnerable, less interesting or less powerful. If knowledge is power, ignorance is weakness. But when we do admit the limitations of our knowledge at the beginning of a dialogue, several things are set free. One of them is trust. People are not afraid of being manipulated or persuaded; they can begin to let down their defenses. An admission of inexperience must, therefore, be one of the first steps in nonviolence. Another quality liberated by this humility in dialogue is spontaneity. If you are free from the need to show how clever or learned you are—the temptation of scholars in dialogue—then you are free to respond immediately and freshly to what is before you. This is precisely what happened at *The Good Heart*. The Dalai Lama did not know much "about" the Gospels. But he did know a great deal through his Buddhist learning, his monastic training, and his own spiritual evolution. And this knowledge allowed him to respond to Christian symbols and ideas as if he actually knew them very well indeed.

As a result of this, the Christians at the Seminar were surprised to discover that a Buddhist was helping them understand and discover in new ways the stories and texts that had been familiar to them perhaps since childhood. The Dalai Lama has often made it clear that he does not advise anyone to change their religion—although he does respect an individual's right to make this choice. Better, he says, to rediscover the deeper meaning and power of your own religious tradition. It was surprising to find that a Buddhist could help Christians deepen their faith, and clarify it in the very process of contrasting it with Buddhist belief—even when there were clear conflicts or untranslatable ideas between the two. This was only possible because the dialogue was exploratory, not declamatory. The Dalai Lama was sincerely curious and stimulated by the intense dialogue. He listened deeply to the questions that were raised in the panel discussions. Above all, people saw that he was listening, that he was curious, that he was *sincerely* interested. Dialogue is more like a piece of experimental theater than a highly polished Broadway musical. Sometimes it works, other times it is less successful. It requires commitment. It demands maximum participation by all concerned. It is not mechanical. It is not dogmatic. The ideas must be bartered and wasted if they are to illuminate.

The Dalai Lama asked many questions. Before each session, I spent some time with him in a quiet room preparing the Gospel texts on which he would then comment for an hour or so. He listened to the background I gave on the texts and my explanation of some of the key terms and ideas. If, as he said, he was "unfamiliar" with the Gospels, his phenomenal receptivity and the alacrity of his mind in constellating new ideas more than made up for this lack of knowledge. I was reminded of a phrase Saint Gregory the Great uses in his *Life* to describe Saint Benedict. Benedict, he said, had dropped out of school in Rome and betaken himself to a hermitage in a state of *wise ignorance*.

The Dalai Lama's intellectual training and brilliance are unobtrusive. He does not flaunt them. But he employs them skillfully in the pursuit of truth.

Christians were particularly aware of these gifts as he uncovered meanings and subtleties in the often overfamiliar Scriptures. Through him, they enriched and renewed their faith in ways that filled them with wonder and gratitude. If knowledge is power, the Dalai Lama's knowledge trained onto the Gospels created a power of insight—an insight that he never used in any manipulative way. He was not arguing with Christians about the meaning of the Gospels. He was, with great detachment, giving them the benefit of his reading, discussing this view with them, and then leaving the use of it entirely up to them.

Like and Unlike

One of Saint Benedict's "tools of good works" (the Christian equivalent to a Buddhist's skillful means) is the injunction "never to give a false peace."[17] It is just as important to avoid the danger of false friendship in dialogue as it is to avoid the traps of caricature, misrepresentation, or dismissive judgment. Professional translators refer to certain words in two different languages that have a formal likeness but very different meanings as "false friends." The Good Heart Seminar stayed faithful to the principle of true friendship and respected the differences as much as the similarities between the participants' beliefs and attitudes.

It is very tempting in dialogue between two religious traditions to opt for a safe zone of generalities. By doing so, both sides avoid conflict and leave with a glowing feeling of mutual congratulation. This struck me strongly a few years ago when I took part in a dialogue with Buddhist and Christian meditators in Canada. We discussed how we had each come to the paths we were on and the ways we dealt with the difficulty of persevering on those paths. It was useful and in its way inspirational. But I felt that we were sharing too safely. We were not risking with each other what was most precious and particular to us personally.

So at the Good Heart Seminar, instead of proceeding with my scheduled afternoon talk, I asked permission to speak about Jesus. I could sense there were suspicions and fears that this would spoil the good atmosphere. I felt a twinge of the post-imperial guilt[18] that Christians today can hardly help but feel, especially when they are talking to people with whom they may share much common ground but who have "left the Church" in anger or disappointment at its human faults and failures. However, I did not think

I could express what meditation means for me as a Christian if I did not also speak about what Jesus means for me. Meditation is such an important part of the way I explore the mystery of Jesus' real presence in my life that it seemed right to speak about a Christian's feelings about Jesus in particular, not just about God or Truth in general. I realized that to stand up and proclaim that "Jesus Christ is my personal savior"[19] might cast a gloom over the proceedings. In any case, I did not feel inclined to present it this way.

What I went on to share was the value and meaning of the *person* of Jesus, not only the *ideas* of Christianity. In doing this, I knew I would throw a spotlight on one of the main differences between Christian and Buddhist meditators. But I sensed that seeing and acknowledging the distance between us would actually bring us closer. Consequently, the atmosphere of friendship that we had risked was actually deepened and strengthened. As Saint Aelred had said, friendship must be tested continually if it is to grow to its full potential.

The Value of Difference

At the Good Heart Seminar, the Dalai Lama led us into this awareness of the *value of difference* immediately and without hesitation. He said from the beginning of the Seminar that the purpose of his commenting on the Gospels was not to assist in the construction of a synthetic universal religion. He does not believe in creating a single universal religion but does believe in respecting, and indeed reverencing, the unique characteristics of each religion. While a number of Christians maintain a more fundamentalist view, many other Christians are in touch with the broader tradition and would agree with this idea of respecting other religious traditions. But the Dalai Lama and these Christian practitioners would believe in this for very different reasons.

The Dalai Lama affirmed several times in the course of the Seminar that he was a Buddhist. There were moments that he needed to remind us (and perhaps himself?) of this. I do not mean that he ever felt he was anything but a complete (a very complete) Buddhist. But, when recognizing some of the real, strong parallels between the teachings of Jesus and of the Buddha, he smelled the danger of certain words intruding as "false friends." Then he would say how important it was to recognize the significance of both parallels and differences. He said that the meaning of these points of convergence and departure between religions is to be found in the spiritual and psychological needs of their respective practitioners. People have different needs, which are met by the unique particularities (the "differences") of each religion. This sounds quite acceptable, tolerant, and liberal. For most people, it would seem an appropriate attitude for the global pluralism of the next millennium. But it raises difficult questions.

Maybe a highly realized practitioner, a very holy person, can practice this degree of tolerance genuinely. For many of us, however, there will always be, in practice, a danger of splitting what we *think* we believe from what we actually *feel* and believe. If, after all, the truth of different religions is valued only by its psychological suitability for an individual's needs, where does that leave the integrity of absolute Truth? If Buddhism and Christianity are relevant only to the subjective circumstances of individual Buddhists and Christians, what is their claim to be truth-full or even universal? I raised this question of religious relativism with the Dalai Lama, and he responded by saying that even within Buddhism there are schools of thought that acknowledge the possibility of different absolute truths existing simultaneously. We did not go into this further, perhaps because we all realized that we were entering upon very technical philosophical territory which was not necessarily an appropriate path for our dialogue. So we laughed and moved on.

However, the question lurks disturbingly at the heart of our dialogue. Christians, for example, are often concerned that total tolerance edges over the borderline of faith. Does acknowledging the truth of the Buddhist's taking refuge in Buddha, Dharma, and Sangha compromise our belief in the nature of Christian faith as a call to discipleship of Jesus? Is faith in Christ one way to find Truth, while belief in the Buddha represents another path? Jung thought so when he said that each represented the True Self for West and East respectively. But, Christians might ask, does this not challenge their central idea of the completeness of the Incarnation of God in the human being of Jesus, in whom the "complete being of the Godhead dwells embodied"?[20]

But does it challenge Christian understanding of Jesus to acknowledge that truth is also to be found in the Buddha, or Moses, or Lao Tsu?[21] The early Christian Fathers were the first practitioners of dialogue between the Gospel and other faiths, and they had to wrestle with this question of "uniqueness" from the start. Dialogue was the anvil on which they formulated their faith in conceptual terms. Because their faith was the new arrival among the already established Jewish and Hellenistic faith systems,[22] and also because they deeply respected the achievements of the pre-Christian philosophers, dialogue was the necessary way to deepen faith, not dilute it. Unfortunately, history did not provide an opportunity for them to dialogue with Buddhists: for Christians the partners in dialogue were the Greeks and Jews. The Christian approach was not to deny or to undervalue the truth that had been discovered and expressed in these other traditions. Instead, the Christian Fathers pondered how these faith systems related to the truth they saw embodied in Jesus. This question, the dialogue of their age, deepened and clarified their insight into Jesus and the Gospels and led to the great theology of the Logos.

Long before Plato, Heraclitus[23] said that the Logos is the wisdom that shapes and governs all things. It is the unified field theory that makes everything fit. Saint John's Gospel, in particular, allowed the early Christians to respond to this view, and they came to see that the Incarnation of the Logos in Jesus need in no way diminish or invalidate other, pre- or non-incarnate epiphanies of Truth. Quite the reverse, a clear perception of Jesus opens windows of insight that permit one to see the Logos more clearly, perhaps where one had failed to see it before. There are, therefore, differences in the manifestations of the Logos, different expressions of the Truth, dialects of the same language. The acceptance of differences (tolerance) and the assertion of uniqueness (faith) may seem contradictory. But they are both integral to the achievement of peace and unity between all people. Uniformity suggests falsehood. The different paths human beings will always follow express, in their very diversity, the unity of Truth. There is one Truth, one God. One Word, but many dialects.

The Problem with Tolerance

One may accept the notion of parallel absolute truths, but this is an idea that does not make the daily work of living with people of other beliefs much easier. Even with this accommodation to the problem of tolerance, difficulties remain.

It can seem to non-Christians that Christianity is smuggling all other faiths under its wing by insisting on the uniqueness of the Incarnation. Judaism is true, but it is prophetic. Krishna is true, but he was mythical. Philosophy is true, but it is cerebral. Buddhism is true, but it is psychological. Christ is true because he is the completely human embodiment of the divine. Many Christians use these precise terms when expressing their faith, or believe in the concept whether they actually express it or not. That is, in fact, part of the uniqueness,[24] the difference, of orthodox Christianity: it *does* believe that Jesus is the embodiment of the divine. The forms of language in which these beliefs must be expressed are renewed constantly through dialogue between people who believe and speak differently. But in that dialogue the Christian hears the Logos sounding and respects and reveres any manifestation of Truth as an epiphany of God's love. Beyond these exchanges in language, however, there is a deeper experience beyond language and thought. In that experience, which is silence, uniqueness and difference, along with all other dualities, coincide: they meet in a unity that respects and fulfills difference and at the same time transcends division. This is love.

Buddhism is also challenged by tolerance and dialogue. It also accommodates to the problem of tolerance in its own unique way and runs the same risk of subtle intolerance in doing so. When a Buddhist, perhaps especially a Western Buddhist, says that all religions are compatible because they represent the different personal or psychological needs of individuals, many may add or think "at different stages of their development." Behind this may be the feeling—which I never sensed at all in the Dalai Lama in either private or public discussion—that the notion of a personal God is acceptable, but that it represents a more immature, perhaps an earlier, stage of spiritual development, a kind of balancing third wheel on a child's bicycle.

Christian theology also recognizes the danger of this kind of infantilism—it calls it anthropomorphism. It recognizes that there are indeed stages of faith in which the symbol of God is understood more maturely. Every believer in God wrestles with idolatry and superstition before coming to the mystery of the divine Other. The Dalai Lama seemed to accept this quite naturally while leaving the question open about, as he called it laughingly in one exchange, the "nature of the Father" that seemed to be causing so much confusion among us. In the same open way, he did not mind using the word *God*, and the term remained flexible during our discussions.

The Purpose of Dialogue Is to Become Silent

If the purpose of dialogue is to get at the answers to these problem areas of difference and similarity, the Good Heart Seminar failed. But the purpose of dialogue is something else. Dialogue is meant to illuminate both the parallels and the divergences of belief in order to dispel the dark forces of delusion, fear, anger, and pride that can lurk in the spaces between people and their religions. To this degree the purpose of dialogue in religion is different from, say, dialogue between political or economic rivals in which some kind of practical answer acceptable to all the contestants is being sought. In religion, when answers of this kind are reached, they are often dangerous achievements. They are like false friends who run out on you as soon as real difficulties start.

Dialogue exposes not only the areas of coincidence and departure between religions, but it also uncovers the hidden inner forces that so readily make religions the most implacable of rivals. In the history of religious intolerance and persecution, Buddhism, like Jainism, has a better record than Christianity. Nevertheless, there are different forms of intolerance, some more political, others more psychological. And they all have their root in the tyranny of the individual ego that clings to its obsession with being special yet shirks the challenge of accepting its uniqueness. The powers at work are ignorance and fear. The less we know about another person or group, the more likely we are to project our worst feelings and prejudices onto them.

When Saint Francis Xavier[25] first landed in India to preach the Gospel, he regarded all Hindus as devil worshipers. He knew nothing of Vedanta[26] or the mystical experience underlying the popular religion of the country. A Westerner can still find it a little scary to be led into the heart of a Hindu temple and witness the chants and rituals of worshipers that have such overwhelming sensory power. On the other hand, when Francis Xavier's contemporary and fellow-Jesuit Matteo Ricci went to China, he soon realized that dialogue and inculturation were the best ways to achieve his mission.[27] Matteo Ricci's superiors in Rome disagreed and removed him. One of the great opportunities for East-West dialogue was thus lost. Today we see the same kind of diverse situations in which people must deal with a very different culture or religion, and we see the same variety of responses to these situations as well. But by recognizing the value of dialogue and minimizing the egotistical arrogance of a biased belief, it is perhaps easier for us than it was for our ancestors to identify prejudice, which is often unconscious, and to correct it with silence. It is easier for us today because we know more about each other. It is also more necessary than ever before in humanity's history to dialogue—and to dialogue in silence.

Certainly, if a more widespread tolerance between religions is to take place, more Christians need to develop a better familiarity with the major texts of other traditions. Reading the *Bhagavad Gita*[28] or the *Dhammapada* might also help to transform the way many Christians read (if they do so at all) their own scriptures. On the other hand, the same determination to overcome ignorance or prejudice challenges Buddhists. In Asia, Christianity is still sometimes negatively identified with memories of Western imperialism or modern economic imperialism. Many Buddhists in the West, especially those who were raised as Christians, have an image of Christianity that may be sadly uninformed or misinformed. And in these cases it is very easy to attribute the faults of individual denominations to the Christian faith itself.

Some Terms of Reference

We are Buddhist or Christian in a meaningful sense, not only because of what we believe, but also by how we act and what we are like. In this way, there will be Christians who are better Buddhists than Buddhists, because they practice mindfulness more seriously or have sharper insight into the impermanent nature of things. And there will be Buddhists who surpass Christians on their claimed turf, because they practice rather than just mouth charity. At this level of authentic religion, it is personal experience and holiness that count rather than objective systems of belief and philosophical or theological niceties. A great deal of (to some people) fascinating conversation can take place over the question, for example, of whether the *triratna*, the Three Jewels of Buddhism, can be compared with the Trinity; or whether the *dharmakāya* expresses the Christian's Holy Spirit. But this sort of philosophical conversation may bear no relation whatever to the personal behavior or attitudes of the people engaged in it so passionately.

Anityatā (impermanence), *duḥkha* (suffering), *anātman* (no-self), *dharmatā* (naturalness), *śūnyatā* (emptiness), and *tathatā* (thusness) can all be paralleled with Christian terms such as poverty, repentance, loss of self, in-Christ, simplicity, Spirit, and mystery.[29] One of Buddha's parables reminds us, however, not to divert the energy of our spiritual practice to theory for its own sake. We will be no closer to *nirvana* if we achieve philosophical certainty for just a few blissful moments before self-questioning resumes. In the story, the Buddha responds to a challenge from Mālun-kyaputta[30] regarding his not having taught about speculative issues. If, the Buddha responds, a man is shot with a poisoned arrow, is he likely to waste time asking who shot it, where it came from, and what kind of poison it is? Is he not more likely to remove the arrow as quickly as possible?

Jesus, in an ecstatic moment in the Gospel, lifts his eyes to heaven and thanks his Father for revealing the mysteries of the Kingdom to the simple and unlearned and for hiding them from the learned and the "wise."[31] Saint Paul berates some of the early Christians for their interminable wrangling over words and for splitting hairs when they should be living out the meaning of the terms they are arguing about.[32] He himself, he says, speaks of the folly of the Cross, and even with learned Greeks he avoids philosophical argument. His authority is Spirit, not logical artistry. "We demolish sophistries," he says proudly, "and all that rears its proud head against the knowledge of God."

Buddhist and Christian perspectives here are fundamentally the same. There is experience and there is reflection on the experience. If you are going to reflect, they both suggest, at least make sure you are reflecting on your own experience directly, rather than on someone else's reflection on someone else's reflection on . . . and so on.

Nirvana and the *Kingdom* are not interchangeable terms, yet they both refer to an event-in-life, not to an after-death experience. *Salvation* and *liberation* are not exactly synonymous either, but both concepts indicate a goal of human life that demands commitment and perseverance. Both Buddhists and Christians must work it out for themselves "with diligence." The hindrances or vices that they confront along the way—in their own personalities, as well as in the collective *karma* or *sin* in the universe—are existentially the same but conceptually different. After all, a proud or angry Buddhist is very much the same as a proud or angry Christian.

Differences Need Not Be Divisions

To express the meaning of these existential realities, we require many different languages, certainly between traditions, and even within the same tradition. In a sense, these different languages then create their own divisions within a common tradition. Even the Catholic Church, compared with its pre-modern self, does not offer a very united front to the world today. Its diversity is in painful tension with its unity: this is the precise challenge of catholicity. The debates in Buddhism may be less public than those sparked by papal encyclicals, but they are no less intense. For instance, there are tensions of intolerance and stereotyping between the Mahayana and Theravadan schools of thought. Even within the same national tradition, tensions of belief are felt deeply. In Thailand, the great teacher Buddhadasa Bhikkhu shocked the establishment by rejecting the whole question of rebirth, declaring that it was foolish and had nothing to do with Buddhism at all. Buddhists argue whether *nirvana* (liberation) is the goal of mind or the original mind, just as Christians argue about the meaning of Original Sin or the divinity of Jesus.

God was not a part of the Buddha's idea of liberation. He felt that questioning and pondering the existence and nature of God did not help the practical work of freeing oneself from ignorance. Like Jesus, he attacked ritualism and the empty religiosity that requires intense beliefs and polemic about God for its survival. Still, the Buddha did not reject the concept of God. He was simply silent about it. His silence was neither agnostic nor atheistic. It is a significant approach to the question, the mystery, of God.[33]

The Buddha's approach may be somewhat different from that of many Christian saints, mystics, and theologians, but it would certainly be understandable to many of them. Saint Augustine doubtlessly believed in God, but he was also sure that God is unknowable to the thinking mind alone. "If you can understand it," he said, "then it is not God." His contemporary Saint Gregory of Nyssa, a great mystical teacher of the Eastern Church, said that all ideas about God run the risk of becoming idols.

The *apophatic* traditions of Christian prayer—prayer without thought or image of any kind—are profoundly and existentially true to the basic biblical idea of the mysteriousness of God. As expressed in *The Cloud of Unknowing*,[34] a medieval English treatise on contemplative prayer, we can know God not by thought but only by love. The most systematic and *cataphatic* of theologians, the great Thomas Aquinas, said that all we can say about God is *that* God is, not *what* God is. Toward the end of his life, after a transforming mystical experience, Aquinas dismissed all he had thought and written as straw. Nicholas of Cusa also spoke of a "learned ignorance," stating it was a form of awareness that does not have an intellectual root but has the greatest power to lead us into truth. Meister Eckhart, a friend to Buddhism, emphasizes the unknowability and no-thingness of God, at times to a delightful excess: "Let thy soul be de-spirited of all spirit; let it be spiritless. Love God as he is: a not-God, a not-spirit, a not-Person, a not-image; as sheer, pure, limpid unity, alien from all duality."[35]

Paradox rather than simple logic thus becomes the key to mystical theology as well as to a dialogue between theists and nontheists on the meaning of God. What may seem like the crude, offensive dualism of theism to the Buddhist perspective is actually just as unfaithful to the heart of Christian theology, which seeks to reconcile the absolute otherness of God with the divine universality as the ground of being, the transcendence with the immanence of God, the Creator with the Creation. "With Thee Creation and existence are the same" is a key Christian insight into the meaning of God.[36]

The eightfold path and the Ten Commandments or the Beatitudes illuminate the path of daily practice we all tread toward this time-devouring and thought-transcending experience. As the Dalai Lama frequently points out, it is in the nature of these paths to require deep personal commitment and concentration. The paths themselves are the external training required for an even deeper commitment—that of the practice of meditation itself. While each path can help to illuminate the other, and while each leads to the silence inherent in a mind whose activities have been stilled, they are still separate ways to be followed with dedication, fidelity, and single-mindedness. Beyond a certain point in one's practice, one cannot be authentic and continue to straddle different paths. One cannot ride two horses at the same time. In time, one's steady practice must settle into a single-minded dedication. This single-mindedness, however, is not narrow-mindedness. It actually strengthens tolerance and receptivity toward other paths and thus fosters equanimity of mind. Jesus said that the road that leads to life is narrow, and few there are who find it. The narrowness of the path to life is not the result of exclusion but of convergence and concentration. There is even a genuine tolerance, actually fostered by single-mindedness, that is bursting with curiosity about other ways and paths.

To love one's own tradition and religion is perhaps a requirement of the spiritual life, and it is certainly a prerequisite for loving other paths and traditions. It is no more fanatical to love your own Christian or Buddhist tradition than it is to love the place where you were born or the home in which you live. However, love of country can become a jealous and exclusive nationalism, fearful of foreigners. And love of religion can create bigotry. But neither has to degenerate in this direction. The serious inner practice of silence and stillness, overcoming the egotistical forces of self-centeredness, allows us to remain deeply rooted in the soil of our tradition, while openly branching outward and upward into the great spaces of truth.

Holy Scriptures

The scriptures of a religion obviously belong to their particular tradition. They have a "nationality." But they also constitute a meeting place between neighbors of distant traditions, like the duty-free zones in airports where all nationalities mingle equally. They are the space of symbolic truth between the land of philosophical or theological debate and the realm of the pure experience of truth where thought is subsumed in vision. Philosophers and theologians may delve into their scriptures in order to find the material for their craft. Ordinary practitioners feed off scriptures as spiritual food, ingesting and assimilating their wisdom.

Christians revere the Holy Scriptures of the Bible—the Gospels and the Letters of the New Testament—not only for what they say but for what they are. If the Word became flesh, as the Gospels affirm, there is also a sense in which the flesh becomes Word again in the Holy Scriptures. When they celebrate the Eucharist, for example, many Christians believe and feel that the presence of Christ is not restricted to the bread and wine. It is also accessible in the faith of the worshiping community, in the way we are present to each other, and in the reading of the Scriptures, which forms the first part of the sacramental rite. Early Christians attributed great importance to the *breaking of the Word* in the private or communal reading of the Gospels.[37] The act of interpretation was sensed to be something far richer than a merely intellectual achievement. It was a work of wisdom. It led to insight.

Insight is an experience of the truth that cannot be simply given to another person in the way that one may communicate ideas or beliefs. Insight is spontaneous and has the nature of a gift. It is surprising when it comes and yet obvious. It is joyful and yet calm. The monastic tradition practices a form of spiritual reading (*lectio divina* as Saint Benedict called it), which is not the same as study or analytical reading and which is dedicated to the progressive awakening of insight in the practitioner. Like the Jewish tradition of reading the Bible, quality is preferred to quantity, depth to breadth. Reading in this way, one chooses a short passage and then continues to ruminate or "chew" over it. You go back over it many times, homing in more and more until you are left with a single word or short phrase, simultaneously arresting and awakening the mind to meaning. In this way, as the mind is stilled, one is brought to the threshold of meditation.

How to Read the Word

Origen, a third-century Christian teacher in the Alexandrian school of Christian philosophy, was the first to systematically describe the act of reading and interpreting Scripture as well as the first to describe how the mind's encounter with the Scriptures lifts the mind above itself. He identified the different levels of meaning (an exercise that was anathema to fundamentalists then as it is now) waiting to be experienced in the Scriptures.

He saw the reading of Holy Scripture as a process of deepening consciousness and insight. The process begins with the literal meaning of the text, a meaning that requires both a sense of grammar and of history. But, beyond the "letter that killeth,"[38] which goes no further than its surface meaning, Origen pushed on toward the level of moral meaning. This level is reached by seeing the stories and characters of Scripture as "types" or symbols that teach us lessons within the context of our personal or social circumstances. Then, Origen said, the "allegorical" or mystical meaning waits to be discovered as we are lifted above ourselves and absorbed into the Logos itself. A good example of how this process works can be seen by exploring the different levels of meaning in the Bible of the term *Jerusalem*: the word, the place, and the symbol. Jerusalem has a literal historical meaning. As the center of sacred presence and worship for three religions, it symbolizes the spiritual realities of the pilgrimage of our lives. As the "heavenly Jerusalem" it represents the goal of the spiritual journey.

Origen applied his method to many passages of the Bible. "You must not think," he said of the stories from the Old Testament, "that all these things happened only in earlier times. In fact, all these things come true in *you* in a mystical way." The Book of Joshua, for example, tells the story of Rahab the harlot who made it possible for the Israelites to capture the city.[39] In Origen's imagination she becomes a *type* or symbol of the Church, a harlot turned virgin. The blood of Christ, which saves us from damnation, is foreshadowed in the scarlet cord that Rahab tied to the window to identify her family and protect them from the attacking Israelites. In another example, the crossing of the Jordan was a prefiguring of Baptism—and Baptism, as a rite of passage, is a symbol in its turn of something yet to be achieved: "We have been promised a passage through the very air itself." The goal of reading the Bible is for the reader ultimately to be incorporated into the highest reality into which the humanity of Jesus has already been assumed. And so, as Origen said, in reading the Gospels and being open to all levels of consciousness and meaning, we come "to gallop through the vast spaces of mystic and spiritual understanding."[40]

Saint Bernard, a twelfth-century monk and teacher, was another major influence on the Christian tradition of reading the Gospels. He spoke of Scripture as a window through which we glimpse the divine reality. In reading Scripture, we pursue the timeless Word of God back to its source: what Saint Bernard called the "endless following of the Word." On the way, we undergo the experience of *inverbation* by which the Word actually becomes part of us and we of it.

And so, in the Christian tradition, we see that one does not read the Gospels merely to learn about the facts of the life of Jesus or the answers to catechism questions. It is an awakening of the mystical intelligence. One could say that reading the Gospels in this way is the strengthening of *buddhi*, spiritual intelligence. And this strengthening is not limited to times of formal spiritual practice, but enters into and transforms all the activities and situations in our lives. Concentrating on the swirling patterns of scriptural meaning can also be seen as a practice of focusing consciousness that is similar to the visual attention employed to center the mind with a mandala.

Attention Leads to Wisdom

Reading the Gospels requires the work of attention and concentration. It can be immensely rewarding and enriching. But there is more effort asked from us in reading Scripture than is required of us by many of the ancient systems of divination and prediction, some of which—such as the Tarot, Runes, or the I Ching—have again become popular today. There is additional work demanded from us in reading Scripture, including an interaction with the text and its many meanings. We are not passive before the Word. Hearing the Word energizes us and causes us to spring to our feet, ready for action. Through the Word we win a more personal ownership of the meaning of the texts, as well as of the process and its fruits. The wisdom we seek in reading the Gospels is no longer felt to be located magically in the actual process of reading. The words of the Scriptures are not spells; the Word is not magic.

Wisdom is found to reside within the person who follows the practice of reading Scripture. The inner Spirit is realized by interacting with the accumulated wisdom of the tradition that supports the reading. When people in therapy want the therapist or their therapy session to do the work for them, they have lost their own authority. An egotistical therapist can encourage this, and so promote a dependency that traps a patient in an infantile awareness. However, the Spirit, who is the guide, the real therapist, in the act of reading Scripture, encourages the reader to do the work. We are only asked a simple registration fee to read Scripture well: we are asked to give our undivided attention to it. Attention alone is necessary to build our journey, our practice, on the twin pillars of spiritual authority: the authority of personal insight and of the living, transmitted tradition.

We develop mystical intelligence by reading the Gospels in this way. Progressively, this intelligence illuminates and enriches ordinary life. This is quite different from attributing magical power to the literal meaning, a mistake that can distort and disrupt ordinary life rather than enhance it. A fundamentalist reader of the Bible once appealed to his well-thumbed book for advice in a dilemma. He flicked the pages and placed his finger blindly on a verse. It read "and Judas went and hanged himself." Thinking something had gone wrong with his divination, he thought he would try again. This time the verse he alighted on read "go thou and do likewise." It was perhaps the beginning of his learning the true way to read the Holy Book.

Reading the Gospels is an artistic activity of the heart. Recovering the lost art of reading Scripture is one of the great tasks for Christianity today. When I thanked the Dalai Lama at the end of the Good Heart Seminar for his gift to those present as well as, in some way, to the Church in the West, I was thinking partly of our need to recover this art of reading Scripture. His Holiness restores to religion a self-confidence and integrity that has been lost for many Westerners. And in addition, he shows how many of the traditional practices of religion, such as the reading of Scripture, can be regained even at this late stage in our Western alienation from the spiritual.

Meditation

Discovering how to truly read and experience the Gospels is one of the first fruits of meditation. Even people who have no habit of spiritual reading develop an unexpected thirst for the Word in Scripture as a consequence of their meditation practice. Others who have been reading Scripture for many years become aware of a substantial change in the quality of the reading, in the way they are now read *by* Scripture.

Meditation is a way of faith, and so it strengthens faith. With the *eye of faith*[41] opened and clarified, an entire other dimension of consciousness is awakened. We read the Gospels, the *sutras*, and all the sacred scriptures of humanity with this eye of faith. The dimension of consciousness that it opens does not compete with scientific reason or philosophical logic. But it is distinguished from them by its air of freedom. Faith is not logical certainty. With logic there is no personal freedom. The mind must impose the truth of a logical statement. But with faith, the deeper levels of truth call forth a personal response that we are eternally free to give or to retain. If, with your rational mind, you see that ten divided by five equals two, you are not really free to believe it or not. To deny it is absurd. If, however, with the eye of faith, you realize that you are in love, then you are confronted with the vast space of human freedom in which that truth can be lived or denied, accepted or evaded.

What I have just written is a very Christian way of putting it. The word *faith* may make some Buddhists uncomfortable. But it is important that we share an understanding of this word if meditation together is to be the common ground from which dialogue can penetrate deeper than merely scholarly or diplomatic encounters. Jesus said that faith saves us, that it moves mountains, and that by faith we are healed. An act of faith, such as one we make toward another human being or a community, is an act that advances the healing process of human integration. Without acts of faith to nourish and challenge our lives, we feel less alive, less whole.

It is in this sense that I say meditation is a way of faith. Because we were meditating together three times a day, it was possible for the Dalai Lama's commentaries on the Gospels to be delivered and shared in an atmosphere of a common faith. From the beginning it was clear to us all that these periods of silence were crucial to the success of the experiment. The Dalai Lama showed this by agreeing, as I think only a few major religious leaders would, to come over to the meditation hall early in the morning each day—a trip that necessitated his returning to his residence for breakfast and making the same long journey back for the first session an hour later.

We meditated each in our own way. There was no discussion about methods or techniques and, of course, no analysis about what happened (or did not) during the meditation. This experience of silence and thought-free *being* together, *for* each other, was the underlay of the dialogue. I think that this was the essential act of dialogue that took place during the Seminar. This book conveys the words we used, but I hope it makes clear that the words were charged with the power of silence. Maybe it was due to this silence that there was also so much laughter and goodwill. The Good Heart Seminar was a remarkable lesson in the nature of silence as a medium that penetrates language and discourse. Ramana Maharshi,[42] a great Indian sage of this century, once said that silence is not turning off the tap of communication but turning it full on.

If *The Good Heart*—as seminar, video, book, or living tradition—has a single, crucial point to make, it is the value of silence.

In the United Nations building in New York, a Christian Meditation group has established weekly meetings that welcome people of all faiths and cultures. The building itself is one of the great modern icons of hope. Its architecture and spaciousness express the desperate human longing after a millennium of war for a time of rest, when swords can finally be beaten into plowshares. The building is also a labyrinth of bureaucracy and talk. Everyone is talking, and talking about talking. It is all necessary. But it is also incomplete. There are some there, like the woman who started the meditation group, who sense that silence would not be a suspension of dialogue between nations. Silence would facilitate dialogue and the understanding and friendship that we need for peace.

And why do we need peace? Why not fight each other and make an art of war, as we have done for so long? The answer to that, of course, is beyond words. It is found in the meditation itself. Buddhists and Christians and people of all faiths would agree that the reason for peace is not badly described as *love* or *goodness*. If the human heart is basically good—what hope is there if we think it is not?—it is good because it can love.

This book is an expression of that love, a love that is unsentimental and unselfish. The dialogue between Christianity and Buddhism can be a model of how it is possible for human beings to love each other *because* they are different, not just despite their differences. This goal will be enriched and strengthened for the next century by meetings of mind and heart—such as the meeting of mind and heart that occurred when the Dalai Lama laughingly accepted, with deep reverence, the challenge of reading the Gospels with a group of contemplative Christians.

This book expresses a generous experience of friendship shared by many people whose unique talents and energies facilitated the Seminar, the videos, and now the book. From the beginning of *The Good Heart*, Mrs. Kesang Y. Takla and her team at the Office of Tibet in London have been exemplars of positive cooperation. Robert Kiely generously took on the whole task of editing the transcripts, which derived from the masterly recordings made by Peter Armstrong of WordPictures and Mark Schofield of our Community. Gregory Ryan's transcription of the Seminar gave a clear and accurate record from which to work. Giovanni Felicioni, director of Medio Media, and Judith Longman, a friend and advisor of its work, gave valuable time and insights at all stages. Teresa O'Neill and Sadie Summers at our International Centre in London contributed secretarial skills and kept in contact all the far-flung parties involved in the book. Thupten Jinpa's precise but human translation at the Seminar lies behind his contribution to making the Buddhist terminology of the book accessible to the general reader. Timothy McNeill of Wisdom Publications has been a delight to work with and has led the coordination of the project with eponymous wisdom and prudence. Susanna Ralli's editing and John Dunne's reading of the translations and his own translation of the Tibetan prayers have also added inestimably to the accuracy and usefulness of the book. Connie Miller of the Wisdom staff has made a valuable contribution in helping to develop the glossaries and read the Buddhist references for the precision and clarity of their meaning. All these people, inspired by various traditions, have made the book of *The Good Heart* something more than a book: it is a sign of friendship between people who have discovered that, in the modern world, differences need no longer be divisions but sources of a greater unity than human beings have known so far.

Laurence Freeman, OSB

THE GOOD HEART

I

A WISH FOR HARMONY

The lecture room in Middlesex University in North London was not grand: it was a rather narrow, cramped space with a steeply rising bank of creaky wooden seats that banged and scraped whenever anyone moved. Large posters of calligraphed sayings of John Main were patched between windows opening out to the gray English sky. A few chairs, a little carpet, and a bunch of flowers looked forlorn on a wobbly temporary platform. The whole place looked makeshift, as though it had been thrown together the night before and nothing of importance could possibly happen there.

The audience fidgeted in anticipation. Mixed in among English, Canadian, and American laypeople were Buddhist monks and nuns in saffron or crimson robes, their shaven heads still in the bobbing throng. In the front rows were Benedictine monks and sisters, some in black, Olivetans in white. Cameras and microphones were adjusted. Throats were cleared. No organ played, no horns sounded. A little group of people climbed onto the platform from a side entrance. In their midst was His Holiness the Dalai Lama, wearing sensible shoes and wrapped in his crimson and yellow habit, grinning, nodding, and waving a little shyly but with obvious pleasure.

He had made an entrance without an entrance. There had been no procession. Indeed, his arrival was a Buddhist non-procession. One moment, he wasn't there; the next he was. Very much there.

Several welcoming speeches were made, including one by the Lady Mayor of Enfield, who described her borough as "multiracial, multicultural, multireligious." This northern suburb of London, with a strong commitment to harmony in pluralism, was an appropriate meeting place for a Seminar gathering two great religious traditions.

Following the Mayor's remarks, Dom Laurence Freeman, OSB, rose to welcome His Holiness. As the spiritual director and teacher of the World Community for Christian Meditation, Father Laurence had extended the invitation to the Dalai Lama and was serving as host for the Seminar's proceedings. Gentle and mild of manner, Father Laurence nonetheless conveyed an intellectual and spiritual energy that the guest of honor clearly found congenial and intriguing. As the conference went along, the rapport and affection between the two monks increased visibly. When Father Laurence spoke, His Holiness, as he did with everyone who addressed him, fixed his gaze and attention on him.

Father Laurence, in his very first remarks, sounded what was to become a theme of the Seminar—the reciprocal nature of the event.

IT IS A great honor, Your Holiness, to welcome you. You told me you would like to learn from us and we are here to learn from you as well. It is a great privilege for us that you are going to lead this John Main Seminar on the theme you chose, The Good Heart, and that you have accepted with openness and generosity our invitation to comment on the Gospels, the Christian Scriptures.

In the Christian tradition, we call the scriptures the Holy Scriptures because we believe that the presence of Christ can be found in them, even in the reading of the words. They are human words, and they are subject to understanding and, of course, also to misunderstanding. These words need to be interpreted through the mind so that the heart can see their meaning. We know that you represent a rich and wonderful Buddhist tradition which has refined the instruments of the mind for the perception of truth. And so we feel eager to read our Holy Scriptures through your mind, and, with you, to see them in a fresh way.

Just as we are sure that we Christians will be enriched, we hope that all the Buddhists here with you, and people here of all faiths, will also be enriched. We know that the search for understanding is not just intellectual but that it is about true insight, *vipaśyanā*, the experience of the meaning of sacred words. One of the great teachers of Christian theology, Thomas Aquinas, said that we put our faith not in propositions but in the realities that the words point to. What matters is the experience, not merely the ideas by themselves. We understand that the way of meditation we will share during this Seminar in silence with Your Holiness will be a universal, unifying way into that experience beyond words.

John Main understood the unifying power of silence to lead us beyond words. That is why, in this Seminar, perhaps the most important time that we will spend together will be the time of silence. After His Holiness speaks to us, he will lead us in a period of meditation. For each of these periods, we will be able to go beyond words into that truth that lies at the heart of reality. Meditation enriches us in so many ways. One of these ways is in the power of meditation to enable us to read the holy scriptures of the world more wisely and perceptively than we otherwise could.

We appreciate the gift of your presence, Your Holiness. If we can be open to the reality of *presence*—to the presence that we will experience in the Scriptures, the presence that we will experience as you open your mind and heart to us—let us also grow in a spirit of peace and friendship.

On behalf of our entire Community worldwide, I would like to assure you that we hold in our minds and hearts the Tibetan people. We feel them here with you today. The Cross and the Resurrection of Christ lie at the heart of Christian faith. Perhaps in the history of Tibet and in your own personal history, we can see that the Cross and Resurrection are human realities that belong to all people, and not to one religion alone. We have seen Tibet crucified, but we have also seen the resurrection of Tibetan wisdom and teaching, particularly through Your Holiness, as a gift to the whole world.

We are open to the mystery of reality. We hope and pray that in the silence of meditation, as well as in the words through which you will guide us, we will be able to enter into the fullness of consciousness and light.[44]

When Father Laurence had finished, the audience applauded enthusiastically while the Dalai Lama beamed, acknowledging the clarity of the welcoming remarks and the obvious warmth of his reception. He began speaking in English, speaking in Tibetan intermittently when it became necessary to clarify a point.

Spiritual brothers and sisters, it is a great joy and privilege for me to have the opportunity to participate in this dialogue and to open the John Main

Seminar entitled "The Good Heart." I would like to express my deep appreciation to all those who have helped to organize this event.

I am grateful for the warm words of welcome from the Lady Mayor, and I am very encouraged by her reference to the harmony and understanding that exists among the various communities and religious traditions in this borough, which she described as multicultural, multi-ethnic, and multireligious. I would like to express my thanks for that.

I met the late Father John Main many years ago in Canada and was impressed to meet a person in the Christian tradition who emphasized meditation as a part of spiritual practice. Today, at the beginning of this Seminar, I think it is very important for us to remember him.

I am also happy to see so many familiar faces and to have the opportunity to meet new and old friends here.

Despite many material advances on our planet, humanity faces many, many problems, some of which are actually of our own creation. And to a large extent it is our mental attitude—our outlook on life and the world—that is the key factor for the future—the future of humanity, the future of the world, and the future of the environment. Many things depend on our mental attitude, both in the personal and public spheres. Whether we are happy in our individual or family life is, in a large part, up to us. Of course, material conditions are an important factor for happiness and a good life, but one's mental attitude is of equal or greater importance.

As we approach the twenty-first century, religious traditions are as relevant as ever. Yet, as in the past, conflicts and crises arise in the name of different religious traditions. This is very, very unfortunate. We must make every effort to overcome this situation. In my own experience, I have found that the most effective method to overcome these conflicts is close contact and an exchange among those of various beliefs, not only on an intellectual level, but in deeper spiritual experiences. This is a powerful method to develop mutual understanding and respect. Through this interchange, a strong foundation of genuine harmony can be established.

So I am always extremely happy to participate in religious dialogue. And I am particularly happy to spend these few days talking with you and practicing my broken English! When I spend a few weeks on retreat in Dharamsala, my residence in India, I find that my broken English becomes even poorer, so these days of exchange will give me a much-needed opportunity to practice.

Since it is my belief that harmony among different religious traditions is extremely important, extremely necessary, I would like to suggest a few ideas on ways it can be promoted. First, I suggest we encourage meetings among scholars from different religious backgrounds to discuss differences and similarities in their traditions, in order to promote empathy and to improve our knowledge about one another. Secondly, I suggest that we encourage meetings between people from different religious traditions who have had some deeper spiritual experiences. They need not be scholars, but instead genuine practitioners who come together and share insights as a result of religious practice. According to my own experience, this is a powerful and effective means of enlightening each other in a more profound and direct way.

Some of you may have already heard me mention that on a visit to the great monastery at Montserrat[45] in Spain, I met a Benedictine monk there. He came especially to see me—and his English was much poorer than mine, so I felt more courage to speak to him. After lunch, we spent some time alone, face to face, and I was informed that this monk had spent a few years in the mountains just behind the monastery. I asked him what kind of contemplation he had practiced during those years of solitude. His answer was simple: "Love, love, love." How wonderful! I suppose that sometimes he also slept. But during all those years he meditated simply on love. And he was not meditating on just the word. When I looked into his eyes, I saw evidence of profound spirituality and love—as I had during my meetings with Thomas Merton.

These two encounters have helped me develop a genuine reverence for the Christian tradition and its capacity to create people of such goodness. I believe the purpose of all the major religious traditions is not to construct big temples on the outside, but to create temples of goodness and compassion *inside*, in our hearts. Every major religion has the potential to create this. The greater our awareness is regarding the value and effectiveness of other religious traditions, then the deeper will be our respect and reverence toward other religions. This is the proper way for us to promote genuine compassion and a spirit of harmony among the religions of the world.

In addition to encounters among scholars and experienced practitioners, it is also important, particularly in the eyes of the public, that leaders of the various religious traditions occasionally come together to meet and pray, as in the important meeting at Assisi in 1986.[46] This is a third simple yet effective way to promote tolerance and understanding.

A fourth means of working toward harmony among the world's religions is for people of different religious traditions to go on pilgrimages together to visit one another's holy places. A few years ago, I started doing this practice myself in India. Since then, I have had the opportunity to travel as a pilgrim to Lourdes, the holy place in France,[47] and to Jerusalem. In these places, I prayed with the followers of the various religions, sometimes in silent meditation. And in this prayer and meditation, I felt a genuine spiritual experience. I hope this will set an example, serve as a sort of precedent, so that in the future it will be regarded as quite normal for people to join together in pilgrimages to holy sites and share the experience of their different religious backgrounds.

Finally, I would like to come back to the subject of meditation and to my Christian brothers and sisters who practice meditation in their daily lives. I believe this practice is extremely important. Traditionally in India, there is *samādhi* meditation, "stilling the mind," which is common to all the Indian religions, including Hinduism, Buddhism, and Jainism. And in many of these traditions, certain types of *vipaśyanā*, "analytical meditation," are common as well. We might ask why *samādhi*, "stilling the mind," is so important. Because *samādhi*, or focusing meditation, is the means to mobilize your mind, to channel your mental energy. *Samādhi* is considered to be an essential part of spiritual practice in *all* the major religious traditions of India because it provides the possibility to channel all one's mental energy and the ability to direct the mind to a particular object in a single-pointed way.

It is my belief that if prayer, meditation, and contemplation—which is more discursive and analytic—are combined in daily practice, the effect on the practitioner's mind and heart will be all the greater. One of the major aims and purposes of religious practice for the individual is an inner transformation from an undisciplined, untamed, unfocused state of mind toward one that is disciplined, tamed, and balanced. A person who has perfected the faculty of single-pointedness will definitely have a greater ability to attain this objective. When meditation becomes an important part of your spiritual life, you are able to bring about this inner transformation in a more effective way.

Once this transformation has been achieved, then in following your own spiritual tradition, you will discover that a kind of natural humility will arise in you, allowing you to communicate better with people from other religious traditions and cultural backgrounds. You are in a better position to appreciate the value and preciousness of other traditions because you have seen this value from within your own tradition. People often experience feelings of exclusivity in their religious beliefs—a feeling that one's own path is the only true path—which can create a sense of apprehension about connecting with others of different faiths. I believe the best way to counter that force is to experience the value of one's own path through a meditative life, which will enable one to see the value and preciousness of other traditions.

In order to develop a genuine spirit of harmony from a sound foundation of knowledge, I believe it is very important to know the fundamental differences between religious traditions. And it is possible to understand the fundamental differences but at the same time recognize the value and potential of each religious tradition. In this way, a person may develop a balanced and harmonious perception. Some people believe that the most reasonable way to attain harmony and solve problems relating to religious intolerance is to establish one universal religion for everyone. However, I have always felt that we should have different religious traditions because human beings possess so many different mental dispositions: one religion simply cannot satisfy the needs of such a variety of people. If we try to unify the faiths of the world into one religion, we will also lose many of the qualities and richnesses of each particular tradition. Therefore, I feel it is better, in spite of the many quarrels in the name of religion, to maintain a variety of religious traditions. Unfortunately, while a diversity of religious traditions is more suited to serve the needs of the diverse mental dispositions among humanity, this diversity naturally possesses the potential for conflict and disagreement as well. Consequently people of every religious tradition must make an extra effort to try to transcend intolerance and misunderstanding and seek harmony.

These are a few points that I thought would be useful at the beginning of the Seminar. Now I am looking forward to the challenge of exploring texts and ideas that are not familiar to me. You've given me a heavy responsibility, and I will try my best to fulfill your wishes. I really feel it a great honor and privilege to be asked to comment on selected passages of the Holy Scripture—a scripture I must admit I am not very familiar with. I must also admit that this is the first time I have tried to do such a thing. Whether it will be a success or failure, I don't know! But in any case, I will try my best. Now I'll chant a few verses of auspiciousness and then we will meditate.

The modesty, like his smile, was genuine. When the audience laughed, the laughter seemed partly out of surprise at the lack of self-importance in the man and also a gesture of friendly encouragement. It was the beginning of a rapport that, in the next few days, would lead to a climax of shared feeling and thought in an atmosphere of respect and love.

The lights in the hall were turned out, and in the soft light coming only through the windows, the audience collected itself as His Holiness closed his eyes and intoned an ancient Tibetan prayer:

Replete with excellence like a mountain of gold,
The triple worlds' saviors, freed from the three taints,
Are the buddhas, their eyes like lotuses in bloom;
They are the world's first auspicious blessing.

The teachings they imparted are sublime and steadfast,
Famed in the triple worlds, honored by gods and humans alike.
That holy teaching grants peace to all sentient beings;
This is the world's second auspicious blessing.
The sacred community, rich with learning, is honored
By humans, gods, and demi-gods.
That supreme community is modest, yet the site of glory;
This is the world's third auspicious blessing.

The Teacher has come into our world;
The teaching shines like the sun's rays;
The teaching masters, like siblings, are harmonious;
Let there thus be auspicious blessings for the teachings to
    remain for a long time.[48]

Song: "All shall be well. All shall be well. And all manner of things shall be well."

After thirty minutes of silent meditation, Father Laurence rose to speak:

To conclude our first session, we are going to ask His Holiness to light one of the candles in this symbol of unity and then different members of the guests representing other traditions will light other candles from his.[49] These candles will burn during the Seminar as a symbol of the unity and friendship of our different beliefs.

2

LOVE YOUR ENEMY
Matthew 5:38–48

In the morning, His Holiness arrived promptly and took up his task of commenting on a passage from the Gospel according to Matthew with a few brief prefatory remarks. Throughout the Seminar he stressed that his aim was not to make Buddhists of the Christians in the audience, but to offer a Buddhist monk's perspective on the Gospel passages.

SINCE THIS DIALOGUE has been organized by the World Community for Christian Meditation and the main audience attending here is practicing Christians who have a serious commitment to their own practice and faith, my presentation will be aimed primarily toward that audience. Consequently I shall try to explain those Buddhist techniques or methods that can be adopted by a Christian practitioner without attaching the deeper Buddhist philosophy. Some of these deeper, metaphysical differences between the two traditions may come up in the panel discussion.

My main concern is this: how can I help or serve the Christian practitioner? The last thing I wish to do is to plant seeds of doubt and skepticism in their minds. As mentioned earlier, it is my full conviction that the variety of religious traditions today is valuable and relevant. According to my own experience, all of the world's major religious traditions provide a common language and message upon which we can build a genuine understanding.

In general I am in favor of people continuing to follow the religion of their own culture and inheritance. Of course individuals have every right to change *if* they find that a new religion is more effective or suitable for their spiritual needs. But, generally speaking, it is better to experience the value of one's own religious tradition. Here is an example of the sort of difficulties that may arise in changing one's religion. In one Tibetan family in the 1960s, the father of the family passed away, and the mother later came to see me. She told me that as far as this life is concerned she was Christian, but for the next life there was no alternative for her but Buddhism. How complicated! If you are Christian, it is better to develop spiritually within your religion and be a genuine, good Christian. If you are a Buddhist, be a genuine Buddhist. Not something half-and-half! This may cause only confusion in your mind.

Before commenting on the text, I would like to discuss meditation. The Tibetan term for meditation is *gom*, which connotes the development of a constant familiarity with a particular practice or object. The process of "familiarization" is key because the enhancement or development of mind follows with the growth of familiarity with the chosen object. Consequently it is only through constant application of the meditative techniques and training of the mind that one can expect to attain inner transformation or discipline within the mind. In the Tibetan tradition there are, generally speaking, two principal types of meditation. One employs a certain degree of analysis and reasoning, and is known as contemplative or analytical meditation. The other is more absorptive and focusing, and is called single-pointed or placement meditation.

Let us take the example of meditating on love and compassion in the Christian context. In an analytical aspect of that meditation, we would be thinking along specific lines, such as the following: to truly love God one must demonstrate that love through the action of loving fellow human beings in a genuine way, loving one's neighbor. One might also reflect upon the life and example of Jesus Christ himself, how he conducted his life, how he worked for the benefit of other sentient beings, and how his actions illustrated a compassionate way of life. This type of thought process is the analytical aspect of meditation on compassion. One might meditate in a similar manner on patience and tolerance.

These reflections will enable you to develop a deep conviction in the importance and value of compassion and tolerance. Once you arrive at that certain point where you feel totally convinced of the preciousness of and need for compassion and tolerance, you will experience a sense of being touched, a sense of being transformed from within. At this point you should place your mind single-pointedly in that conviction, without applying any further analysis. Your mind should rather remain single-pointedly in equipoise; this is the absorptive or placement aspect of meditation on compassion. Thus both types of meditation are applied in one meditation session.

Why are we able, through the application of such meditative techniques, not only to develop but to enhance compassion? This is because compassion is a type of emotion that possesses the potential for development. Generally speaking, we can point to two types of emotion. One is more instinctual and is not based on reason. The other type of emotion—such as compassion or tolerance—is not so instinctual but instead has a sound base or grounding in reason and experience. When you clearly see the various logical grounds for their development and you develop conviction in these benefits, then these emotions will be enhanced. What we see here is a joining of intellect and heart. Compassion represents the emotion, or heart, and the application of analytic meditation applies the intellect. So, when you have arrived at that meditative state where compassion is enhanced, you see a special merging of intellect and heart.

If you examine the nature of these meditative states, you will also see that there are different elements within these states. For example, you might be engaged in the analytic process of thinking that we are all creations of the same Creator, and therefore, that we are all truly brothers and sisters. In this case, you are focusing your mind on a particular object. That is, your analytic subjectivity is focusing on the idea or concept that you are analyzing. However, once you have arrived at a state of single-pointedness—when you experience that inner transformation, that compassion within you—there is no longer a meditating mind and a meditated object. Instead your mind is generated in the form of compassion.

These are a few preliminary comments on meditation. Now I will read from the Gospel.

> You have heard that they were told, "An eye for an eye, a tooth for a tooth." But what I tell you is this: Do not resist those who wrong you. If anyone slaps you on the right cheek, turn and offer him the other also. If anyone wants to sue you and takes your shirt, let him have your cloak as well. If someone in authority presses you into service for one mile, go with him two. Give to anyone who asks, and do not turn your back on anyone who wants to borrow.
>
> *[Matthew 5:38–42]*

The practice of tolerance and patience that is being advocated in these passages is extremely similar to the practice of tolerance and patience that is advocated in Buddhism in general. And this is particularly true in Mahayana Buddhism in the context of the *bodhisattva ideals* in which the individual who faces certain harms is encouraged to respond in a nonviolent and compassionate way. In fact, one could almost say that these passages could be introduced into a Buddhist text, and they would not even be recognized as traditional Christian scriptures.

> You have heard that they were told, "Love your neighbor and hate your enemy." But what I tell you is this: Love your enemies and pray for your persecutors; only so can you be children of your heavenly Father, who causes the sun to rise on good and bad alike, and sends rain on the innocent and the wicked. If you love only those who love you, what reward can you expect? Even the tax-collectors do as much as that. If you greet only your brothers, what is there extraordinary about that? Even the heathens do as much. There must be no limit to your goodness, as your heavenly Father's goodness knows no bounds.
>
> *[Matthew 5:43–48]*

This reminds me of a passage in a Mahayana Buddhist text known as the *Compendium of Practices* [50] in which Shantideva asks, "If you do not practice compassion toward your enemy then toward whom can you practice it?" The implication is that even animals show love, compassion, and a feeling of empathy toward their own loved ones. As we claim to be practitioners of spirituality and a spiritual path, we should be able to do better than the animals.

These Gospel passages also remind me of reflections in another Mahayana text called *A Guide to the Bodhisattva's Way of Life*, in which Shantideva states that it is very important to develop the right attitude toward your enemy. If you can cultivate the right attitude, your enemies are your best spiritual teachers because their presence provides you with the opportunity to enhance and develop tolerance, patience, and understanding. By developing greater tolerance and patience, it will be easier for you to develop your capacity for compassion and, through that, altruism. So even for the practice of your own spiritual path, the presence of an enemy is crucial. The analogy drawn in the Gospel as to how "the sun makes no discrimination where it shines" is very significant. The sun shines for all and makes no discrimination. This is a wonderful metaphor for compassion. It gives you the sense of its impartiality and all-embracing nature.

As I read these passages, I feel that the Gospel especially emphasizes the practice of tolerance and feelings of impartiality toward all creatures. In my opinion, in order to develop one's capacity for tolerance toward all beings, and particularly toward an enemy, it is important as a precondition to have a feeling of equanimity toward all. If someone tells you that you should not be hostile toward your enemy or that you should love your enemy, that statement alone is not going to move you to change. It is quite natural for all of us to feel hostility toward those who harm us and to feel attachment toward our loved ones. It is a natural human feeling, so we must have effective techniques to help us make that transition from these inherently biased feelings toward a state of greater equanimity.

There are specific techniques for developing this sense of equanimity toward all sentient creatures. For instance, in the Buddhist context, one can refer to the concept of rebirth to assist in the practice of generating equanimity. As we are discussing the cultivation of equanimity in the context of Christian practice, however, perhaps it is possible to invoke the idea of Creation and that all creatures are equal in that they are all creations of the same God. On the basis of this belief, one can develop a sense of equanimity. Just before our morning's session, I had a brief discussion with Father Laurence. He made the point that in Christian theology there is the belief that all human beings are created in the image of God—we all share a common divine nature. I find this quite similar to the idea of buddha-nature in Buddhism. On the basis of this belief that all human beings share the same divine nature, we have a very strong ground, a very powerful reason, to believe that it is possible for each of us to develop a genuine sense of equanimity toward all beings.

However, we should not see equanimity as an end in itself. Nor should we feel that we are striving for a total state of apathy in which we have no feelings or fluctuating emotions toward either our enemies or our loved ones and friends. That is not what we are seeking to achieve. What we aspire to achieve is, first of all, to set the foundation, to have a kind of clear field where we can then plant other thoughts. Equanimity is this even ground that we are first laying out. On the basis of this, we should then reflect on the merits of tolerance, patience, love, and compassion toward all. We should also contemplate the disadvantages and the negativities of self-centered thinking, fluctuating emotions toward friends and enemies, and the negativities of having biased feelings toward other beings.

The crucial point is how you utilize this basic equanimity. It is important to concentrate on the negativities of anger and hatred, which are the principal obstacles to enhancing one's capacity for compassion and tolerance. You should also reflect upon the merits and virtues of enhancing tolerance and patience. This can be done in the Christian context without having to resort to any belief in rebirth. For example, when reflecting upon the merits and virtues of tolerance and patience, you can think along the following lines: God created you as an individual and gave you the freedom to act in a way that is compatible and in accordance with the Creator's wishes—to act in an ethical way, in a moral way, and to live a life of an ethically disciplined, responsible individual. By feeling and practicing tolerance and patience toward fellow creatures, you are fulfilling that wish: you are pleasing your Creator. That is, in a way, the best gift, the best offering that you can make to the divine Creator.

There is an idea in Buddhism of something called *offering of practice* (*drupai chöpa*): of all the offerings you can make to someone that you revere—such as material offerings, singing songs of praise, or other gifts—the best offering you can make is to live a life according to the principles of that being. In the Christian context, by living life in an ethically disciplined way, based on tolerance and patience, you are, in a way, making a wonderful gift to your Creator. This is in some sense much more effective than having only prayer as your main practice. If you pray but then do not live according to that prayer, it is not of much benefit.

One of the great yogis of Tibetan Buddhism, Milarepa, states in one of his songs of spiritual experience, "As far as offerings of material gifts are concerned, I am destitute; I have nothing to offer. What I have to offer in abundance is the gift of my spiritual practice." We can see that, generally, the person who has a tremendous reserve of patience and tolerance has a certain degree of tranquility and calmness in his or her life. Such a person is not only happy and more emotionally grounded, but also seems to be physically healthier and to experience less illness. The person possesses a strong will, has a good appetite, and can sleep with a clear conscience. These are all benefits of tolerance and patience that we can see in our own daily lives.

One of my fundamental convictions is that basic human nature is more disposed toward compassion and affection. Basic human nature is gentle, not aggressive or violent. This goes hand in hand with Father Laurence's statement that all human beings share the same divine nature. I would also argue that when we examine the relationship between mind, or consciousness, and body, we see that wholesome attitudes, emotions, and states of mind, like compassion, tolerance, and forgiveness, are strongly connected with physical health and well-being. They enhance physical well-being, whereas negative or unwholesome attitudes and emotions—anger, hatred, disturbed states of mind—undermine physical health. I would argue that this correspondence shows that our basic human nature is closer to the wholesome attitudes and emotions.

After you have reflected upon the virtues of tolerance and patience and feel convinced of the need to develop and enhance them within you, you should then look at different types and levels of patience and tolerance. For example, in the Buddhist texts three types of tolerance and patience are described. The first is the state of resolute indifference—one is able to bear pain or suffering and not be overwhelmed by them. That is the first level. In the second state, one is not only able to bear such sufferings, but is also, if necessary, prepared and even willing to take upon oneself the hardships, pain, and suffering that are involved in the spiritual path. This involves a voluntary acceptance of hardships for a higher purpose. The third is a type of patience and tolerance arising from a sound conviction about the nature of reality. In the context of Christian practice this kind of patience would be based on a firm faith and belief in the mysteries of the Creation. Although the distinctions between these three levels of tolerance are found in Buddhist texts, they are also applicable in the Christian context. This is especially true of the second type of tolerance and patience—deliberately taking upon yourself the hardships and pains that are involved in your spiritual path—which seems to come up in the next passage: the Beatitudes from the Gospel of Matthew.

The Sermon on the Mount:
The Beatitudes
Matthew 5:1–10

When he saw the crowds, he went up the hill. There he took his
seat, and when his disciples had gathered round him, he began to
address them. And this is the teaching he gave:

How blest are those who know their need of God;
    the Kingdom of Heaven is theirs.
How blest are the sorrowful;
    they shall find consolation.
How blest are those of a gentle spirit;
    they shall have the earth for their possession.
How blest are those who hunger and thirst to see right prevail;
    they shall be satisfied.
How blest are those who show mercy;
    mercy shall be shown them.
How blest are those whose hearts are pure;
    they shall see God.
How blest are the peacemakers;
    God shall call them his children.
How blest are those who have suffered persecution for
    the cause of right;
    the Kingdom of Heaven is theirs.
[Matthew 5:1–10]

WHEN I READ these lines from the Beatitudes, the first thing that
comes to mind is the following point. This passage seems to indicate

the simple fact that those who are willing to embark on a path and accept the hardships and the pain involved in it will reap the rewards of their commitment. When we speak of a kind of tolerance that demands that you accept the fact of hardships, pain, and suffering, we should not have the erroneous notion that these spiritual teachings state that suffering is beautiful, that suffering is what we all must seek. Needless to say, I do not subscribe to such a view. Personally, I believe that the purpose of our existence is to seek happiness, to seek a sense of satisfaction and fulfillment. However, since we do experience hardships, pain, and suffering, it is crucial that we develop an outlook toward them that allows us to deal realistically with these trials of life so that we gain some benefit from them.

If we examine the nature of suffering, we will find that there are certain types of suffering that are amenable to solutions and can thus be overcome. Once we realize this, we should seek their solution and the means to overcome the suffering. But there are also other types of suffering that are inevitable and insurmountable. In such cases, it is important to develop a state of mind that will allow you to deal with this suffering in a realistic way. By doing so, you may be able to accept these difficulties as they arise. Such an attitude will protect you, not necessarily from the physical reality of suffering, but from the unnecessary, added psychological burden of struggling against that suffering.

One of the most effective approaches to deal with suffering is found in *A Guide to the Bodhisattva's Way of Life*: If the problem is such that there is a way out, a solution, there is no need to worry about it. If, on the other hand, there is no way out or no solution, there is also no point in worrying about it!

These verses of the Beatitudes also seem to point to the principle of causality. While the Sanskrit technical term *karma* would not be used in the biblical context, the general principle of causality, which is behind the doctrine of karma, seems to be suggested here. The verses imply that if you act in a certain way, then you experience a certain effect, and if you do not act in a certain way, then you will not experience a certain effect. So the principle of causality is clearly embedded in the teaching here.

Although all of the major spiritual traditions of the world may not speak of causality in terms of many life cycles, there seems to be a central message based on the principle of causality common to all of these traditions. That is to say, if you do good, then you experience desirable results, and if you do evil, then you experience undesirable results. This fundamental ethical message seems to be inherent in all major spiritual traditions.

As an aside, it is also very interesting to see certain striking stylistic similarities between the Christian and Buddhist scriptures. In the preamble to the Beatitudes, the Gospel states that when Jesus saw the crowds he went up the hill, took his seat, and so on. This is very similar to the way that some of the sutras, the holy scriptures of the Buddhists, begin. The Buddhist sutras state that at a particular time the Buddha was visiting such and such a place, he was surrounded by so many disciples, he sat down, and thus he began his teaching. So there is an interesting similarity in the way these passages unfold.

One of the most difficult concepts involved here, especially for Buddhists, is the concept of a divine being, God. Of course, one can approach this concept in terms of something which is inexpressible, something which is beyond language and conceptuality. But one must admit that, at the theoretical level, the conceptions of God and Creation are a point of departure between Buddhists and Christians. However, I believe that some aspects of the reasoning that leads one to such a belief are common to both Buddhists and Christians.

For example, if one examines the nature of all natural occurrences, common sense tells us that every event must have a cause. There must be certain conditions and causes that give rise to an event. This is not only true of one's own individual life and existence but also of the entire cosmic universe. To our common sense, to accept something as uncaused—whether it is the universe or our own individual existence—is unacceptable. Then here is the question that follows: if this is the case, if one's own existence must have a cause—if even the cosmic universe on that scale must have a cause—where does that cause come from? And if it follows that *that* cause must also have a cause, then we have an infinite regress.

In order to surmount this problem of infinite regress, it is helpful to posit a beginning, a Creator, and to accept certain truths regarding the nature of the Creator: it is independent, self-created, all-powerful, and doesn't require any other cause. Accepting such a beginning is one way to answer the problem of infinite regress.

If one posits such a Creator, and then examines the process of evolution starting from the Big Bang and the whole mystery of the universe, one can quite plausibly accredit the Creator with omnipotence. In addition, if you examine the nature of the universe, you will see that it does not operate in total chaos or randomness. There seems to be an inherent order, an inherent causal principle in operation. Through that, again, it is possible to accredit the Creator with a sort of omniscience, as if the whole process or procedure was planned. From that point of view, all creatures are in some sense a manifestation of this divine force. One could say that the Creator is the *ultimate* and the creation is the *relative*, the ephemeral. In that sense, the Creator is absolute and ultimate truth. But I don't know what Christian theologians would say to this!

Personally, when I look at the idea of Creation and the belief in a divine Creator, I feel that the main effect of that belief is to give a sense of motivation—a sense of urgency in the individual practitioner's commitment to becoming a good human being, an ethically disciplined person. When you have such a concept or belief, it also gives you a sense of purpose in your existence. It is very helpful in developing moral principles.

That is my understanding of Christian theology!

DISCUSSION ABOUT THE GOSPEL READING

Father Laurence: Your Holiness, I would like to thank you most sincerely for your teaching this morning. I speak for myself, and I think for all of us here, when I say that it was very moving for me as a Christian to hear you read the words of Jesus with such purity and deep understanding of their meaning. As we have come to the time for the first panel discussion, I would like to present to you each speaker. The panelists are Robert Kiely, an oblate of our Community and a professor of literature at Harvard University, and Isabelle Glover, also a Benedictine oblate of our Community, and a teacher of Sanskrit. The purpose of the panel discussion is to enable all of us to listen more deeply to the Word that we have already been touched by this morning. The idea of the panel is not to look for differences, but simply to contemplate, with minds as open and generous as possible, both the similarities and the rich differences between our faiths. I shall ask Bob Kiely to begin with a few introductory words, and then we'll begin the discussion.

Robert Kiely: Your Holiness, I would like to add to Father Laurence's words of gratitude for your commentary and readings of the Christian scriptures this morning. Knowing something of your own life story and the history of your people in the twentieth century, I was particularly touched when you read from the Beatitudes, and especially the lines "How blest are the sorrowful; they shall find consolation" and "How blest are those who have suffered persecution for the cause of right; the Kingdom of Heaven is theirs." It is a Christian belief that when Scripture is read by someone with a good heart, it comes to life for all of us again. For me, and I think for many of us here, hearing you read those words did that for us.

One of the things that I wanted to talk a bit about, and ask for your response to, has to do with the Jewish and Christian idea of God, the Absolute, entering into the relativity of history, of time and space. When Christians hear the words that you read today, or any of the teachings of Jesus, the context in which they place those teachings is composed of at least three stories. One is the story of the life of Jesus. No Christian can hear his teaching without remembering that Jesus was born poor, that he was a Jew in an occupied country, that he had a very brief public life of teaching, that he was persecuted, that he was crucified as a common criminal, and that he rose again from the dead. For Christians hearing the words you read, that is the primary context, I think.

Secondly, when we listen to the Gospels, we are aware of our heritage of the history of the Jewish people whose story is also part of our Scripture. It is a history marked by slavery in Egypt, bondage, liberation under the leadership of Moses, who was the giver of the Law, and ultimately of dispersal throughout the world. The third story is always the story of our own lives. So when we think about the words of Jesus, they come to us through narratives that occur through time and in history—personal, national, and theological in the life of Jesus himself. I wonder if you would reflect, as a Buddhist monk, on your reaction to that temporal aspect of Christianity and any possible parallels or similarities with Buddhism.

The Dalai Lama: When we compare two ancient spiritual traditions like Buddhism and Christianity, what we see is a striking similarity between the narratives of the founding masters: in the case of Christianity, Jesus Christ, and in the case of Buddhism, the Buddha. I see a very important parallel: in the very lives of the masters, the founding teachers, the essence of their teachings are demonstrated. For example, in the life of the Buddha, the essence of the Buddha's teaching is embodied in the Four Noble Truths: the truth of suffering, the truth of the origin of suffering, the truth of the cessation of suffering, and the truth of the path leading to this cessation. These Four Noble Truths are very explicitly and clearly exemplified in the life of the founding teacher, the Buddha himself. I feel this is the same case with the life of Christ. If you look at the life of Jesus, you will see all the essential practices and teachings of Christianity exemplified. Another similarity that I see is that in both the lives of Jesus Christ and the Buddha, it is only through hardship, dedication, and commitment and by standing firm on one's principles that one can grow spiritually and attain liberation. That seems to be a central and common message.

Isabelle Glover: Your Holiness, you mentioned "rebirth." In the early days of the Christian church there are many signs that rebirth may have been an accepted belief which is no longer operative in Christian thinking.[51] Could you speak more about that? How important is the teaching on rebirth and karma?

The Dalai Lama: I have heard about this point that you raise, that in the teachings of the early Church there are certain parts of the Scriptures that could be interpreted as implying that a belief in rebirth need not be incompatible with Christian faith. Because of that I have taken the liberty to discuss this point with various Christian priests and leaders—of course, I haven't had the opportunity to ask His Holiness the Pope directly. But otherwise, I've asked many different Christian practitioners and Christian priests about this. I was told by all of them, quite unanimously, that this belief in rebirth is not accepted in Christian doctrine—although no specific reason was given as to why the concept of rebirth would not fit in the wider context of Christian faith and practice. However, about two years ago in Australia, at my last meeting with Father Bede Griffiths (I have met him on several occasions and know him personally), I asked him the same question. I vividly remember the meeting; he was dressed in his *sadhu* saffron-yellow robes, and it was a very moving encounter. He said that, from the Christian point of view, a belief in rebirth would undermine the force in one's faith and practice. When you accept that this life, your individual existence, has been directly created and is like a direct gift from the Creator, it immediately creates a very special bond between you as an individual creature and the Creator. There's a direct personal connection that gives you a sense of closeness and an intimacy with your Creator. A belief in rebirth would undermine that special relationship with the Creator. I found this explanation deeply convincing.

Father Laurence: Your Holiness, I see a connection between the question that Robert Kiely raised and the one that Isabelle just asked, about the relationship between time and eternity, the absolute and the relative. One of the names that Christians give to God is Truth. And all human beings know through experience that truth is something we discover by stages. Truth is emergent; it comes about through phases in an individual's life—whether it is one life or several lives. We also see that there is a historical evolution of religion. There is an absolute core to the teachings of the Buddha and the teachings of Jesus, but the truth of them emerges through history, through reflection. Otherwise there would be no point in having a Seminar like this one. There is always more truth to be discovered. Would you comment on this idea of truth as something which is here-and-now in its fullness, but also as that which is experienced little-by-little in stages?

The Dalai Lama: Buddhist teachings also address the question of how ultimate truth manifests in stages and has a historical evolution, while at the same time it is absolute or ultimate. There's a particular passage in the *Prajñāpāramitāsūtra*, one of a collection of Buddhist scriptures known as the *Perfection of Wisdom Sutras*, that deals specifically with this concept. The passage states that whether the buddhas of the past or future have come to the world, or whether there is even a buddha existing in the world or not, the truth of the ultimate mode of being of things and events will always remain the same. This truth is ever-present; it is always there. However, this does not imply that all living beings will share in that truth—that is, will attain liberation—spontaneously or without any effort, because individuals must experience that truth in a gradual way. So we must make a distinction between the actual existence of the truth on the one hand, and the experience of that truth on the other. It is here that the point of contact between the historicity and the absolute nature of truth can be understood.

You raised an interesting point. How can an absolute principle like the divine Creator manifest in a historical figure like Christ? What exactly is the nature of the relationship, and what are the mechanics that would explain the relationship of the absolute, which is timeless, and a historical figure, which is time-bound? In the Buddhist context, this question would be regarded in terms of what is known as the doctrine of the *three kāyas*, the three embodiments of an enlightened being. Within this framework, the physical, historical manifestations of enlightened beings are seen, in some sense, as spontaneous emergences from the timeless, ultimate state of the *dharmakāya*, or Truth Body of a buddha.

Robert Kiely: Perhaps another way of thinking about this, especially in terms of day-to-day practice and worship, would be to recall the titles or names that Christians give to Jesus and Buddhists give to the Buddha. One of the seeming paradoxes of Christianity is that we call Jesus our Brother and our Redeemer, or our Brother and our Savior. In personal terms, this can mean that we are invited to love Jesus as a human being, as a brother or spouse. At the same time, we believe that he is our savior, our redeemer, so we also worship him as God. These names remind us that Jesus endows us with the capacity to love him both ways, that he brings his divinity into our hearts. Does this correspond at all to the feelings Buddhists have for the Buddha and the names they give to him?

The Dalai Lama: Given that there is such a diversity even among the Buddhist traditions, we should not have the impression that there is one homogeneous tradition, one definitive path as it were. Personally, I prefer to relate to Buddha as a historical figure and personality—someone who has perfected human nature and evolved into a fully enlightened being. However, according to certain schools of thought in Buddhism, Buddha is not just seen as a historical figure, but also shares a timeless, infinite dimension. In this context, although Buddha is a historical figure, the historicity of Buddha Shakyamuni would be seen as a skillful display of Buddha's compassionate action manifesting from the perfected, timeless state of the *dharmakāya*, or Truth Body. Buddha Shakyamuni as a historical figure is known as the *nirmāṇakāya*, which means Emanation Body: an emanation that is assumed in order to suit the mental dispositions and needs of a particular time, place, and context. That emanation comes from a preceding emanation, the *sambhogakāya*, or perfect resourceful state, which has arisen from the timeless expanse of the *dharmakāya*. However, if we go into all of these specifics now, we would have plenty of material for headaches and confusion!

The simplest way to regard Buddha Shakyamuni as a historical figure is as follows. For Buddhists—especially for those who are following a monastic way of life—Buddha was the founder of the Buddhist monastic tradition. He is the origin of the lineage of Buddhist monasticism. Fully ordained monks and nuns within that lineage must maintain complete acceptance of their vows of ordination. In order for someone to be a *bhikṣu*, a fully ordained monk, or a *bhikṣuṇī*, a fully ordained nun, he or she must be a human being. So if you relate to Buddha as a fully ordained monk then that means you relate to him as a historical, human person.

Isabelle Glover: Your Holiness, I would like to ask about your frequent use of the phrase "examine the nature of . . . ." Most of us are not so systematic, I think, as to "examine the nature of" things. How, for example, can we "examine the nature of" a lack of compassion?

The Dalai Lama: For the sake of convenience, a typical Buddhist approach to understanding a particular topic is to classify and subdivide that phenomenon into different classes and categories. For example, mental phenomena may be categorized into various classes: conceptual and nonconceptual, distorted and nondistorted, and so on. Consequently, in Buddhist literature you will find whole lists of various modalities and aspects of the mind, based on its various functions. To give another example, when you examine the nature of compassion, you would first try to define it, try to understand what exactly we mean by "compassion." Then you may ask yourself specific questions in order to enhance the classification. What are the ramifications of compassion in terms of all possible experiences in the human state, its phenomenology? What are the causes and conditions that give rise to such an emotional state? What are the typical emotional responses when you experience compassion? What are the effects of your compassion on others? And so on. And through these analyses you begin to get a sense of what compassion might be like, or *is* like.

When you delve further into Buddhist literature, you also find discussions of different types of compassion. For example, in one type of compassion there is not only a sense of empathy toward the object of compassion, but also a sense of responsibility in that you want to relieve that suffering yourself. That's a more powerful compassion than mere empathy. And degrees of compassion vary according to what concomitant states of mind you have. For example, in the Buddhist context, if you have a deep and profound understanding of the transient nature of life, then your compassion will be all the more powerful because of that wisdom. Similarly, if the sense of self-grasping[52] within yourself is significantly diminished, then of course your compassion would be again more powerful.

In order to make such distinctions, you first need a degree of discernment to perceive the different subtleties. Also, when you examine a phenomenon like compassion, you should not assume that it is just one entity. Just as one condition of mind has multiple aspects. For example, compassion, being an emotional state, shares the nature of consciousness. It is not a physical object; it is an affective state. Thus it is in the nature of experience and so shares the same nature as all emotional states. To use another example, let us examine the identity of a single individual. When you begin such an evaluation, you can immediately appreciate the complexity of that person. One facet of that person's identity is derived from a cultural background, which may be European or American. Based on gender, a person is identified as a man or a woman. Identity is also based on one's country of origin or on religious affiliation. So you see how there are many distinctions, even within the identity of a single person. This is how you examine the nature of any given thing.

Father Laurence: Buddhist training and practice seem to require a great deal of rational analysis, and Your Holiness has said that the great gift of human birth is the mind. Yet one can be compassionate without being clever. Could you help me to understand this? Is it necessary to be very clever and to have a well-trained, educated, and precise mind in order to be enlightened?

The Dalai Lama: No, of course not! As in all things, extremism is always a fault. The Buddhist scriptures describe three categories of people according to individual aptitude in spiritual practice, demonstrating the types of people most suited to derive the greatest benefits from profound spiritual practice. Although I cannot remember the exact quotation, it runs something like the following: ideally, individuals who are best suited for practice are those who are not only intellectually gifted, but also have single-pointed faith and dedication and are wise. These people are the most receptive to spiritual practice. Individuals in the second group are those who may not be highly intelligent, but they have a rock-solid foundation in faith. The unfortunate are those in the third category. Although these individuals may be highly intelligent, they are always dogged by skepticism and doubts. They are clever, but they tend to be hesitant and skeptical and are never really able to settle down. These are the people listed as the least receptive.

When we speak about levels of intelligence, we are talking about a relative phenomenon. A person may be more intelligent when compared to some people, but less intelligent in relation to others. Generally speaking, what seems to be true is that in one's own spiritual practice, any faith or conviction that is based on an understanding attained through a process of reasoning is very firm. Such a conviction is firm because you have convinced yourself of the efficacy or validity of the idea in which you have placed your faith. And this conviction is consequently very powerful in motivating you into action. This is why, according to Buddhism, intelligence is considered to be very important in one's spiritual path. In this tradition, you find intelligence cooperating with the heart, the emotional side. When faith and compassion—which are more in the nature of emotional states—are backed by a powerful conviction arrived at through reflection and investigation, then they are very firm indeed, whereas a faith or compassion that is not based on such powerful reasoning, but is more affective and instinctual, is not very firm. It is prone to being undermined and shaken when you meet certain situations and circumstances. There is even a Tibetan expression that states, "Someone whose faith is not grounded in reason is like a stream of water that can be led anywhere."

Robert Kiely: On the subject of emotional affect and reason, I wonder, Your Holiness, if you might reflect with us on the place of ritual in religion. Ritual has been a source of great disagreement among Christians for centuries. Some believe that ritual, song, incense, candles, colorful robes, and certain prescribed forms make a positive difference in the way we worship. Others see such things as obstacles to worship. Can you tell us about the place of ritual in your tradition?

The Dalai Lama: When reflecting upon the role and importance of ritual in one's spiritual practice, it is important to examine how human beings are affected by their environment. For instance, it seems to be true that certain formalities like rituals assist us in creating an atmosphere that is most conducive to the spiritual state of mind we are aspiring to achieve, and, in that sense, they do have an important role to play. For example, though one may wish to accomplish a particular thing, another person who has made a formal pledge based on such a wish will have a stronger motivating factor, which will have a greater effect on his or her action. Similarly, when through rituals and formalities you create that spiritual space or atmosphere that you are seeking, then the process will have a powerful effect on your experience. When you lack the inner dimension, that spiritual experience that you are aspiring to, then rituals become mere formalities, external elaborations. In that case, clearly, they lose their meaning and become unnecessary customs—just a good excuse for passing time. The great Tibetan yogi Milarepa always criticized formalities and rituals. His writings are full of sarcastic comments on various aspects of rituals here and formalities there!

Father Laurence: I would like to ask you a question, Your Holiness, that arises out of this discussion of ritual as a physical expression of faith, as a way we express belief through our bodies and with our senses. In the past Western Christianity was very dualistic. There was an assumption that body and spirit were in conflict, that the body had to be controlled and dominated by the spirit. Today we see the beginning of a recovery among Christians of an original Christian sense of the friendship of body and spirit. We cannot separate body, mind, and spirit in this life, and therefore they must be friends. I wonder if you might help us to understand the relationship between body and mind from a Buddhist perspective. I may be wrong, but sometimes it seems as if there is even a greater opposition between mind and body in Buddhism than in Christianity.

The Dalai Lama: You are right. In certain passages of Buddhist scriptures, there are statements by the Buddha that give the impression of a dualistic view of body and mind. He states in one of the sutras that the five aggregates are like a burden or load, and the person is the carrier of that load. So the Buddha does demonstrate a sense of dualism between the person and his or her psychophysical constituents. But it does not follow that this is the Buddhist standpoint. The traditional Buddhist interpretation is that the passage really addresses someone who has a philosophical inclination toward a belief in an *ātman*, an eternal, abiding soul-principle. However, the Buddha's own standpoint on the nature of the mind-body relationship versus the identity of the person is the *anātman* doctrine. That principle states that, apart from the psychophysical aggregates or the *skandhas* that constitute the being, there is no separate, autonomous, eternally abiding soul-principle. That is a doctrine that is common and universal to all schools of Buddhism.

Although this is a universal teaching, there are such diverse philosophical viewpoints even among Buddhists that we find there are again divergences of opinion as to what exactly is the nature of the self or the person. Some Buddhist schools identify the person among the psycho-physical aggregates, either as the consciousness or the totality of aggregates and so on, whereas other schools of thought adopt a more nominalist position, maintaining that person or self is a mere designation.

Father Laurence: This may be a good point to pause and meditate. If His Holiness will light the candles, we can all stand, and then we can begin our meditation.

EQUANIMITY
Mark 3:31–35

Then his mother and his brothers arrived, and remaining outside sent in a message asking him to come out to them. A crowd was sitting around and word was brought to him: "Your mother and your brothers are outside asking for you." He replied, "Who is my mother? Who are my brothers?" and looking round at those who were sitting in a circle about him he said, "Here are my mother and my brothers. Whoever does the will of God is my brother and sister and mother." *[Mark 3:31–35]*

THE FIRST THOUGHT that comes to my mind in reading these passages from the Gospel of Mark is that not only do they give us a definition of what compassion is, but they also describe the stages in the development of a consciousness generating that compassion. For example, this passage shows on the part of Jesus a certain attitude of unimportance accorded to his own mother and brothers and sisters. To my mind, this tells us that true and genuine compassion is a compassion that is free from attachment, free from the limitations of personal bias. This is very close to the Buddhist idea of compassion in which, again, there is an understanding that in compassion there is a certain freedom from attachment. As I pointed out in our earlier discussion on the nature of compassion, the precondition for genuine compassion is to have a sense of equanimity toward all sentient beings.

Our normal state of mind is heavily biased. We have an attitude of distance from people that we consider as unfriendly or enemies and a disproportionate sense of closeness or attachment toward those whom we consider to be our friends. We can see how our emotional response toward others is fluctuating and biased. Until we overcome these prejudices, we have no possibility of generating genuine compassion. Even though we might be able to feel a certain amount of compassion toward some people, that compassion, as long as it is not based on profound equanimity, will remain biased, for it is mixed with attachment.

If you look at compassion that is mixed with attachment, no matter how intense and strong that mixed emotion may be, you will realize that it is based on your projection of certain positive qualities onto the object of your compassion—whether the object is a close friend, a family member, or whomever. Depending upon your changing attitudes toward that object, your emotional feelings will also change. For example, in a relationship with a friend, suddenly one day you may no longer be able to see in that person the good qualities that you had previously perceived, and this new attitude would immediately affect your feelings toward that person. Genuine compassion, on the other hand, springs from a clear recognition of the experience of suffering on the part of the object of compassion and from the realization that this creature is worthy of compassion and affection. Any compassionate feeling that arises from these two realizations cannot be swayed—no matter how that object of compassion reacts against you. Even if the object reacts in a very negative way, this won't have the power to influence your compassion. Your compassion will remain the same or become even more powerful.

If you carefully examine the nature of compassion, you will also find that genuine compassion can be extended even to one's enemies, those whom you consider to be hostile toward you. In contrast, compassion mixed with attachment cannot be extended to someone whom you consider to be your enemy. Conventionally speaking, we define an enemy as someone who either directly harms or hurts us, or someone who is motivated to or has the intention to harm or hurt us. The realization that such a person is fully intent on hurting and harming you cannot give rise to a feeling of closeness and empathy as long as such feelings require an attachment to the person. However, this realization that another person wishes to harm and hurt you cannot undermine genuine compassion—a compassion based on the clear recognition of that person as someone who is suffering, someone who has the natural and instinctual desire to seek happiness and overcome suffering, just as oneself. In the Christian spiritual context, this could be extended by thinking along the following lines: just as myself, this enemy shares the same divine nature and is a creation of the divine force. So on these grounds, that person is worthy of my compassion and a feeling of closeness toward him or her. This kind of compassion or feeling of empathy is genuine compassion free from attachment.

The last sentence of this Gospel passage states that "Whoever does the will of God is my brother and sister and mother." According to the literal reading, it seems to give a sense of partiality, a discrimination based on a condition: only those who obey the will of God are my brothers and my sisters and my mother. However, in the Christian context, I think you can approach this passage in a more interpretive way by extending the meaning. Although in literal terms it says that "whoever obeys the will of God are my brothers and sisters and mother," it could also imply that all those who share the divine nature, who have the capacity or potential to follow the will of God, are also my mother and brothers and sisters. This would include or embrace the whole of humanity and underline the unity and equality of all human beings.

In this context, I would like to point out a particular element in the practice of the bodhisattva path that might be suitable for a Christian to practice. There is a special category of teachings and practices known as *lo jong*: thought transformation, or mind training. There is a special way of reflecting upon the kindness of all sentient beings, in this context all human beings, that is described in some of the literature. For example, we can easily perceive the kindness of someone who is directly involved in our life and our upbringing. But if you examine the nature of your existence, including your physical survival, you will find that all the factors that contribute to your existence and well-being—such as food, shelter, and even fame—come into being only through the cooperation of other people.

This is especially true in the case of someone who lives an urban life. Almost every aspect of your life is heavily dependent upon others. For example, if there is an electricians' strike for even just one day, your whole city comes to a halt. This heavy interdependency upon others' cooperation is so obvious that no one needs to point it out. This is also true of your food and shelter. You need the direct or indirect cooperation of many people to make these necessities available. Even for such an ephemeral phenomenon as fame you need others. If you live alone in a mountainous wilderness, the only thing close to fame that you could create would be an echo! Without other people, there is no possibility of creating fame. So in almost every aspect of your life there is the participation and involvement of other people.

If you think along these lines, you will begin to recognize the kindness of all others. And if you are a spiritual practitioner, you will also be aware that all of the major spiritual traditions of the world recognize the preciousness of altruism and compassion. If you examine this precious mind or emotion of altruism, of compassion, you will see that you need an object to generate even this feeling. And that object is a fellow human being. From this point of view, that very precious state of mind, compassion, is impossible without the presence of others. Every aspect of your life—your religious practice, your spiritual growth, even your basic survival—is impossible without others. When you think along such lines, you will find sufficient grounds to feel connected with others, to feel the need to repay their kindness.

In light of these convictions, it becomes impossible to believe that some people are totally irrelevant to your life or that you can afford to adopt an indifferent attitude toward them. There are no human beings who are irrelevant to your life.

I would like to clarify my use of the word "emotion." I've been told that the word "emotion" often has a very negative connotation—a rather base, instinctual, almost animalistic connotation—for many people. However, several years ago during discussions with biologists and psychologists as part of a scientific conference, we discussed the nature of emotion and how we could define it. As a result of long discussions, the consensus was that emotion could be positive, negative, or even neutral. In this way, even from a Buddhist point of view, there is no contradiction in attributing emotion to a fully enlightened buddha. It is in this broader sense that I use the word emotion.

THE KINGDOM OF GOD
Mark 4:26–34

He said, "The Kingdom of God is like this. A man scatters seed on the land; he goes to bed at night and gets up in the morning, and the seed sprouts and grows—how, he does not know. The ground produces a crop by itself, first the blade, then the ear; but as soon as the crop is ripe, he plies the sickle, because harvest time has come."

He also said, "How shall we picture the Kingdom of God, or by what parable shall we describe it? It is like a mustard seed, which is smaller than any seed in the ground at its sowing. But once sown, it springs up and grows taller than any other plant, and forms branches so large that the birds can settle in its shade."

With many such parables he would give them his message, so far as they were able to receive it. He never spoke to them except in parables; but privately to his disciples he explained everything.

[Mark 4:26–34]

THE LAST SENTENCE reminds me of a particular expression in Tibetan called *me ngag pe khyü*, which means imparting the most profound essence of the teachings to only a select few. One could almost interpret this to mean that the speaker is reluctant to reveal the secret because others will then know it. There are several distinct approaches to teaching in the Tibetan Buddhist tradition. One is known as *tsog she*, which is teaching performed in a more public exposition, something that is accessible and open to all. Then there is another type of teaching known as *lob she*, literally meaning "teachings to the disciples." Here the commentary would be much more selective, directed to a select few who can really understand the depth and the import of the messages.

This passage is directly related to the idea of the Kingdom of God. The metaphor used here is that of a seed, and the sprout and plant that the seed gives rise to. The combination of the two—the idea of the Kingdom of God and the metaphor of the seed—indicates to me the possibility of understanding the various stages in the enhancement and perfection of our divine nature that we spoke of earlier. Immediately preceding or succeeding these Gospel passages, there are passages that state that the degree of growth depends upon a number of factors, such as the fertility of the soil and where you plant the seeds. In some locations you will have a greater yield, in other locations the plant grows faster. In some places the plant may grow faster, but it will also die faster. And so on. For a Buddhist like myself, these passages seem to point to a parallel teaching in Buddhism that discusses the diversity among sentient beings and the various degrees of receptivity on the part of individual sentient beings. For example, our belief that buddha-nature is universal and that Buddha's compassion is unbiased and encompasses all sentient beings is similar to the metaphor in the Gospel of Matthew of the sun that rises on good and bad alike. However, while this is true, as there is a difference in the degree of receptivity on the part of individual sentient beings, spiritual growth will also differ from individual to individual.

I find this idea—which is so emphasized and explicitly pointed out in Buddhist literature—very attractive: that there is a diversity of mental dispositions and receptivity, interests, and spiritual inclinations existing among humanity. In Buddhist literature, all Buddhist schools of thought follow the same teacher, Buddha Shakyamuni. However, there is such diversity in the teachings that are attributed to the Buddha—some of them may even seem to contradict each other—that we are prevented from falling into dogmatism. All these various teachings are aimed toward sentient beings' diverse mental dispositions, needs, and spiritual inclinations. And when I understand the truth of this, I am able to truly appreciate the richness and value of other traditions, because it enables me to extend the same principle of diversity to other traditions as well. Given the variety of doctrines that are taught in Buddha's own scriptures, Buddhists make a distinction between the subject matter of a particular scripture and the intention of the speaker. A statement found in a particular scripture does not necessarily correspond to the position of the speaker.

Within Christianity there seem to be a number of diverse interpretations or understandings of the concept of God. During an earlier discussion with Father Laurence on this subject, it emerged that there seem to be not only diverse views in the Christian perspective but also a profound mystical understanding of the concept of God, a way of looking at God not so much in terms of a personal deity but rather as a ground of being. Yet qualities such as compassion can also be attributed to that divine ground of being. Now if we are to understand God in such terms—as an ultimate ground of being—then it becomes possible to draw parallels with certain elements in Buddhist thought and practice, as well as parallels with aspects of the Sāṁkhya school of thought and the notion of Great Brahman (*mahābrahman*) in Hinduism.

We should also be careful not to reduce everything to a set of common terms so that at the end of the day we have nothing left to show that is distinct about our specific traditions. As I mentioned earlier, I feel that it is much more beneficial and useful if the major religions maintain their uniqueness, their distinctive beliefs, visions, and practices. For example, if one were to try hard to draw parallels between Buddhism and the idea of the Trinity, the first thing that might come to mind would be the idea of the three *kāyas*, the doctrine of the three embodiments of the Buddha: *dharmakāya*, *sambhogakāya*, and *nirmāṇakāya*. But while it is, of course, possible to draw parallels and show similarities, I feel we should be careful not to push these lines of comparison too far. Interestingly enough, Father Laurence pointed out that there are many cases in Christian theology in which the Son of God is equated with the Word of God in a discussion of the Trinity: the Father, Son, and Holy Spirit. I immediately thought of a parallel in Mahayana Buddhism in which the *sambhogakāya*, one of the three buddha bodies, is often defined in terms of the perfected speech of the Buddha.

But there is a Tibetan expression which says that an intelligent person can make *anything* sound plausible! So if one is always trying to look at things in terms of similarities and parallels, there is a danger of rolling everything up into one big entity. As I mentioned earlier, I do not personally advocate seeking a universal religion; I don't think it advisable to do so. And if we proceed too far in drawing these parallels and ignoring the differences, we might end up doing exactly that!

Therefore it is crucial that religious teachers teach according to the receptivity, the spiritual inclination, and the mental disposition of each person. One cannot eat a particular food and then say, "Because it is nutritious for

me, everyone must eat it"; each person must eat foods that are suitable for
the best physical health according to his or her own physical constitution.
One must maintain a diet that is most suited to one's individual health
because the very purpose of eating food is to seek bodily nourishment. It
would be stupid or foolish for someone to insist upon eating a specific dish,
when it is not suitable or may be harmful, merely because it is highly prized
or the most expensive.

Similarly, religion is like nourishment for your spirit and your mind.
When embarking upon a spiritual path, it is important that you engage in a
practice that is most suited to your mental development, your dispositions,
and your spiritual inclinations. It is crucial that each individual seek a form
of spiritual practice and belief that is most effective for that individual's
specific needs. Through this one can bring about inner transformation, the
inner tranquility that will make that individual spiritually mature and a
warm-hearted, whole, and good and kind person. That is the consideration
one must use in seeking spiritual nourishment.

The belief in creation and divinity is not universal to all major religious traditions. While there are many traditions that base their practice
and belief on that central premise, there are also certain traditions that do
not. However, what *is* common to all religions is the importance of a firm
grounding of one's spiritual practice on a single-pointed faith, or confidence,
in an object of refuge. For instance, in the case of Buddhism, which is a
nontheistic religion, one single-pointedly entrusts one's spiritual well-being
to the three objects of refuge, the Three Jewels—Buddha, Dharma, and
Sangha—as a foundation for practice. In order to have such single-pointed
confidence and a sense of entrusting your spiritual well-being, one needs to
develop a feeling of closeness and connectedness with those objects of faith.
In the case of theistic religions, in which there is a belief that all creatures
are created by the same divine force, you have very powerful grounds for
developing that sense of connectedness, that sense of intimacy, on which
you can ground your single-pointed faith and confidence that enable you
to entrust your spiritual well-being to that object.

DISCUSSION ABOUT THE GOSPEL READING

Father Laurence: Thank you very much, Your Holiness. The more clearly you define the subtle differences in our religious traditions, the more I feel a kind of unity. I think there is a paradox of unity and difference, and I thank you for sharing your thoughts with us so wisely and with such humanity.

I'd like to introduce the participants in our next panel discussion. Ajahn Amaro, a Buddhist monk from Amaravati, a Buddhist monastery not far from here, and Sister Eileen O'Hea, a sister of Saint Joseph, who works as a therapist in Minnesota in the United States. Ajahn Amaro will make the first comment in our discussion.

Ajahn Amaro: Your Holiness, I'd like to pick up on several themes that were discussed. First of all, I was very impressed by your explanation of detachment in relationship to compassion and how the incident between Jesus and his mother, Mary, was an expression of true compassion. As a Buddhist monk living in the West, I am often asked about non-attachment, as people are very concerned that it is a kind of callousness or hardheartedness. Your explanation is very helpful and one that I hope to use in the future. Rather than *detachment*, however, one way of translating this Buddhist concept might be more a sense of *non-possessiveness* toward other people and things. People can immediately recognize that possessiveness is inherently unwholesome and that a sense of ownership has a sticky quality that brings delusion, division, and other problems. That quality of detachment, which you have described as being invested with compassion and clarity, has that non-possessive nature.

It was also very helpful for us to hear you explain how detachment is actually a non-attachment to the illusory aspect of things and an attachment to truth, so that one is really letting go of a limiting view. I was struck by a very close parallel in this Gospel passage to a Buddhist principle in the Theravadan tradition. In this tradition, when an individual sees the truth, when they enter upon the path and see the Dhamma [Pali for Dharma], then that seeing, that change of attitude, is called the "change of lineage." And what is expressed in the passage from Mark is a change of attitude or "lineage" in which Jesus no longer relates to himself merely as a person whose mother is Mary. When he says "God is my Father," Jesus changes the perspective from one that is based on the individual person to one that is based on ultimate truth.

It is also very striking to see you express that perception as you describe all people as your brothers and sisters. When one stops seeing in a personal way and experiences this kind of detachment, it is like the change of attitude that comes with an awakening. The similarities struck me very deeply. I've also been very touched by your care in saying we must keep Buddhist things Buddhist and Christian things Christian and mustn't try to mix it all together. But I must admit I keep finding myself saying, "Yes, but perhaps they *are* talking about the same things." Having grown up in the West with Christian conditioning but having now spent a number of years as a Buddhist, I have a sort of equal mixture of both sets of principles in my perceptions. And what I find over and over again—partly through the use of contemplative meditation as a basis rather than just scriptural study—is that I am drawn more and more to the possibility that these different ways of speaking are actually referring to identical experiences.

I wonder if you would comment on the value of this view. For example, you brought together the Father, Son, and Holy Spirit, as *dharmakāya, sambhogakāya,* and *nirmāṇakāya.* From my tradition, I would have brought them together as Buddha, Dhamma, and Sangha. In this way, Dhamma represents the ground of being, the *dharmakāya* or refuge in Dhamma. The Buddha is like the manifestation of Dhamma. The words of the Buddha are also called the Dhamma, so the Buddha is the manifestation of this. The Buddha is also called the "One Who Knows," the "One Who Is Aware," and he describes himself as "born of the Dhamma." Then the result of this relationship where the Buddha knows and embodies the Dhamma, the result of that presence of the enlightened mind in the world, is the Sangha, which one can describe as the spiritual community or, we might say, holy communion. It is a communion of many different beings together in harmony. I've considered that perhaps I simply have the kind of mind that likes to make everything fit. But now I have the opportunity to ask! Through my discussions with other Christians over the years, it does seem that we are talking about—if not identical occurrences—very similar phenomena. So when a Christian quotes Jesus as saying "Whoever does the will of God . . . ," can we maintain that practicing the Dhamma is the same as doing the will of God? Or is even thinking that way a misstatement? That was a long preamble, but, finally, there is the question!

The Dalai Lama: Generally speaking, many aspects of spiritual realization—which in the Tibetan tradition are categorized as the method side of the path—compassion, love, tolerance, and so on—seem to be equal in both Christianity and Buddhism. In order to approach your question in a way that contextualizes it in the Buddhist tradition, it must be addressed in a language that is common to all schools of thought within this tradition.

All Buddhist philosophical schools of thought speak about the Four Noble Truths, and they all speak of two realities: the ultimate and the relative. Even the Sāṃkhya school, which is a non-Buddhist ancient Indian school of thought, also speaks of ultimate and relative realities. But when it comes to actually defining the Four Noble Truths and the two realities—their definitions, specific characteristics, and so on—we see profound differences.

For example, from the point of view of the Prāsaṅgika-Madhyamaka school of Mahayana Buddhism, which is based on the interpretation of Nagarjuna's thought by Chandrakirti and Aryadeva, the description of *arhathood*—that is, the state of nirvana or spiritual liberation—as found in the Buddhist Abhidharma literature would not be accepted as a complete or final description of nirvana. From the Madhyamaka view, the characterization of liberation, nirvana, according to the other schools of thought—in terms of identifying the fundamental ignorance, misknowledge, and delusory states that obstruct the attainment of arhathood—is not sufficiently subtle. Therefore, if the delusory states obstructing the attainment of liberation are not properly identified, then the antidotes that are advocated will also not be final. Thus the result that is characterized as liberation or arhathood again will not be final. You can see that even within the Buddhist schools, although they may all use the same terms—arhathood; *śūnyatā,* or emptiness; *mokṣa,* or nirvana; *kleśa,* the obstructing emotions and delusions; and so on—those terms do not always have the same meaning. The terms are the same; the *general* meanings may even be the same. However, because the way you individually recognize and identify them differs in the context of different Buddhist schools of thought, your resulting understanding will be quite different.

So to cut a long story short—just like your preamble!—I feel that there are significant distinctions in the different approaches. And I firmly believe that at a very profound level there is value in the distinctness and uniqueness of these different approaches. One can especially appreciate this in looking at the profound writings of the great masters, such as the great Indian Buddhist writers of the past. These masters were not mere scholars who indulged in abstract intellectual discussion; they were true and dedicated followers of the Buddha who engaged in profound meditative practices. And they not only gained deep realizations and experiences but had tremendous compassion toward their fellow sentient beings. Therefore I believe that the subtleties they have perceived and articulated arose out of their compassion, out of their feeling the need to share with others what they have themselves experienced and realized. I feel certain they did not write about these things to add to our confusion!

Sister Eileen: Your Holiness, it is a great privilege to be in your presence. My question concerns what may be a difference in our traditions. One of the ways we experience the person of Jesus is as a historical figure. But one of the missions of Jesus was to shift our way of relating to God from that of fear or mere doctrine to one of a relationship of love and intimacy. As Christians, we believe in the Risen Christ, the Christ who still lives among us. We believe that we can experience the Christ who is still among us and that this experience is a personal one of love and devotion. As our religious practice deepens, our devotion to Christ deepens. That is why many of us meditate. This experience first begins as any other relationship with another person would begin: we try to get to know that person. In the beginning we tend, even if we admire that person, to see them as an object. Then we come to understand not merely the outward personality but the inner person of Christ. Eventually, we are called to become one with the same consciousness that Christ had. For Christians, this spiritual journey is very personal and intimate. Is there an analogue to this in Buddhism?

The Dalai Lama: There is definitely a parallel in Buddhist practice. As I pointed out earlier, it is just as important in Buddhism as it is in the Christian context that one's spiritual practice be grounded in a single-pointed confidence and faith, that there is a full entrusting of one's spiritual well-being in the object of refuge. In Buddhism, one's practice must be grounded in taking refuge in the Three Jewels—the Buddha, Dharma, and Sangha—and in particular, in the Buddha. In that relationship, there is not only a sense of entrusting your spiritual well-being to the guidance of the Buddha—a fully enlightened, perfected being who has fully realized the enlightened state—

but you are also aspiring to realize that state within yourself. So there are several aspects to the act of taking refuge. Sometimes the phrase "attaining the state of inseparability" with the Buddha is also used. This is not to say that you lose your individual identity, that your identity becomes one with that of the Buddha. Instead it is meant to emphasize that you have reached a stage in which you are like a buddha, a fully enlightened being. So there is that intimacy in the relationship.

Father Laurence: Your Holiness, it seems to me that we are not trying to create one religion, though we are discovering a deep unity. And where there is unity, there are also differences. For example, as you have just said, the Buddhist takes refuge in the Buddha. The Buddha is his or her teacher. The Christian follows Jesus and, like the Buddhist, has devotion and dedication to a particular teacher. The differences exist, I suppose, in the way we understand and describe the nature of the Buddha and the nature of Jesus.

Still, in practical terms, in following a spiritual path or being a disciple, there are many similarities. For example, Jesus tells us that to follow him, we must leave self behind. Now I have personally found in Buddhism great wisdom and clarity in understanding what it means to leave self behind, to go beyond egoism. And I find the same wisdom when Jesus tells us to love one another and to love our enemies. Your talk this morning beautifully and wonderfully explored how that works from a Buddhist perspective.

In the film we saw yesterday, we observed you working on a watch in Dharamsala. Sometimes, it seems to me, through Buddhism, I understand how the watch works. But what we all face, Buddhist and Christian, is the meaning of time. That is not so easily expressed in words. How would you see that image as a way of understanding the relationship between different religions? It seems to me, finally, essential that we understand how Buddhism and Christianity speak to one another, how we understand each other today, because the meeting of these two traditions is so important for the world.

The Dalai Lama: To achieve a meaningful dialogue, a dialogue which would mutually enrich the two traditions, I feel we need a foundation that is based on the clear recognition of the diversity that exists among humanity, the diverse mental dispositions, interests, and spiritual inclinations of the people of the world. For example, for some people, the Christian traditions, which are based on belief in a Creator, have the most powerful effect on their ethical life and serve to motivate them to act in an ethical and sound way. However, this might not be the case for every person. For others, the Buddhist tradition, which does not emphasize belief in a Creator, may be more effective. In the Buddhist tradition, there is an emphasis on a sense of personal responsibility rather than on a transcendent being.

It is also crucial to recognize that both spiritual traditions share the common goal of producing a human being who is a fully realized, spiritually mature, good, and warm-hearted person. Once we have recognized these two points—commonality of the goal and the clear recognition of the diversity of human dispositions—then I feel there is a very strong foundation for dialogue. It is with these convictions, these two principal premises, that I always enter into dialogue with other traditions.

Father Laurence: I think there is a wonderful truth in the idea that a person's individual disposition conditions his or her spiritual journey. But it raises the question whether, if that is the case, any of the traditions can claim an absolute perception of the truth. It seems to me a very modern and perhaps necessary stage of evolution in religious history that we are now exploring the implications of what Your Holiness has been saying. But this is very different from what religions have said in the past!

The Dalai Lama: I would say that even truth need not have only one aspect, but we can have a conception of truth that is multidimensional. This is the case especially from the Madhyamaka philosophical standpoint, in which even the very notion of truth has a relative dimension. It is only *in relation to* falsity, it is only *in relation to* some other perception that anything can be said to be true. But to posit a concept of truth that is atemporal and eternal, something that has no frame of reference, would be quite problematic.

Let us take the case of the diverse teachings given by the Buddha on different occasions, some of which may seem on the surface to be contradictory. For example, Buddha's teachings of "self" (*ātman*) to those who have strong inclinations toward selfhood conflicts with the basic Buddhist teaching on "no-self" (*anātman*). And even the version of the doctrine of *anātman*—the doctrine of no-soul or selflessness of a person—that the Buddha taught to the followers of the lower Buddhist philosophical schools, such as the Vaibhāṣika and Sautrāntika schools, must be regarded as true. This is because, taking into consideration the perception and under-standing of his audience of that particular time, environment, and context, *that was the truth.* That is how the concept of truth has to be understood in Buddhism. A higher philosophical school, such as the Madhyamaka school, would argue that this version of no-self contradicts reason, that that partic-ular view of *anātman* is not the complete, final truth. However, the Mad-hyamaka school would not go to the next step and say that Buddha gave a false teaching. Even they would say that this is a true statement because it is true as far as that particular context and situation is concerned.

But perhaps this is just too complicated!

To sum up all that we've discussed, I feel there is tremendous conver-gence and a potential for mutual enrichment through dialogue between the Buddhist and Christian traditions, especially in the areas of ethics and spiritual practice, such as the practices of compassion, love, meditation, and the enhancement of tolerance. And I feel that this dialogue could go very far and reach a deep level of understanding. But when it comes to a phil-osophical or metaphysical dialogue I feel that we must part company. The entire Buddhist worldview is based on a philosophical standpoint in which the central thought is the principle of interdependence, how all things and events come into being purely as a result of interactions between causes and conditions. Within that philosophical worldview it is almost impossible to have any room for an atemporal, eternal, absolute truth. Nor is it possible to accommodate the concept of a divine Creation. Similarly, for a Christian whose entire metaphysical worldview is based on a belief in the Creation and a divine Creator, the idea that all things and events arise out of mere interaction between causes and conditions has no place within that world-view. So in the realm of metaphysics it becomes problematic at a certain point, and the two traditions must diverge.

However, I do feel that dialogue could promote a better understanding and mutual respect in the areas of ethics, conduct, and metaphysics—in other words, in the areas in which there are many parallels and compatibil-ities, as well as the areas in which there are many diversities and differences. This can be easily appreciated in the area of ethics and conduct, in which there are many similarities and parallels that could enrich the dialogue and give rise to better understanding and mutual reverence. Even in the case of the metaphysical realm, where there are fundamental differences, through dialogue it is possible to transcend those differences by clearly recognizing that those differences exist and yet simultaneously appreciating their common ground in terms of their purpose and effectiveness. While the Christian and Buddhist metaphysical standpoints seem so far apart, they can both lead to the creation of similarly good human beings, who are spiritually mature and ethically sound. Hence, these differences need not divide us.

Sister Eileen: My question is simple, I think . . . . If a meeting between Your Holiness and Jesus could be arranged, would you like that? And what do you think you would ask or discuss during your time together?

The Dalai Lama: For a Buddhist, whose main object of refuge is the Buddha, when coming into contact with someone like Jesus Christ—whose life clearly demonstrates a being who has affected millions of people in a spiritual way, bringing about their liberation and freedom from suffering—the feeling that one would have toward such a person would be that of reverence toward a fully enlightened being or a bodhisattva.

Sister Eileen: Would Your Holiness have certain questions you would like to ask him?

The Dalai Lama: The first question I would ask is, "Could you describe the nature of the Father?" Because our lack of understanding concerning the exact nature of the Father is leading to so much confusion here!

Sister Eileen: Well, now we think it's both Father and Mother![53]

Father Laurence: Perhaps Mary could be at the meeting as well!

The Dalai Lama: Whenever I see an image of Mary, I feel that she represents love and compassion. She is like a symbol of love. In Buddhist iconography, the goddess Tara occupies a similar position.

Ajahn Amaro: Your Holiness, I don't know if I dare ask another metaphysical question . . . . But speaking of differences in our traditions, as a Westerner I've always found it hard to accommodate the uniqueness of Jesus

Christ, to understand him as a completely unique human being, different from all others that have ever appeared in the world. I wonder if you have any reflections that you'd like to offer, since this idea comes across regularly in the Christian scriptures. How do you relate to the idea of the unique, special nature of Jesus?

The Dalai Lama: If you are asking how a practicing Christian should understand the claims of uniqueness of Jesus Christ, then my answer is that it is only by relying on the authoritative scriptures of the spiritual fathers of the past that one may understand the uniqueness that is being described in the Scriptures. But if you are asking my own personal opinion, then I have given it earlier. For me, as a Buddhist, my attitude toward Jesus Christ is that he was either a fully enlightened being or a bodhisattva of a very high spiritual realization.

The following anecdote may not be directly related to your point, but I would like to mention my visit to Lourdes last year as a pilgrim. There, in front of the cave, I experienced something very special. I felt a spiritual vibration, a kind of spiritual presence there. And then, in front of the image of the Virgin Mary, I prayed. I expressed my admiration for this holy place that has long been a source of inspiration and strength, that has provided spiritual solace, comfort, and healing to millions of people. And I prayed that this may continue for a long time to come. So my prayer there was not directed to any clearly defined object, like Buddha or Jesus Christ or a bodhisattva, but was simply directed to all great beings who have infinite compassion toward all sentient beings.

Father Laurence: Your Holiness, I have a question for you from one of the groups who were discussing your talks earlier this afternoon. It is a question arising from what you said about suffering, that certain types of suffering can be surmounted and others cannot. The question from the group is this: how do you tell the difference? Could you comment, from your own experience, about the process of discernment?

The Dalai Lama: I think this is fairly obvious. When you face a problem and try your best to overcome it, and yet at the end you find that the problem is still there, then that is an indication that it is insurmountable. In this sort of discernment, you do not begin with a clairvoyance that allows you to determine that a particular suffering can be overcome or not. That is not the way.

Father Laurence: Thank you. And now I have four very simple questions. They are not only the shortest questions of the day, but also the most difficult. I'll say them all. What is reborn? What is divine in us now? What occurs after death? Does our consciousness create our reality?

The Dalai Lama: I'd like to address the last question first. Individual experiences of pain, suffering, pleasure, and happiness are often, to some degree, creations of our mind. Many of these experiences are actually created by our consciousness; but to go on from there and state that reality is a construct of the mind is to make a very different point. In Buddhism there are certain schools of thought that maintain this view, but there are other opinions as well. From the Madhyamaka point of view, which is the worldview that I personally embrace, the idea that everything is created by consciousness cannot be accepted.

At this point, His Holiness laughingly indicated that each of the different panel members—Ajahn Amaro, Father Laurence, and Sister Eileen—should respond to the remaining three questions: What is reborn? What is divine within us? What is after death?

Ajahn Amaro: What is reborn? From the Theravadan Buddhist perspective there is no fixed doctrinal position. The Buddha described the process of rebirth quite clearly, but he also said that all knowledge is based on personal experience. So when he talks about the idea of death and rebirth in a different realm of existence, this is like a map that he laid out. It is not handed out as something that we as individuals must believe, but more as a pattern that can help describe our experience of reality.

Generally speaking, what is reborn are our habits. That is the essence of it. Whatever the mind holds onto is reborn: what we love, hate, fear, adore, and have opinions about. Our identification with these aspects of the mind has a momentum behind it. Attachment is like a flywheel. Enlightenment is the ending of rebirth, which means a complete non-attachment or non-identification with all thoughts, feelings, perceptions, physical sensations, and ideas. So that when we talk about escaping from birth and death, or the ending of rebirth, enlightenment is really the natural condition of the mind when it's not confused, identified, or caught up with any internal or external object.

What is being reborn from life to life is that in us which identifies with objects blindly. Or in the case of a bodhisattva within the Mahayana tradition—which is stepping slightly outside my tradition, so I stand to be corrected by the people from the northern tradition—he or she is one who chooses to be born out of a sense of compassion, caring for the welfare of other beings. Normally, for most human beings, the process of rebirth happens more by accident than by design. But the conditions of an uncontrolled rebirth are determined by what one clings to. So if a bodhisattva is deliberately born, this will result from the act of deliberately holding onto something. Now, I can pick this leaflet up and hold it, but that holding can be done peacefully. Or, I can cling to it, saying, "This is *my* leaflet!" The latter is identification and possessiveness; it is a blind holding. Rebirth can occur simply by picking up a body and holding it without attachment, and a bodhisattva would pick up a body or a human life in this way. I tend to be a wordy person, but that's as brief as I can make it!

Father Laurence: What is divine in us now? I'll share this question with Sister Eileen to show that Christians have diverse traditions as well. I think the divine is our source, our origin. Saint Paul describes God as the source, the guide, and the goal of all that is. He also says in the Letter to the Ephesians that God knew us and chose us—individually, each human being—before the world began. God is the source of time and space and creation and cosmos; all of this exists in the mystery of God. And so we exist for eternity in the mystery of God. We have come into manifestation, we exist, out of the nature of God, which is to express and to love. I think what is divine and holy in us is our source and origin. We are always one with our origin. Anything that has existence is always one with its origin. That is our holiness and our divinity. That is our goal. The journey from our source to our goal—which is the same place, the same point—is the journey that we are on now. It is the journey of liberation or enlightenment.

Sister Eileen: The Christian teaching has always been that we are made *in* God's image, that we are temples of the Holy Spirit, and that we are already in union with God. But because of our human condition, we don't experience it fully because we are still caught in our minds and our patterns. That is why we meditate and follow our spiritual practice so that we can return to what in Zen Buddhism is called our "original face," to that original experience of who we were created to be. As you were saying, Your Holiness, this does not involve a loss of identity, but it is the experience of oneness in God.

Father Laurence: We'll prepare for meditation now with the lighting of the candles.

In preparation for the chant and meditation, His Holiness and representatives of the audience lit five candles signifying harmony among diverse religious traditions. This was repeated each day. Though extremely modest and simple as a gesture, and performed without pomp or ceremony, the candle lighting took on a curious life of its own, somewhere between improvisation and the most familiar of rituals. Since all cultures and, as far as anyone knows, all religions have always regarded light and especially flame with awe and reverence, the act was charged with a sense of the sacred. Yet precisely because in this instance there was no prescribed ritual context and because candles often have a way of refusing to stand straight or stay lighted, there was about the little moment, as with the entire conference, something spontaneous, not quite perfect, but touchingly human and natural.

When His Holiness resumed his place on a straight chair in the center of the raised platform, the lights were dimmed in the auditorium. He tucked and folded various ends and corners of his robes, shifted and settled his body into a quiet position, took out his beads, closed his eyes, and began to pray. It must have struck many members of the audience who have Catholic mothers and grandmothers how the Dalai Lama's small preparations and especially his completely familiar, comfortable, easy, and tender way with the beads seemed to cut across the divisions of culture and language. The chant itself did not sound at all like a Hail Mary, but the reverence with which it was sung and listened to was unmistakable.

Regarding all sentient beings
As excelling even the wish-granting gem
For accomplishing the highest aim,
May I always hold them most dear.
When in the company of others
I shall always consider myself the lowest of all,
And from the depth of my heart
Hold them dear and supreme.

Vigilant, the moment a delusion appears,
Which endangers myself and others,
I shall confront and avert it
Without delay.

When I see beings of wicked nature
Overwhelmed by violent negative actions and suffering,
I shall hold such rare ones dear,
As if I have found a precious treasure.

When others, out of envy, treat me with abuse,
Insult me or the like,
I shall accept defeat,
And offer the victory to others.

When someone I have benefited
And in whom I have great hopes
Gives me terrible harm,
I shall regard him as my holy spiritual friend.

In short, both directly and indirectly, do I offer
Every benefit and happiness to all sentient beings, my mothers;
May I secretly take upon myself
All their harmful actions and suffering.

May they not be defiled by the concepts
Of the eight profane concerns,
And aware that all things are illusory,
May they, ungrasping, be freed from bondage.[54]

6

THE TRANSFIGURATION

Luke 9:28–36

About eight days after this conversation he took Peter, John, and
James with him and went up into the hills to pray. And while he
was praying the appearance of his face changed and his clothes
became dazzling white. Suddenly there were two men talking
with him; these were Moses and Elijah, who appeared in glory
and spoke of his departure, the destiny he was to fulfill in Jerusalem. Meanwhile Peter and his companions had been in a deep
sleep; but when they awoke, they saw his glory and the two men
who stood beside him. And as these were moving away from Jesus,
Peter said to him, "Master, how good it is that we are here! Shall
we make three shelters, one for you, one for Moses, and one for
Elijah?" But he spoke without knowing what he was saying. The
words were still on his lips when there came a cloud which cast
a shadow over them; they were afraid as they entered the cloud,
and from it came a voice: "This is my Son, my Chosen; listen to
him." When the voice had spoken Jesus was seen to be alone. The
disciples kept silence and at that time told nobody anything of
what they had seen.   *[Luke 9:28–36]*

THESE PASSAGES of transfiguration point toward certain themes
that, again, seem to be common to the major religious traditions of
the world. These common themes include the possibility of having mystic
visionary experiences and the importance of metaphors such as rainbows
and clouds,[55] although in the context of these Gospel passages, the meaning
of these themes may be slightly different because of the uniqueness that is
accorded to Jesus as the Son of God. But generally speaking, from the Buddhist point of view when an individual practitioner reaches a high degree

of realization in his or her spiritual evolution, it is possible that such a transformation can manifest at the physical level as well. We find such stories
about the Buddha in the sutras. As in the Gospel, such stories begin with
Buddha residing at a particular place, at a particular time. His disciples—
principally the two chief disciples, Shariputra and Maudgalyayana—notice
a physical change in Buddha's appearance. A radiance shines from his body
and a distinct smile illuminates his face. Then one of the disciples asks the
Buddha, "I see these changes in you. Why are these changes taking place?
What are the reasons? What thoughts are occurring in your mind? Please
tell us." These parables are similar to the ones we find in the Gospel passages
on the Transfiguration.

The vision of the two prophets Moses and Elijah also corresponds to
the many references in Buddhist literature to mystical incidents in which
an individual comes face to face with certain historical figures. These are
known as *pure visions*. In some cases, these could be genuine contacts at the
mystical level with these historical figures. Or in other instances, they could
be encounters with other beings who assume the appearance or the physical
form of these historical figures. Such contacts can take place.

In order to understand these mysterious phenomena, we must have a
basic understanding of the whole phenomenon of emanation. For example,
the degree of autonomy of an emanation depends upon the level of realization of the individual who is creating the emanation, that is, the emanator.
At a lower level, an emanation created by an individual is to a great extent
monitored and controlled by the emanator, almost as if by computer. On
the other hand, in the case of an individual who has very high spiritual realizations, then the emanated beings may be fairly autonomous. A passage
in one Buddhist text states that emanations created by a fully enlightened
being will also enjoy a very high degree of autonomy. However, this is not
to say that emanations are real, living beings. They are, in some sense, mere
creations of that highly evolved mind. For instance, in the monastic precepts there are four cardinal rules, one of which is not to murder. In the
definition of murder, however, there is the qualification that the object of
killing should be a human being, not an emanated being: thus emanated
persons are not regarded as real living beings.

Even to this day individuals experience mystical visions. Some people
have had mystical experiences in which they have come into contact with
great masters of India and Tibet. I wish that I had such mystical experiences

myself, but—no luck! There are quite a few questions that I would like to ask! If I were to have such mystical visionary experiences, there is much that I would do. For example, if I succeeded in having a visionary encounter with one of the great Indian masters of the past, I would take the side of a scientist, be the devil's advocate, and ask a lot of questions! Even though individuals at highly evolved spiritual states have the capacity to emanate and manifest in various forms, that is not to say that everyone will be able to perceive this vision and presence. For a person to be able to apprehend such visions, he or she needs a certain degree of spiritual maturity, receptivity, and openness. For example, in the passage that recounts the incident in which Peter sees Moses and Elijah, if there had been other people with Christ, it is perfectly possible that some of them would not have seen Moses and Elijah.

If such phenomena of emanations are possible, we may naturally question the mechanics of them. On what grounds can one explain such occurrences? In the Buddhist context, if we explain such phenomena from the viewpoint of *tantra*, which is the esoteric aspect of Tibetan Buddhism, it is possible to give an explanation based on the dynamics of the subtle energies, called *prāṇa*. By means of various meditative techniques, a practitioner is able to gain a high degree of control over these psychophysical energies. In the *sutra* system, which is the non-tantric system, the explanation of these phenomena would be given more in terms of the power of concentration, or the power of meditation. Frankly speaking, these are very mysterious phenomena, and I cannot claim to have any competence in explaining them in detail. I feel these are areas that require a great deal of study and research, as well as experimentation.

Such visionary encounters are experienced on many different levels and may be divided into three principal types. The first type is experienced more at the mystical, intuitive level, in which the encounter is not really actual or tangible but is more like a *sense* or intuition of a presence. The second is a more tangible encounter, but not at the sensory level; it is experienced more at the mental, conceptual level. The third type is the most tangibly real and is a sensory experience. It is like seeing someone face to face with your eyes open. So in terms of degree, the latter is more actual and real than are the former.

There is a similar phenomenon involving mystical visions at the sacred lake of Lhamö Lhatso in Tibet.[56] I have even heard of cases in which foreign tourists have had visions at that lake. However, if there are ten people view-ing the lake at the same time, it is possible that each individual will have a different vision. Or it is even possible that all ten people will see the same image. In certain cases people have even succeeded in capturing the images in photographs. Why are there such differences? It is deeply mysterious. Yet there must be some explanation.

In these passages of the Gospel, there is a reference to *destiny*. This made me wonder whether, in the Christian context, there is a belief that every human being has a unique destiny to be fulfilled.

Father Laurence: Yes. Everyone has a destiny, ultimately, to share in the being of God.

The Dalai Lama: Can one say that, due to certain circumstances, an indi-vidual's destiny could evolve and change?

Father Laurence: Yes, because the individual is free to accept that destiny, or "call," or not. There is a relationship between destiny and free will.

The Dalai Lama: In the Buddhist context, although one might not use the word "destiny," there is the concept of karma, which might be the closest equivalent. Although karma implies a certain degree of compulsion, it also does not rule out the need for certain circumstantial conditions to cause the fruition of the karma. As I mentioned earlier, there are special images—such as clouds and rainbows—that are commonly used in many religious traditions. Of course, there is a scientific explanation as to why rainbows come into being—because of certain conditions of moisture, temperature, and so forth. But I've always been curious to learn about those particular rainbows that do not have different textures of color, that are like a pure white light and lie in a straight line instead of forming an arch. I've always wondered why this is the case!

In the Tibetan Buddhist context, the imagery of the rainbow performs two functions. First, the rainbow is often associated with signs of auspi-ciousness, of good luck and good fortune. In addition, the rainbow is often used as an image to illustrate the illusory and non-substantial nature of all things and events. Interestingly, this Gospel passage mentions a voice com-ing from space. Again, in the Buddhist teachings, we find similar references to a voice coming from nowhere. In Tibet, it is widely believed that around the seventh century, during the reign of King Lha Tho-thori, certain Buddhist scriptures fell from the sky. Some scholars have argued that this was not the case, that these scriptures were actually imported from India. But if the true Indian origin of the scriptures had been revealed at that time, the people would not have revered them. Therefore this myth of the scriptures having fallen from the sky came into being and had a specific function in their spiritual tradition.

THE MISSION
Luke 9:1–6

He now called the twelve together and gave them power and
authority to overcome all the devils and to cure diseases, and sent
them to proclaim the Kingdom of God and to heal. "Take nothing for the journey," he told them, "neither stick nor pack, neither
bread nor money; nor are you each to have a second coat. When
you are admitted to a house, stay there, and go on from there. As
for those who will not receive you, when you leave their town
shake the dust off your feet as a warning to them." So they set out
and traveled from village to village, and everywhere they told the
good news and healed the sick.   *[Luke 9:1–6]*

I THINK THESE PASSAGES point to a very important spiritual ideal that
is common to all religions. That is, that a spiritual practitioner who has
gained a certain degree of realization as a result of his or her long practice
should not rest content. Instead this practitioner should set out and attempt
to communicate it to others, so that they too can share in the experience.
Since the essence of all spiritual practice is the practice of love, compassion,
and tolerance, once you have had a profound experience of these it is natural
that you should wish to share it with others.

In the Buddhist context, when we speak of teachings or doctrines, we
speak of two levels, or two types. One is scriptural, the other is realizational. And just as there are two kinds of teaching, there are different ways
to uphold each doctrine or teaching. The scriptural teachings are upheld
by disseminating them, by teaching them, by explaining their meanings to
others. The realizational teachings are upheld by cultivating that experience within yourself. It is very important that an individual who teaches
others have at least some experience in the teaching, some deeper spiritual

realization. This is totally different from other sorts of communication, such as a person telling a story or a historian narrating some aspect of history. In these cases the individual, based on his or her knowledge, can tell the stories without actually having experienced them. However, in the case of spiritual teachings it is crucial for the teacher to have at least some degree of realization and personal experience.

In this Gospel passage Jesus tells his disciples to take nothing for their journey, not food, stick, pack, or money. Perhaps this reference points to an important spiritual ideal: simplicity and modesty. In fact, in the Buddhist monastic order the very word referring to a monk or a nun connotes someone who possesses nothing and lives on alms. The alms bowl carried by the monks is called a *lhungse*, which means "the container that receives what is being dropped." This name shows that a monk who is living on alms has no authority to express his preference regarding what is given to him. I once had a discussion on the question of vegetarianism with a very learned Sri Lankan monk, and he said that Buddhist monks cannot be categorized as vegetarians or non-vegetarians given that they must live on alms. Whatever food is given must be accepted. This passage also reminds me of a Tibetan expression: if the meditator who is high up on the mountain does not come down, then his food and provisions will climb up to him.

There is a passage in the *Vinaya Sutra*, the scripture that outlines the codes of the monastic way of life, in which the Buddha states that the ideal way for a monk to live is to walk from village to village begging alms. After receiving alms in one village, he should leave and go to another village. The metaphor used here is that of the honeybee who goes from flower to flower, taking honey from each flower in turn without harming any of them. So should monks go from village to village, never causing any damage or destruction.

There are references in this Gospel passage to such phenomena as devils and healing diseases. Similar ideas come up in the literature of other religious traditions as well. I feel that these are terms and ways of speaking that are used at a particular time, in a particular environment, and that take into account a people's belief systems. But an important spiritual ideal is pointed out here: spiritual practitioners should not be complacent about their own levels of realization. It is critical to serve others, to contribute actively to others' well-being. I often tell practitioners that they should adopt the following principle: regarding one's own personal needs, there should be as little involvement or obligation as possible, but regarding service to others, there should be as many involvements and obligations as possible. This should be the ideal of a spiritual person.

The reference in this passage to healing the sick need not be taken literally, in the sense that sickness refers only to physical ill health. Sickness can also be understood in terms of psychological and emotional illness. For me, the association of healing the sick with the telling of good news implies that it is through sharing one's spiritual experiences, through giving teachings and communicating this good news, that one can help others overcome their sicknesses and illnesses. This admonition is quite similar to certain passages found in some of the Buddhist sutras. In some texts, for example, the Buddha, at the conclusion of his teaching, states, "Those who uphold the teachings that I have given you today by putting them down on paper and by reading them and explaining them to others will acquire great merit." This is a similar idea.

Related to this is another very important issue. It is crucial for us as modern-day readers to be able to make a distinction between conversion and the concept of mission. As we discussed earlier, there is great diversity in human dispositions and spiritual inclinations. So if someone tries to impose certain religious beliefs onto a person whose inclination is clearly opposed to it, then this action will not be beneficial, it will be harmful. This sensitivity is very clearly reflected in the Mahayana bodhisattva ideals. For example, according to one of the eighteen bodhisattva precepts, one should not teach the profound doctrine of emptiness to someone whose mental faculty is not suited to it. For if, out of insensitivity, one insists on teaching the doctrine of emptiness to such a person, there is a danger of adverse consequences: instead of helping that person and enhancing his or her spiritual practice, this teaching could lead the person to confusion and possibly even to nihilism. In such cases, rather than accumulating merit by teaching the Dharma, one would accumulate negativity by being insensitive to the needs and suitability of the other person.

In Buddha's own teachings we see this sensitivity to the receptivity of an audience very clearly reflected. For example, there is a list of questions known as *the fourteen questions unanswered by the Buddha*. Needless to say, there are many different interpretations as to how this whole phenomenon of unanswered questions should be understood. For example, one of the questions is "Is there such a thing as a 'personal essence,' or self?" The Buddha did not reply to this either positively or negatively. The question came from a person who had a very strong belief in the identification of the self with an eternally abiding soul-principle. Consequently the Buddha sensed that denying the selfhood of person would lead that individual to experience discomfort and also lead to a nihilism—a total denial of the existence of persons or agents. On the other hand, to affirm the self would again be damaging to that person because it would reinforce his or her clinging to an egoistic, isolated notion of self. Given this situation, Buddha did not give any conclusive response. This shows the Buddha's sensitivity in choosing words that suit an individual's needs.

Once I spoke to an Indian Buddhist monk about the Buddhist doctrine of *anātman*, the theory of no-self, or no-soul. He was a serious practitioner and, in fact, had taken ordination from me. When he first heard that expression, he was so uncomfortable, he was literally shivering; he simply could not relate to the concept. I had to soften the impact with further explanation. It took him a long time to truly grasp the meaning of the *anātman* doctrine. So you see, it is crucial to judge the suitability of what you are teaching to a person's mental dispositions and spiritual inclinations. We do not find in Buddhism a tradition of active conversion—apart from the story of King Ashoka in India who seems to have actively sent out several missionary expeditions in the surrounding countries. Generally speaking, the Buddhist attitude about the issue of spreading its message is this: unless someone approaches a teacher and requests specific teachings, it is not right for a teacher to impose his or her views and doctrines onto another person.

I would also like to comment on another important point related to this Gospel passage. When one is thinking about devils—because this word crops up quite often in many scriptures—it is important not to have a notion of some independent, autonomous eternal force "out there" existing as a kind of absolute negative force. The term should be related more to the negative tendencies and impulses that lie within each of us. I discussed this with Father Laurence earlier today, and he seemed to agree with this interpretation. Otherwise this whole idea of Satan becomes a large area of confusion. Personally, I am quite curious to hear the traditional Christian interpretation of the nature of Satan. I simply cannot imagine it!

DISCUSSION ABOUT THE GOSPEL READING

Father Laurence: Your Holiness, I would like to introduce to you the two panelists who will be discussing with us this morning. First, Lady Maureen Allan, who has been a meditator for thirty years and has been of great assistance as our liaison with the Office of Tibet in London in the organization of this Seminar. And also, Peter Ng from Singapore, who is the chief investment officer of the Singapore Investment Corporation and who, on a more spiritual level, is one of the directors, along with his wife Patricia, of the Christian Meditation Center in Singapore. I would like to ask Peter to raise the first point for discussion.

Peter Ng: Your Holiness, the question I want to put to you is a rather basic one. It concerns the goal and the way of the spiritual life from the Buddhist perspective, as well as how you see single-pointed meditation as helping spiritual development. From the Christian perspective, the goal of our spiritual life, our destiny, as Father Laurence has mentioned, is to share in the being of God. For us the way is Jesus. The supreme commandment or value by which we follow Jesus is the way of love. In fact, as Christian meditators, we understand meditation as a way of love. This is what Father John Main taught us about meditation. Through meditation we come into a personal relationship with Jesus and expand our love so that we can come into the fullness of love, which is God.

From the Buddhist perspective, could you comment on the goal of the spiritual life: is there an equivalent Buddhist teaching of love as the way, and do you see meditation as an aid in that spiritual life?

The Dalai Lama: Perhaps in this context it may be useful to speak about what are known as the *four factors of goodness* and the two goals toward which an individual aspires. One goal is material, worldly well-being on the mundane level; the other goal is the attainment of spiritual perfection or liberation, nirvana. The means by which one attains mundane well-being is through the accumulation of material wealth and comforts, whereas the appropriate means for attaining spiritual liberation and perfection is the practice of Dharma. In your case, these two seem to converge because you are a banker! When Buddhists speak of Dharma, the Tibetan equivalent is *chö*, which means "transformation" or "transforming power." Compassion is, in many ways, the fundamental principle of the Dharma; however, compassion must be combined inseparably with wisdom. It is the union of wisdom and compassion that is the way, or the Dharma.

When speaking of compassion and wisdom, compassion and intelligence, or knowledge, it must be understood that we are talking again about different levels and types of knowledge and wisdom. Generally speaking, there is conventional knowledge that relates to the everyday world of experience, and then there is ultimate knowledge that pertains to deeper aspects of reality. Of course, in the Buddhist context, "ultimate truth" refers to the ultimate nature of reality, which is described as *anātman* (selflessness or essencelessness). In short, when Buddhists speak of the ultimate nature of reality, we are speaking about the doctrine of *śūnyatā*, emptiness.

Generally speaking, there is nothing uniquely Buddhist regarding the meditative practice of single-pointedness and the various techniques that are used to develop this ability. They are common to all the major spiritual traditions in India, both Buddhist and non-Buddhist. What is unique about the application of this faculty of single-pointedness is that it enables and assists the spiritual practitioner to channel his or her mind onto a chosen object without distraction. We need to be clear in our understanding that the *single-pointedness of the mind* is a very generic term, whereas *śamatha*, in Sanskrit, or tranquil abiding, refers to a heightened state of mind. In our daily life, we all experience occasional glimpses of this single-pointedness, and on this basis we can develop this faculty by applying the appropriate techniques in meditation. The fully enhanced and developed state of that faculty is *śamatha*. By applying meditative techniques, and cultivating and enhancing this single-pointedness within you, you may develop not only profound stability in the mind—thus freeing you from the normal state of distraction in which the whole of your mental energy is dissipated and dispersed—but a profound alertness as well. Hence, these techniques allow you to channel your mental energies and develop both stability and clarity. Once you have achieved these two factors, you are able to direct your mind toward the object of your meditation most effectively—compassion, wisdom, or whatever that object may be.

If we look carefully, we find that within our mind there are two principal factors that obstruct us from fully developing this inherent faculty of single-pointedness. One is a distracted, scattered state that keeps your mind in an excited state, thus preventing you from having any stability. This is the principal obstacle to maintaining a profound stability. The other obstacle is mental laxity. Even though you may have overcome mental scattering and found a degree of stability, your mind still may sometimes lack alertness. So you have reached a withdrawn state of mind that may be temporarily free from mental distraction, but there is no dynamism or vitality. It is a "spaced-out" type of mind. In Buddhist terminology, this is called "mental sinking" or laxity. Both of these obstacles must be overcome. When you overcome mental sinking, you attain, in addition to stability, a profound clarity and vitality. And when you are able to join these two forces together, you have the required stability to fix your mind on the object as well as the required alertness to focus all your mental energy on penetrating the nature of the object.

Lady Allan: I'm a perfect description of the scattered mind sitting here, I'm afraid!

The Dalai Lama: Yes, everyone feels this! When we are participating in the panel discussion, I feel that most of our minds are in the realm of scattering. And when we are meditating, they are in the realm of mental sinking!

Lady Allan: One thing I think we have all appreciated so very much in the discussion today is how Your Holiness is an embodiment of happiness. It is a great blessing for Christians who grew up with a legacy of being miserable sinners! Your Holiness spoke of spiritual nourishment, spiritual food, and we would like to thank you for giving us a feast. As regards a question, I would be very grateful if you would take further this idea of the cosmic universe. In the past, science and religion became so very separate, but at the present time it seems there is a possibility of their coming together. In Western Christianity, there is a difficulty in defining or redefining God. I don't think that the people in this room any longer have a picture of an old man high up with a long white beard, though I'm afraid this is probably quite current in parts of the world. Yesterday Your Holiness gave us a wonderful modern description of God, so we're very grateful for that, too. Could you say something more about interdependence, since it's very obvious that we, all of humanity, are physically interdependent now? We've seen the world from the moon. And science is talking more and more about interdependence in nature. But we still don't understand what it means to be interdependent as one mind—mentally and emotionally. I feel that we would benefit from Your Holiness speaking more on that.

The Dalai Lama: In this context, I feel that it is, first of all, quite important to understand what we mean by consciousness. The nature of consciousness, or awareness—*shepa* in Tibetan—is such that it is not at all material; it has no material form or shape or color whatsoever. As such, it is not quantifiable in scientific terms, and it thus does not lend itself to current scientific investigation. Instead of having some material nature, consciousness is by nature "mere experience" or "mere awareness."

When I say, "I know" or "I am aware," there seems to be an agent, "I," who engages in the activity of knowing or being aware; but what we mean by consciousness is that capacity in dependence upon which one knows or is aware. It is, in other words, the activity or process of knowing itself, and as such, it is "mere awareness" or "luminous cognizance." This is because, generally speaking, we associate it with an external object or with a pleasant or unpleasant sensation. That is, whether we are thinking conceptually or simply having a sensory experience, awareness itself arises with the form or appearance of an object, and as a result, we usually do not recognize it as "mere awareness" or "clear, luminous cognizance." In short, in our ordinary experience consciousness becomes caught up with the dualistic appearances of "object" and "subject."

So we could say that we only experience consciousness as colored by the object; the perception is almost inseparable from the object. We know that when we have a perception of a blue object, it is almost as if the perception itself is blue. However, it is possible to bring about an experience of this essential nature of consciousness—this mere luminosity, this mere experience, this mere knowingness, or cognizance, that I spoke of—by consciously trying to empty the mind of its various patterns, concepts, memories, and, most importantly, preoccupations with sensory experiences. So while maintaining a profound alertness, if you are able to put a stop to this turbulence within the mind—the conceptual thought processes and thought patterns chasing after sensory experiences—you can begin to perceive the deeper level. If you are totally withdrawn, that does not help in this process. You must maintain an alertness and gradually stop the fluctuations of thought and sensory experiences within your mind. Then it is possible to have a glimpse of the nature of the mind. Initially, when you first experience this nature, you experience it as only a type of vacuity. But it is possible, through practice, to extend that period. Slowly, as you progress in your meditation, you are able to extend the duration of the experience. And then the nature of mind, this clarity and cognizance, will become more and more apparent. This is how it is possible to recognize the nature of consciousness in contrast to the consciousness that is linked to physical reality.

As to the interdependence of consciousness and matter, Buddhists would explain it is the mind and the motivations that come from the mind that actually determine an individual's actions and behavior. Any action, regardless of its significance, has an effect and leaves an imprint in the mind. And this action immediately affects the experience and the very world in which the individual is living. As far as that individual is concerned, the world has changed. It is on this basis that Buddhists explain the interdependent nature of mind and matter, or mind and body. Of course, in Buddhism, the term *karma* would be used. Although the doctrine of karma itself speaks about the imprint, or potential, left on the mind—how the potential is carried, and how the dynamism of that potential works—the crucial point is really the action or the behavior that is motivated by a state of mind.

In Buddhism, especially in Madhyamaka Buddhism, the principle of interdependence is understood in three ways. The first is in terms of cause and effect. In this case interdependence is linear: certain causes and conditions bring about certain results. This interdependence of causes and conditions is common to all Buddhist schools. There is a second level of understanding in which interdependence is understood more in terms of mutual dependence, in which the existence of certain phenomena is mutually dependent upon other phenomena. There is a kind of interconnectedness. This is very clearly reflected in the idea of "whole" and "parts." Without parts there cannot be a whole; without a whole there cannot be parts. There is a mutual dependence. A third understanding of the principle of interdependence is more in terms of identity: the identity of a particular event or object is dependent upon its context or its environment. In some sense identity is regarded as emergent: it is not absolute, it is relative. Certain things and events possess identity in relation to other things and events. These are the three levels, or three different ways, in which the principle of interdependence is understood.

Father Laurence: I would like to follow up on that wonderful description of consciousness and apply it to Christian understanding, in particular to "the mind of Christ." Christians believe that the human consciousness of Christ is with us and within us. The essential Christian experience that we enter through meditation is the opening of our consciousness to Christ's consciousness. We believe that the mind of Christ *now*, the human consciousness of Christ *now*, is in the condition you describe as one of absolute purity and undistracted oneness. Now if I could just very briefly describe one way that a Christian would understand how this encounter and knowledge of Christ brings about our personal liberation and fulfillment of our destiny, maybe Your Holiness could comment.

The stages by which a Christian comes to know Christ begin in childhood with stories that we hear, reading the Gospel stories that you have been reading with us; then later we come to a theological, philosophical, and historical understanding and knowledge of Jesus. Then, through meditation, we begin to experience the *indwelling*,[57] the fact that Jesus is not only a historical teacher from the past, but now has an inner existence within each human being, as well as a cosmic presence. He is beyond all time and space, and so he is in *all* time and in *all* space. But then to understand fully how Christ is our teacher, our Way, we need to go back to the Scriptures in which Jesus tells us that he is the Way and describes himself as a door. We walk through the door. He is a gate through which we pass. He does not point to himself, but always to the Father. So, for example, we say in the Mass that we go to the Father "in Jesus, with him and through him." In that sense, Jesus would be the teacher, the guru, the Way through the indwelling of his consciousness in us. This is the presence of divine love. His consciousness being fully at one with divine love is an experience of love for us. Could you comment on this exposition of consciousness?

The Dalai Lama: Being very mindful of my comments yesterday about the importance in noting the subtle differences at a very profound level between religious traditions, I definitely see a parallel here in Buddhist practice. However, this parallel should not be taken to the extreme. There is a Tibetan expression that states, "Don't try to put a yak's head on a sheep's body." Similarly, Nagarjuna, a famous second-century Indian master, stated in one of his philosophical writings that if one was determined to equate two things, one could find points of similarity between anything! Carried to the extreme, the whole realm of existence would turn into a single entity, just one thing.

Being mindful of these points, however, I do see a parallel here in the Buddhist practice. In Buddhism there is the idea of buddha-nature called the *tathāgata-garbha*, the seed of perfection. Although there are divergent opinions as to the nature of this seed of buddhahood, or buddha-nature, it points toward the nature of mind, a quality that exists in all of us. And the *tathāgata-garbha* relates to this mere luminosity, the pure nature, the potential that makes it possible for us to overcome imperfections and attain liberation. One of the grounds on which the presence of buddha-nature in all people is argued is the human capacity for empathy. Some people may have a stronger force, others less; but all of us share this natural capacity to empathize. This buddha-nature, this seed of enlightenment, of perfection, is inherent in all of us. It is not something that needs to be newly cultivated; it is there, ever present.

To attain perfection, however, it is not enough that a spiritual practitioner merely possess such a nature; this nature must be developed to its fullest potential. And to accomplish this, you require assistance. In Buddhist practice, you require the assistance of an enlightened guide, a guru or teacher. Interestingly enough, the Buddhist texts often describe one's teacher as the gateway through which you receive the blessings from the Buddha: through this gateway you have communication or contact with the Buddha. It is through a combination of the teacher's experienced guidance and the presence of this buddha-nature within you that this buddha-nature is activated, and you are able to perfect it and answer to its full potential. I feel this is very similar to the idea that Father Laurence just mentioned.

For Christian practitioners—although all of us share this divine nature— it is through the Christ, through Jesus, that you activate, fully utilize, and perfect this divine nature within you. Through Jesus it comes into full bloom and becomes unified, one, with the Father. Interestingly, even in the Buddhist context, the full realization of buddhahood—enlightenment—is sometimes also described as becoming of "one taste" with the expanse of the *dharmakāya*. To become of "one taste" is to become inseparable with the *dharmakāya* state. However, that is not to say that individual identities do not remain.

Father Laurence: Thank you. That is very enlightening, and I think the yak's head stays on the yak.

Peter Ng: Your Holiness, I would like to ask a question that is related to the Gospel passage on the Christian mission. This concerns your encouragement to spiritual practitioners to share spiritual teaching with others to help them to grow spiritually. But, at the same time, you said it is necessary for a person who wants to share the spiritual teaching to have had some experience, to have some deeper understanding of what they are teaching. This is a question of great interest to many of us here who are Christian Meditation Group leaders because we are sharing this teaching with others. How do we know whether we are competent to be a meditation group leader?

The Dalai Lama: Generally speaking, except in cases of self-delusion, it is possible to judge one's level of mind, not necessarily in full detail, but to a great extent. If a person who is leading or teaching is a true and genuine practitioner, it is certain that this person's motivation will be pure—and one's motivation is an extremely important factor. This is how an individual may judge his or her own state of mind and suitability as a teacher. It is extremely difficult for a third person to judge whether or not someone is suited to that role. Generally speaking, it is extremely difficult, if not impossible, for a person to judge the spiritual level of another person. This is because another person's spiritual level or realization is in some sense totally closed to you. However, it is possible to judge that person's level of spirituality in very broad terms. When you associate with a person for a long time, you can occasionally perceive the spiritual level of a person by observing that person's behavior—mannerisms, speech, the way he or she interacts with others, and so on.

And it is not enough that you have seen someone behaving in a very spiritual way just once. This must be a consistent behavior—something that can withstand repeated observation. When you continue to see such characteristics, then you can infer there is a degree of spiritual maturity. In the sutras, Buddha gives the beautiful analogy of the ocean. He says that when you are looking into the ocean trying to locate a fish, you will not be able to find one while the ocean is still and the fish are under the water. But when a wave comes, you will occasionally be able to glimpse the fish. Similarly, he states that a bodhisattva's level of realization, particularly his or her level of compassion, can be glimpsed—perhaps not definitively but through inductive reasoning—by assessing the way he or she responds to particular situations, environments, and instances.

Father Laurence: There is a question from the floor that we might use to end our session now. The question is from one of the discussion groups and has to do with nonviolence. They ask if compassion has an active element, or if it is passive? Could compassion ever require violent action? I suppose the idea is that if you saw someone about to commit an evil act—for example, blow up a building—could you, out of compassion, use violence to stop them?

The Dalai Lama: It is definitely the case that there is an active element in compassion, and the possibility is open to use force, if it is deemed really necessary. This is clearly demonstrated in the *Jataka Tales*, in a story of one of the Buddha's previous lives in which he was born as a merchant. When crossing a river on a ferry, the bodhisattva found himself in a most difficult situation: the ferryman was a murderer and planned to kill all 499 passengers in the night. There was no other possible way that the bodhisattva could deal with the situation except by getting rid of this murderer. He took upon himself the responsibility to do just that. This bodhisattva engaged in an act that not only saved the lives of 499 people, but also, out of compassion, saved the potential murderer from the necessity of facing the negative consequences of killing so many people. For a Buddhist, the bodhisattva's sacrifice was to take upon himself the negative act of killing a person and to face the consequences of that act.

However, having said that, when we talk about violence, we must understand that we are speaking about a phenomenon in which it is almost impossible to predict the outcome. Even though the motivation on the part of the perpetrator of the act may be pure and positive, when violence is used as a means, it is very difficult to predict the consequences. For this reason, it is always better to avoid a situation that may require violent means. Nevertheless, if you find yourself in a situation in which you must clearly act in a forceful way in defense, then you must make the appropriate response. In this context it is important to understand that tolerance and patience do

not imply submission or giving in to injustice. Tolerance, in the true meaning of the word, becomes a deliberate response on your part to a situation
that would normally give rise to a strong negative emotional response, like
anger or hatred. This can be seen in the Tibetan term for patience, *sopa*,
which literally means "able to withstand."

This is especially the case with the tolerance of being indifferent to harms
that are inflicted upon one, which is one of the three kinds of patience discussed earlier. One might misinterpret this to mean that we should give in
or submit ourselves to whatever harm someone else might inflict on us—
one might think it means that we should just say, "Go right ahead and hurt
me!" But this is not what this kind of tolerance is. Rather, it is a courageous state of mind that prevents us from being adversely affected by that
incident; it helps to keep us from experiencing mental suffering when we
encounter harm. It does not mean that we just give up.

It is understandable that people have misconceptions of tolerance. I have
met some Tibetans who have read *A Guide to the Bodhisattva's Way of Life*,
which deals extensively with the practice of tolerance, and they have said
to me, "If we practice tolerance, Tibet will never regain its independence!"
But they are misunderstanding tolerance to mean some kind of submission
or withdrawal.

FAITH
John 12:44–50

Father Laurence: Welcome again, Your Holiness. In this session, His Holiness will be reading and commenting on the last two Gospel passages, both from the Gospel of Saint John. The first concerns faith and the second contains the account of the Resurrection.

Jesus proclaimed: "To believe in me, is not to believe in me but in him who sent me; to see me, is to see him who sent me. I have come into the world as light, so that no one who has faith in me should remain in darkness. But if anyone hears my words and disregards them, I am not his judge; I have not come to judge the world, but to save the world. There is a judge for anyone who rejects me and does not accept my words; the word I have spoken will be his judge on the last day. I do not speak on my own authority, but the Father who sent me has himself commanded me what to say and how to speak. I know that his commands are eternal life. What the Father has said to me, therefore, that is what I speak." *[John 12:44–50]*

THESE PASSAGES FROM the Gospel of John seem to be an important section of the Bible. When I read them, the first thing that strikes me is a close resemblance to a particular passage in the Buddhist scriptures in which the Buddha states that whoever sees the principle of interdependence sees the Dharma and whoever sees the Dharma sees the *Tathāgata*, the Buddha. The implication is that through understanding the nature of interdependence, through understanding Dharma, you will understand the true nature of buddhahood. Another point this raises is that simply having a visual perception of the Buddha's body does not correspond to actually seeing the Buddha. In order to actually see the Buddha, you must realize that the *dharmakāya*—the Truth Body of the Buddha—is suchness. This is what it means to actually see the Buddha. Similarly, these passages point out that it is through the historical personification of the Christ that you are actually experiencing the Father that he represents. Christ is the gateway to this encounter with the Father.

Here again we see the metaphor of light, which is a common image in all the major religious traditions. In the Buddhist context, light is particularly associated with wisdom and knowledge; darkness is associated with ignorance and a state of misknowledge. This corresponds to the two aspects of the path: there is the method aspect, which includes such practices as compassion and tolerance, and the wisdom, or knowledge, aspect, the insight penetrating the nature of reality. It is the knowledge, or wisdom, aspect of the path that is the true antidote to dispelling ignorance.

Since these passages also seem to point out the importance of faith in one's spiritual practice, I think it might be useful here to give some explanation of the Buddhist understanding of faith. The Tibetan word for faith is *day-pa*, which perhaps might be closer in meaning to confidence, or trust. In the Buddhist tradition, we speak of three different types of faith. The first is faith in the form of admiration that you have toward a particular person or a particular state of being. The second is aspiring faith. There is a sense of emulation; you aspire to attain that state of being. The third type is the faith of conviction.

I feel that all three types of faith can be explained in the Christian context as well. For example, a practicing Christian, by reading the Gospel and reflecting on the life of Jesus, can have a very strong devotion to and admiration for Jesus. That is the first level of faith, the faith of admiration and devotion. After that, as you strengthen your admiration and faith, it is possible to progress to the second level, which is the faith of aspiration. In the Buddhist tradition, you would aspire to buddhahood. In the Christian context you may not use the same language, but you can say that you aspire to attain the full perfection of the divine nature, or union with God. Then, once you have developed that sense of aspiration, you can develop a deep conviction that it is possible to perfect such a state of being. That is the third level of faith. I feel that all of these levels of faith are equally applicable in both the Buddhist and Christian contexts.

In Buddhism we find a repeated emphasis on the need for both faith and reason on the spiritual path. Nagarjuna, a second-century Indian master, states in his famous text, the *Precious Garland*,[58] that a spiritual aspirant requires both faith and reason, or faith and analysis. Faith leads you to a higher state of existence, whereas reason and analysis lead you to full liberation. The important point is that the faith one has in the context of one's own spiritual practice must be grounded in reason and understanding.

In order to develop a faith derived through reason or through understanding, a beginning spiritual aspirant should be open-minded. For want of a better word, we can call it a state of healthy skepticism. When you are in that state of openness, you are able to reason, and through reasoning you can develop a certain understanding. When that understanding is strengthened, it gives rise to a conviction, belief, and trust in that object. Then that faith, trust, or confidence will be very firm because it is rooted in reason and understanding. Because of this, we find in Buddha's own scriptures an admonishment to his followers that they should not accept his words simply out of reverence to him. He suggests that his followers put all of his words to the test, just as a goldsmith tests the quality of gold through rigorous procedures. And it is only as a result of one's own understanding that one should accept the validity of his teachings.

In this Gospel passage, there is a reference to light dispelling darkness, which is immediately followed by a reference to salvation. To connect these two ideas, I would say that the darkness of ignorance is dispelled by true salvation, the state of liberation. In this way it is possible to understand the meaning of salvation even in the Christian context.

Determining the exact nature of salvation is a complex issue. Among the various religious schools of thought in ancient India, there were many religious traditions that accepted some form of the notion of salvation. The Tibetan word for salvation is *tharpa*, which means "release" or "freedom." Other traditions do not subscribe to such notions. Some schools maintain that the delusions of the mind are inherent and intrinsic and are thus part of the essential nature of the mind. In their view, there is no possibility of liberation because negativities and delusions are inherent to the mind and cannot be separated from it. Even among those who accept some idea of salvation, or liberation, there are differences between the actual definitions or characterizations of the actual state of salvation. For example, in certain ancient Indian schools the state of salvation is described more in terms of an external space or environment with positive characteristics, shaped like an upturned parasol.

However, while certain Buddhist traditions may accept the notion of salvation, they view it more in terms of a person's individual spiritual or mental state, a state of perfection of the mind, rather than in terms of an external environment. Buddhism does accept the notion of different pure lands of the buddhas, pure states that come into being as a result of the positive karmic potentials of the individual. It is even possible that ordinary people can be reborn and participate in the buddhas' pure lands. For example, from a Buddhist point of view, our physical environment—this earth or planet—cannot be said to be a perfected realm of existence. But within this realm one can say that there are individuals who have attained nirvana and full enlightenment. According to Buddhism, salvation or liberation should be understood in terms of an internal state, a state of mental development.

What is the Christian meaning of heaven?

Father Laurence: Heaven is the experience of sharing the joy, the peace, and the love of God to the fullness of human capacity.

The Dalai Lama: So there is not necessarily an association with a physical space?

Father Laurence: No. Only in dreams.

The Dalai Lama: Similarly can one by extension understand the notion of hell also in terms of a very negative, deluded state of mind?

Father Laurence: Yes, certainly.

The Dalai Lama: So that means that we need not think of heaven and hell in terms of an external environment?

Father Laurence: No. Hell would be the experience of separation from God, which in itself is unreal. It is illusory because nothing can be separated from God. However, if we think we are separated from God, then we are in hell.

The Dalai Lama: In the Gospel passage, Jesus says, "I have not come to judge . . . the word I have spoken will be his judge . . . ." I feel this closely reflects the Buddhist idea of karma. There is not an autonomous being "out there" who arbitrates what you should experience and what you should know; instead, there is the truth contained in the causal principle itself. If you act in an ethical or disciplined way, desirable consequences will result; if you act in a negative or harmful way, then you must face the consequences of that action as well. The truth of the law of causality is the judge, not a being or person who is handing out judgments.

How would you interpret this?

Father Laurence: There is a poetical metaphor in the Bible in which God punishes humanity for its sins. But I think the teaching of Jesus takes us beyond that image of God as one who punishes and replaces it with an image of God as one who loves unconditionally. Sin remains. Sin is a fact. Evil is a fact. But the punishment that is associated with sin is inherent in sin itself. Instead of emphasizing causality, although that seems logical, I think that a Christian would instead emphasize free will. We have free will in these matters, at least to some degree.

9

THE RESURRECTION
John 20:10–18

So the disciples went home again; but Mary stood at the tomb weeping. As she wept, she peered into the tomb; and she saw two angels in white sitting there one at the head, and one at the feet, where the body of Jesus had lain. They said to her, "Why are you weeping?" She answered, "They have taken my Lord away, and I do not know where they have laid him." With these words she turned round and saw Jesus standing there, but did not recognize him. Jesus said to her, "Why are you weeping? Who is it you are looking for?" Thinking it was the gardener, she said, "If it is you sir, who removed him, tell me where you have laid him, and I will take him away." Jesus said, "Mary!" She turned to him and said, "Rabbuni!" (which is Hebrew for "My Master"). Jesus said, "Do not cling to me, for I have not yet ascended to my Father. But go to my brothers, and tell them that I am now ascending to my Father and your Father, my God and your God." Mary of Magdala went to the disciples with her news: "I have seen the Lord!" she said, and gave them his message.   *[John 20:10–18]*

THIS IS A very appropriate passage to read at the ending session of this Seminar. The Buddha's *parinirvāṇa*, or final nirvana, is seen as the last major act of his life, and this reading from the Gospel of John seems to have a similar meaning.

For someone who believes in rebirth, whenever you speak about death you are also speaking about rebirth. Rebirth can only come into being when death has preceded it. We had a brief discussion of this earlier today—what seems again to be common in most of the major religious traditions of the world is that the lives of the founding masters seem to demonstrate the importance of taking upon oneself the experience of suffering and recognizing the value of suffering.

In a discussion with me earlier today, Father Laurence mentioned that Father Bede Griffiths spoke about the distinctions between the physical body, the subtle body, and the spiritual body associated with Jesus. Before Jesus' death his body is the physical body; during the Resurrection, before ascending to the Father, it is the subtle body; and in the aftermath of the Ascension to the Father, it is the spiritual body. In Buddhism there are extensive discussions about various types of embodiments, such as the subtle body, mental body, and spiritual body. However, there is one major difference when comparing the subtle body of Jesus with the one described in Buddhist texts. In the Buddhist descriptions of the degrees of subtleties in one's embodiment, there are stages in the spiritual evolution of an individual, starting from the state of an ordinary being and moving toward a full enlightenment, whereas in the case of Jesus, we are referring to someone who is unique, who is the Son of God. So the process of stages does not apply. Jesus Christ does not progress through a series of spiritual stages, isn't that the case?

Father Laurence: No, the Resurrection is not reincarnation.

The Dalai Lama: We are not talking about reincarnation here. We are talking about an individual practitioner. As his or her spiritual progress advances, even that person's physical embodiment becomes subtler and subtler.

Father Laurence: Before his death Jesus was present to his disciples and to the world in a certain way; and after his death he is present to the world in a different way. We see in his historical presence to the world, in his meeting with Mary, for example, a presence that must be recognized. There must be a new kind of perception on the part of the practitioner to recognize the new presence of Jesus. In the Gospel, we read of an intermediate stage between his death and Resurrection and his Ascension. And the way that Jesus is present now in the world is different still from this description. Today we would say that he is present through the Holy Spirit.

The Dalai Lama: In the case of Buddhism, again, we find a divergence of views in the understanding of Buddha's final nirvana. One school of thought—principally in the ancient Indian *Vaibhāṣika* school—maintains that Buddha's nirvana constitutes the end of Buddha's existence. Just as his coming into being was a historical fact, his passing away was a historical fact; Buddha's life began and ended there. The final nirvana is seen like the last moment of a flame. When you extinguish the flame, that's the end of the flame; there is total nothingness. Even the continuation of the Buddha's consciousness ceases. Followers of the *Vaibhāṣika* school maintain that consciousness, although it is beginningless, has an end. It can cease to exist.

Then the question is raised, if that is the case, what point is there for the followers of the Buddha to venerate and worship and pray to him? What is the benefit? What point is there in doing such a thing if the Buddha is no more? The response given by this tradition is that the Buddha attained full enlightenment as a result of accumulating merits and perfecting his wisdom through innumerable eons. And during this time Buddha developed and cultivated a very forceful, altruistic intention to be of benefit and service to all. The power of that energy and truth is still there. It is this power that assists and helps when you worship and venerate the Buddha. However, insofar as the historical person of the Buddha is concerned, that was the end.

This is not, however, the standpoint of many other Buddhist traditions, including Tibetan Buddhism. According to the Tibetan Buddhist tradition, buddhahood, or full enlightenment, should be understood more in terms of the doctrine of the three *kāyas*, the three embodiments. From that point of view, Buddha Shakyamuni was a historical figure—he existed at a particular time and in a particular space, context, and environment—and his final nirvana at Kushinagar was a historical event. But Buddha's consciousness and mindstream has continued and is ever-present. Buddha, in the emanation form of a human being, may have ceased; but he is still present in the form known as his *sambhogakāya*, the state of perfect resourcefulness. And he continues to emanate and manifest in various forms that are most suited and beneficial to other sentient beings. From that point of view, although Buddha Shakyamuni as a historical figure has ceased to exist, Buddha's presence is still there. From the point of view of this tradition, consciousness is both beginningless and endless in terms of its continuity.

For a practicing Buddhist, Buddha's final nirvana has a very symbolic meaning because the last words uttered by the Buddha were on the doctrine of impermanence and the transient nature of all things. He stated that all things and events are transient, impermanent, and non-enduring.

He also stated that the body of a fully enlightened being—the Buddha, or *Tathāgata*—is also impermanent and subject to the same laws. And with these words, he passed away. So for a practicing Buddhist, the Buddha's final nirvana, the historical act of passing away, reemphasizes the importance of the practice of impermanence.

I am intrigued by the sentence in the Gospel in which Jesus states, "I have not yet ascended to my Father." I am curious to know how the Ascension is explained in Christian theology.

Father Laurence: Earlier in the Gospel of John, Jesus says, "I know where I have come from, and I know where I am going." He describes his life, his mission, as a return to his source. Everywhere he says, "I have come from the Father . . . ." His Ascension is the reintegration of his fully developed humanity with his source in the Father, in God. In a sense, the Ascension is the full integration of the divinity and the humanity of Jesus.

The Dalai Lama: In Buddhism it is thought that there is a special relationship between the emanation and the emanating force, and that an emanation comes to an end when it has fulfilled its destiny. There is an idea that the emanation is reabsorbed into its source, although in some cases the emanation disappears of its own accord. For example, in the case of the historical Buddha Shakyamuni, after his final nirvana the physical body of the Buddha was clearly there; the Buddha's body was cremated, and everybody could see it. A practicing Buddhist would say that the Buddha's consciousness, the Buddha's own transcendent mind, had reentered or been reabsorbed into the *dharmakāya* state. In some Buddhist texts there are also references to another sort of phenomenon—highly evolved spiritual beings who are actually able to go to different pure realms without having to discard their physical bodies.

Father Laurence: As another way of understanding the Resurrection in the Christian sense, these are wonderful insights, which are very inspiring. I think the Christian's understanding of the Resurrection also involves a cosmic dimension. Jesus is the embodiment of God in human form, and through this Word of God, the Creation, or the cosmos, came into being. Now when the human form of Jesus dies, a process takes place that anticipates what is going to happen to the whole cosmos. The human bodily form of Jesus is reabsorbed in its total physical energy and form into the source of the universe, into God. This is eventually going to happen to the whole cosmos. Everything in the cosmos came from God, is an emanation of God, and will return to God. So I think what we see in the Resurrection is a transformation of matter back into its original source. That happens to the body of Jesus in his human form—body, mind, and spirit—but it is also an anticipation of what will happen to the whole cosmos in time, at the end of time.

Your Holiness, as we come to this final session of our Seminar, I speak for all of us when I say it will take us two lifetimes—or more!—to absorb all that you have so wonderfully given us. I would like to put before you some of the questions that the participants have contributed individually and in their small groups. It has been necessary to be somewhat selective and sort them by type, as many of them cover the same ground. I also thought we'd like to begin by giving our attention, as we did at the start of this Seminar, to the people and nation of Tibet that you represent and embody, and to assure you of our wholehearted support for your cause of peace and justice.

One of the questions that was presented touches on the idea of sacred space and of a holy land. It arose out of your previous comments on pilgrimage. You spoke about the benefit of visiting various holy sites. The question we would like to put before you is, what do you think makes a place holy?

The Dalai Lama: I feel that a place initially becomes holy by the power of the individual spiritual practitioner who lives there. The power of an individual's spiritual realizations in some sense "charges" that place, provides it with certain energy; then in turn, that place can "charge" the individuals who visit it. Secondly, these holy places play another important function, especially those sites that are associated with the lives of the founding masters of the major religious traditions. When followers of a particular religion visit these sites, they have an opportunity to reflect deeply upon the example set by these good masters and, with this inspiration and motivation, a chance to follow their example.

Father Laurence: Does Your Holiness think it would be beneficial for people from different faiths to travel in pilgrimage together?

The Dalai Lama: Yes. In fact, this is a project I have been working on. I believe that this practice will have tremendous benefit.

Father Laurence: Another question, which perhaps flows out of this to some degree, concerns Christians and Buddhists of other traditions—non-Tibetans—who have become sensitive to the needs of Tibet and to the scandal of Western indifference to the Tibetan cause. How, in a spiritual way or in other ways you might suggest, can Christians and Buddhists and people of other faiths help you and the cause of the people of Tibet?

The Dalai Lama: Since the issue of Tibet's freedom is intimately linked with the freedom and, in fact, the very survival of spirituality in Tibet, it has implications for the world at large. If Tibet's ancient spirituality can survive under this threat, I feel that it has tremendous potential not only to benefit Tibetans in the future, but also to contribute greatly to the welfare of the Chinese people. So from that point of view, I feel there is a special role to be played by other religious practitioners and organizations—all people who believe in the value of spirituality. I feel that they can play an important role by providing support for our cause.

Father Laurence: For many, perhaps the vast majority of us here, our practice of meditation day by day is the most practical means that we have to grow in compassion and in generous service of causes such as that of Tibet. We would all be inspired and enriched if you could give us encouragement and advice on how to remain steady in the path of meditation each day. Many people living in cities and with the problems of modern life find it very difficult to meditate. That is why our Community of Christian Meditation has grown up, as a support. But it is often difficult for people not living in monasteries—and sometimes for people who *are* living in monasteries!—to meditate. Please give us some encouragement and insight into what we need to develop in order to persevere and to deepen our meditation each day.

The Dalai Lama: If a person has a really deep interest in spiritual growth, he or she cannot do away with the practice of meditation. That is the key! Just a mere prayer or wish will not effect this inner spiritual change. The *only* way for development is through a constant effort through meditation! Of course, at the beginning it is not easy. You may find difficulties, or a loss of enthusiasm. Or perhaps at the beginning there will be *too much* enthusiasm—then after a few weeks or months, your enthusiasm may wane. We need to develop a constant, persistent approach based on a long-term commitment.

Father Laurence: What are the principal means to help us continue when we become discouraged?

The Dalai Lama: One should constantly reflect upon and weigh the pros and cons of meditating and not meditating. One should consider the benefit, value, and effectiveness of meditation, on the one hand, and the negative effects of not pursuing one's meditation, on the other. By constantly weighing these two sides, one can maintain enthusiasm. There are just over five billion people on this planet; generally speaking, we could divide this vast humanity into three categories: those who are believers and spiritual practitioners; those who are not only non-believers, but are actually antireligious; and, in the third category, those who are not necessarily religious practitioners, yet they have no particular antagonism toward religion. They are in a state of indifference. However, all three types of people are fundamentally equal in that everyone has the natural instinct and desire to be happy and to overcome suffering.

If a practitioner or a believer needs a point of contrast, he or she should not compare themselves with the third group. Instead, they should compare themselves with the second category, the people who are antireligious—those who not only do not believe but who think religion is irrelevant and false. You should compare your life with those in the second category and see whose life reflects more contentment and happiness. Of course, in certain aspects, those people who will do *anything* in order to achieve their goal may appear to be more successful. But, in the long run, one should judge the success of a lifestyle by the quality of life and the individual's peace of mind. A life bereft of a spiritual dimension generally leaves less room for inner tranquility. Look at the leaders of the former Soviet Union and China. Of course both leaders want to be happy, as we all do! But everyone adopts a certain method, and according to the method of these leaders, they feel religion is poison. In the other category, the first category, people also have the desire to seek happiness but have adopted religion as their method.

Here we see the true practitioners—not those who merely claim to believe and practice a religion, for whom religion does not actually play an important role in life. When we compare the two categories, we will definitely find that the life of the true practitioner reflects greater happiness, tranquility, and peace. And even in society in general, I am sure these people will be accorded greater trust and respect.

Thinking along these lines will help you see how worthwhile it is to include religion and some form of spirituality in your life. This is like a point of comparison that you make with others to strengthen your conviction. It is also helpful occasionally to compare your own experiences with scriptures. In this way, gradually and slowly, you will eventually be able to see the deeper value of spirituality. The greater the conviction, the greater enthusiasm you will have, and also the greater force in "moving forward."

This *should* be the case, but in the real world, unfortunately, we see quite the opposite. If you have a very forceful desire or wish to obtain something, of course your commitment for obtaining it will be much more forceful. For example, in the case of politicians who are determined to get elected, it often seems that they give almost everything to achieve that goal. They set out on their campaign trail, stopping in one place after another, and even during the campaign you can see them visibly age! Such is their dedication. There is a similar dedication among some business people whose sole aim is to make money and profit. They want it so badly that they will give everything to obtain that goal. This should be the case for a spiritual practitioner as well, but somehow we don't seem to find spiritual practitioners who are *that* dedicated to attaining their goal! My point is that the more clearly you can see the goal you are aspiring to, and the greater your commitment to attaining it, the greater your motivation will be on the path.

Right from the beginning it is very important to have the view that spiritual development is not easy; it takes time. If there is too much expectation at the beginning for radical transformation within a short period, this is a sure sign of potential failure! So mentally you must be prepared for progress to take time.

Father Laurence: Can you tell us how long?

The Dalai Lama: Now to give a Buddhist reply to your question, we are speaking in terms of innumerable eons. And when you think in terms of eons, years and months are nothing. A short life is nothing! A hundred years—nothing! When you think in terms of many eons, that really helps to develop a strong determination. But that is not relevant here. The main point is how to be good during one's lifetime.

Father Laurence: We Christians believe that the Holy Spirit works not only among Christians, but moves throughout humanity and wherever people are seeking truth. Many would perhaps agree with me that the Holy Spirit is at work in the way that you and many of your fellow monks and lay Tibetans have brought the wisdom of Tibet to the West and have been examples of compassion, forgiveness, and generosity at great personal cost and suffering. I think that the visits of Your Holiness to this country and to the West are a great gift to Christianity. You enable people in the West who have lost their spiritual fervor and their determination for spiritual growth to understand religion in a new light, in a new way. I wonder if you can help us understand why it is that in the modern world—though we have more leisure, more time, better health, better living conditions, more affluence than ever—we have lost this sense of true religion and spiritual practice?

The Dalai Lama: Perhaps in your monasteries there is leisure, but outside— especially in the cities—life seems to be running at a rapid pace, like a clock, never stopping for an instant! In fact, just a few days ago, I commented to a friend of mine that if you look at life in an urban community, it seems as if every aspect of a person's life has to be so precise, designed like a screw that has to fit exactly in the hole. In some sense, you have no control over your own life. In order to survive, you have to follow this pattern and the pace that is set for you.

Father Laurence: What would you say, Your Holiness, to the remark that I hear many times when speaking about meditation, when people say, "I would like to meditate, but I'm too busy."

The Dalai Lama: With regard to this question I would like to tell you a story. There were once two monks—a teacher and his student. One day, the teacher said, in order to give some encouragement to his student, "One day we will definitely go for a picnic." After a few days it was forgotten. The student later reminded the teacher of his promise to go on a picnic.

But the teacher responded by saying that he was too busy and could not go to the picnic for a while. A long time passed; no picnic. Again the student reminded him, "When are we going to go on this famous picnic?" The teacher said, "Not now. I am far too busy." So one day the student saw a dead body being carried off, and the teacher asked him, "What is happening?" And the student replied, "Well, that poor man is going on a picnic!"

The point is that in your life, unless you make specific time for something that you feel committed to, you will always have other obligations and you will always be too busy.

Father Laurence: I would like to say a few words, Your Holiness, in conclusion to the Seminar, and then I'd like to ask Sister Eileen O'Hea to speak her words of appreciation on behalf of all the participants. I want first of all to thank you, from the depth of my being—which is a mystery to all of us. But I know it is from that depth that we thank you for what you have made possible and what you have given to us. I have begun to realize over these last few days that we are at a historic event, which has been made possible primarily because of your courage and your remarkable openness. You have been generous in giving us this great space of time in your schedule and have been courageous in daring to explore scriptures with which you are unfamiliar.

What struck me as we listened to you exploring our Holy Scriptures was that your intuitive wisdom and sense of truth, trained in Buddhism, enables you to see very deeply and very clearly into many of the truths of our Scriptures and to reveal them to us in a new way. It also occurred to me that this was possible because we were able to entrust to you what is very precious and sacred to us. Our trust has been more than repaid because you have handled what is precious and sacred to us with reverence, with a sense of the sacred, and with the deepest respect. And so we thank you deeply for that as well.

I think that the way you explored our Scriptures with us also showed me—and all of us—an exercise in nonviolence. It would have been possible for you to have treated these texts rather roughly. (And you would have the strength to do that!) But instead you used your strength of wisdom, insight, intelligence, and spiritual power with wonderful delicacy. That is a lesson in nonviolence that we will treasure. As we moved through these different Gospel texts and finished this afternoon with the Resurrection, the foundational mystery of our faith, I felt that you were using language, thought, and imagery that combined our cultures and brought us to the limit of language. As we end our Seminar and prepare for an interfaith festival, we will move into other forms of expressions—song, music, and dance, as well as words—that will take us into a different dimension of the truth. But your mastery of thought and language has, as I said, brought us to a limit. I don't think this is the end of our exploration. I hope and pray that in some way Your Holiness will be pleased to continue this conversation.

I want to thank you not only on behalf of our own World Community for Christian Meditation, but also on behalf of the Church and the Monastic Order. I think that this Seminar shows that it is possible for different religious traditions to enter into deep dialogue, not just looking for easy similarities, but searching for the truth together. We may be on parallel paths, but the spirit is one of unity. We are encouraged as Christians to understand our role as servants. Jesus describes himself in the Gospels not as a lord and master but as a servant. He says, "I have come among you as one who serves." In the past many of the followers of Jesus have forgotten that. Many Christians, and the Church itself in many historical periods, have pursued temporal power, political power, or religious power over other people through imperialism or other forms of authoritarianism. As human beings we recognize the sinfulness of that. But you have helped us also to understand the nature of humility and the role of the Christian and our particular understanding of ourselves as disciples and servants. And so we pledge ourselves to a continued work of serving the unity of religions.

Finally, I would like to thank the many people who have helped make this Seminar so enriching—the stewards, the film crew, and especially our coordinator, Clem Sauvé who came from Canada eight weeks ago to begin his work for us. Finally, and not in any way least—I hope not to make him laugh again—I would like to thank Thupten Jinpa, your translator.

And now I would like to ask Sister Eileen to say a few words.

Sister Eileen: Your Holiness, I don't know that I can add to what Father Laurence has said, but as a representative of the group here, I would like to say that we can never fully express our gratitude. You have shared the wisdom of your culture and tradition in a way that helps us recognize in you what clarity and purity of mind truly mean. And, in doing so, we recognize our own call to strive for the same. You have taught us not only by your words, but by your presence and the love that you exude and by your compassion. That word will never mean the same thing to me again! I know that for myself—and I suspect it is also true for many people here—my life has been changed because of this meeting.

We say that the Christian Scriptures are the living Word of God. Some days we may look at them, and they don't seem to mean much and are just the same old story. But there is a movement of Grace of the Holy Spirit that guides us through those times. If we persevere, the words live again and take on deeper and deeper meanings. In hearing you read our Scriptures, I found that the words of Jesus have had deeper and deeper meaning for me, and I think the same may be said for all of us here. I regret that we cannot repay the compliment by sharing in your scriptures as you have shared in ours. I would also like you to know—and I have heard it expressed by many here—that we feel a great pain over the atrocities perpetuated against your people. Personally, I feel a deep shame as a United States citizen that our government has not come to your aid. I can assure you that my voice will no longer be silent in that regard.

Someone said that this has been a great feast, and that we eat so that we may live. I think we will all live better because of our contact with you. I don't know if we will ever meet again, or if I will ever have the privilege of being as close to you as I have been over the last few days. But I do believe that in our meditation, in that place where we meet in prayer and meditation, we are joined. We may leave here, separating, but in that experience, we will always meet in that place of communion-consciousness.

And so, Your Holiness, I give great thanks to you for being here. I extend to you our prayers, our good wishes, our gratitude, and our blessings on all you seek to do in the future. I would like to leave with a quote from Thomas Merton, who said, "At the center of our being is a place of pure light, a place untouched by sin or illusion." I thank you because through this event you have enabled us to see that place of pure light in you.

The Dalai Lama: I would like to express my joy in having the opportunity to share these few very precious days with you. My friendship with Father Laurence has grown during these days. I would also like to take this opportunity to express my deep appreciation for all the concerns, sympathies, and support for my work, my country, and my people that you have expressed.

These sentiments were expressed from an open heart, without any veils. It made me feel both joyous and deeply moved. Thank you.

I would also like to express my deep appreciation to all of you who have attended these readings and discussions. Although what I had to say was quite "sketchy" and rather extemporaneous, I noticed that all of you demonstrated so much attention and concentration. I was really touched by this. So if you experience even a small benefit in your life from these few days as a result of anything that was said or from participating in this Seminar, I will feel fulfilled. My appeal to all of you is this. Please ensure that you make the precious human life you have as meaningful as possible.

The Christian Context
of the Gospel Readings in *The Good Heart*

by Father Laurence Freeman

THE EIGHT GOSPEL passages that were chosen for *The Good Heart* are representative of the particular style of each of the four canonical Gospel writers: Matthew, Mark, Luke, and John. The passages also offer a broad survey of the spectrum of the Christian understanding of Jesus, his teaching, his nature, his power deriving from his knowledge of the Father, and finally, the linchpin of Christian faith, his Resurrection. There are, of course, enormous areas of Gospel meaning that are of value for Christians, such as the Eucharist, that are omitted in the selection of texts. The selection is not meant to be more than a representative slice of the Christian faith. But these passages offer stimulating parallels and differences that we may reflect upon in a dialogue emerging from and returning to silence, the sacred experience of meditation within one's own faith and tradition.

The videos of the Good Heart Seminar have already shown how the dialogue that commenced there can and has been continued. Groups of Buddhists and Christians meet, meditate, view part of a video, and then discuss it. We hope this book will take this dialogue even further.

In this section I offer a short Christian context for each of the Gospel passages that the Dalai Lama commented on. This is meant to give those who may be altogether unfamiliar with the Gospels a simple position from which to understand better where the text is coming from and what its language means. The Buddhist response is of course the substance of the book, His Holiness's commentary. To locate where each of the eight Gospel passages are discussed, please refer to the table of contents.

I have avoided technicalities in these brief introductions to the extremely rich and densely meaningful texts of the Gospels. Any dialogue based on such passages will be unique and will allow a particular interweaving of

beliefs and attitudes sincerely held by Buddhists or Christians. As he prepared to read the Gospel texts, the Dalai Lama said that he did not wish to
challenge or to undermine a Christian's faith in them. Indeed, what resulted
from his insight was a deepening and clarifying of faith for Christians and
a broadening of sympathy and understanding for Buddhists. The point of
the exercise of dialogue is not to come up with final answers but to find
a deeper and fuller vision of the Truth, which contains and fills all—and
which ultimately, as Jesus said, will set us all free from fear and ignorance.

LOVE YOUR ENEMY
Matthew 5:38–48

You have heard that they were told, "An eye for an eye, a tooth for
a tooth." But what I tell you is this: Do not resist those who wrong
you. If anyone slaps you on the right cheek, turn and offer him
the other also. If anyone wants to sue you and takes your shirt, let
him have your cloak as well. If someone in authority presses you
into service for one mile, go with him two. Give to anyone who
asks, and do not turn your back on anyone who wants to borrow.

You have heard that they were told, "Love your neighbor and
hate your enemy." But what I tell you is this: Love your enemies
and pray for your persecutors; only so can you be children of
your heavenly Father, who causes the sun to rise on good and bad
alike, and sends rain on the innocent and the wicked. If you love
only those who love you, what reward can you expect? Even the
tax-collectors do as much as that. If you greet only your brothers,
what is there extraordinary about that? Even the heathens do as
much. There must be no limit to your goodness, as your heavenly
Father's goodness knows no bounds.

The Christian Context

The Sermon on the Mount occurs early in the Gospel of Matthew, which
is the first of the four Gospels. Like all the Gospels, it was written and
should be read not as historical reporting, but as the experience of Resurrection applied to history. The Gospels are understood, therefore, in

the light of the Resurrection. The word *gospel* in Greek (*evangelon*) means "good news."

The writer of each Gospel, or *evangelist*, approaches the life and teaching of Jesus from a unique perspective because he was writing for a different kind of audience. This explains the diversity between the Gospels, which were all originally oral (Aramaic) traditions before being committed to writing (in Greek). The Gospel of Matthew, for example, was probably written for a Jewish group of Christians about seventy years after the death and Resurrection of Jesus.

This passage is an extract from the Sermon on the Mount, a teaching of Jesus which is recorded in all four Gospels. Buddhists will think of the Buddha's Deer Park sermon. The Sermon on the Mount was preached by Jesus in the open air to a large crowd. It contains the essence of his religious and ethical teaching. For example, he stresses the importance of moving beyond merely external ritual observance to the religion of the heart.

The first part of Jesus' teaching in this passage instructs his followers not to take revenge on those who harm them. This idea is in contrast to the ancient law of revenge in the Near East. Jesus even says we should not resist those who harm us. In the traditional Jewish style of exaggeration, he strengthens this point by saying that we should turn the other cheek and always give whatever we are asked to give. His followers are told not only to give way but to go beyond even what is asked.

The reference to the shirt and the cloak is understood better when it is realized that the Palestinian peasant of the time would wear *only* these two items of clothing.

The principle of nonresistance and yielding could not be more clearly stated. There have, nevertheless, been many rationalizations of these teachings in Christian history.

The second part of this passage is about loving your enemies. Your "neighbor" means anyone in your village or group. "Enemy" can mean someone who harms you or simply a stranger or foreigner. So, to "love your neighbor" is not enough. It is not realizing the full human potential of being "like God."

The early Christian thinkers said that God became man so that man could become God. This teaching of Jesus shows that we become "children of God" by loving all people as impartially as God does. The goodness of

God is without limit, and human goodness must be the same. The Hebrew word for *goodness* here means "whole" or "integral."[59] It is the love of our enemies that ensures the integrity of human life.

"Tax-gatherers" were those who collaborated with the Roman forces who had occupied Palestine—just as Chinese forces have occupied Tibet today.

THE SERMON ON THE MOUNT: THE BEATITUDES
Matthew 5:1–16

When he saw the crowds, he went up the hill. There he took his seat, and when his disciples had gathered round him, he began to address them. And this is the teaching he gave:

"How blest are those who know their need of God;
　　the Kingdom of Heaven is theirs.
How blest are the sorrowful;
　　they shall find consolation.
How blest are those of a gentle spirit;
　　they shall have the earth for their possession.
How blest are those who hunger and thirst to see right prevail;
　　they shall be satisfied.
How blest are those who show mercy;
　　mercy shall be shown them.
How blest are those whose hearts are pure;
　　they shall see God.
How blest are the peacemakers;
　　God shall call them his children.
How blest are those who have suffered persecution for the
　　cause of right;
　　the Kingdom of Heaven is theirs.
　　How blest you are, when you suffer insults and persecution
and every kind of calumny for my sake. Accept it with gladness
and exultation, for you have a rich reward in heaven; in the same
way they persecuted the prophets before you.
　　You are the salt of the world. And if salt becomes tasteless,
how is its saltness to be restored? It is good for nothing but to be
thrown away and trodden underfoot.

You are light for all the world. A town that stands on a hill cannot be hidden. When a lamp is lit, it is not put under the meal-tub, but on a lamp stand, where it gives light to everyone in the house. And you, like the lamp, must shed light among your fellows, so that, when they see the good you do, they may give praise to your Father in heaven."

The Christian Context

This passage is from the beginning of the Sermon on the Mount. The Beatitudes are the teaching of Jesus that show the nature of blessedness and happiness. This is in line with the entire biblical tradition, which emphasizes that virtue and true happiness go hand in hand. The Greek word *makarios* means both "blessed" and "happy." In these eight Beatitudes Jesus is showing the true nature of human well-being. They are paradoxical in nature and describe a moral revolution in human nature that has not yet been completed. Hence, the Kingdom of God is both "here" and "yet to come."

1. "Those who know their need of God" refers both to the materially poor of the world, with whom Jesus was especially concerned, and to the universal human condition of dependence on God. When we know we are not self-sufficient but interdependent and responsible for each other, then we "know our need of God," or are "poor in spirit." In this sense the term also denotes non-possessiveness or a non-clinging attitude to everything.

2. The "sorrowful" are blessed because they have confronted the essential separation from God in the present realm of experience. Here sorrow refers not only to external suffering but to the nature of the human condition itself as it struggles toward fulfillment. Consolation is the state of salvation or liberation.

3. The "gentle" will inherit the earth. Nonresistance is the best way to overcome evil. The "earth" does not necessarily mean this present life. Evil is always self-destructive. Its failure is in its finitude. Gentleness triumphs because it is endless.

4. The love of the right, of justice, brings true happiness. Righteousness

means uniting one's will with the will of God. It is inseparable from compassion applied to real life.

5. Showing mercy to others forms them into merciful people. Two of the great works of mercy in the New Testament are giving to the poor and forgiving one's enemies.

6. The "pure of heart" will see God. Purity of heart is the capacity to see reality as it is without the distortion of egotism. This is different from religious ritual purity and even "moral purity" in the usual sense.

7. The "peacemakers" are children of God. Reconciliation of enemies is a Christian work that is often recommended in the Gospels. Such people share in the divine nature, as Saint Peter says in one of his letters, because it is the nature of God to bring peace and unity to discord and division. A child shares the being of the parent.

8. In the next saying in this passage, Jesus reassures his followers that suffering accepted "for the cause of right" will lead to rich reward. There is a statement about discipleship here. The Christian's individual suffering is related in a personal way to Jesus. The early Christians were also a persecuted minority.

Finally, Jesus tells his followers of their importance to the world—to be the salt of reality and the light of Truth. Their mission is to be seen and heard for the works that result from consciousness of the essential goodness of human nature—the good heart.

EQUANIMITY
Mark 3:31–35

> Then his mother and his brothers arrived, and remaining outside sent in a message asking him to come out to them. A crowd was sitting around and word was brought to him: "Your mother and your brothers are outside asking for you." He replied, "Who is my mother? Who are my brothers?" and looking round at those who

were sitting in a circle about him he said, "Here are my mother and my brothers. Whoever does the will of God is my brother and sister and mother."

The Christian Context

The Gospel of Mark is the shortest Gospel. It is traditionally said that it was written by a disciple of Saint Peter, who was the leader of the twelve main disciples, or *apostles*, of Jesus. It is the earliest written Gospel, dating from about A.D. 65, and was probably written for new Christians of non-Jewish stock in Rome, where Saint Peter was executed.

Mark believes that a new age of the world has been introduced by the teaching of Jesus on the Kingdom of Heaven. This Kingdom is not merely doctrinal teaching but a mystery or secret of ultimate reality (God), which Jesus himself embodies and reveals to his disciples.

Therefore the mission of Jesus is primarily to reveal his own true, deepest identity. This takes place through his act of teaching and through the relationship between himself and his disciples. In this Gospel the disciples of Jesus are frequently shown as unable to understand what Jesus was teaching.

This passage follows the account in which Jesus selects his twelve main disciples and sends them out to proclaim the Kingdom. He returns home, where his family thinks he has gone crazy. From the beginning of his public preaching, Jesus had angered the religious authorities, the Pharisees, because he spoke against their hypocrisy with such strong personal authority. They and others accused him of being possessed by a devil.

Jesus is engaged in teaching when he is told that his mother and family members have come to see him. Presumably they do not come in to him because of their disapproval or fear of what he is doing. His reply is not a rejection of them as his kin but a rejection of their misunderstanding of his teaching and mission.

He replaces the natural-blood bond with the bond that unites people who "do God's will," as he does. We see here again the idea that the "children of God" share in the universal nature of the divine.

The "Kingdom of God" makes radical demands on us as individuals. To be a "child of God" means to see that every human relationship is dependent on our relationship to God. For the Christian, this relationship to God is comprehensible within our relationship to Jesus. God is unknowable and invisible, but our relationship to God is expressed in the way we relate to one another. Therefore our relationship to the Risen Jesus also leads us to a fuller relationship with one another. This is the origin of the idea of the church as the "Body of Christ," the harmonious totality of all his disciples and, inasmuch as he is the universal Logos, the totality of the cosmos.

This passage is one of a number in which Mary, the mother of Jesus, appears, for whom Catholics in particular have a strong tradition of reverence. Mary is not a divine being but a historical person of unique holiness and receptivity to God. For many Christians, she continues to exercise a special ministry of love. Her concern for suffering humanity is a way to bring people into the Body of Christ, her son.

The Kingdom of God
Mark 4:26–34

He said, "The Kingdom of God is like this. A man scatters seed on the land; he goes to bed at night and gets up in the morning, and the seed sprouts and grows—how, he does not know. The ground produces a crop by itself, first the blade, then the ear; but as soon as the crop is ripe, he plies the sickle, because harvest time has come."

He said also, "How shall we picture the Kingdom of God, or by what parable shall we describe it? It is like a mustard seed, which is smaller than any seed in the ground at its sowing. But once sown, it springs up and grows taller than any other plant, and forms branches so large that the birds can settle in its shade."

With many such parables he would give them his message, so far as they were able to receive it. He never spoke to them except in parables; but privately to his disciples he explained everything.

The Christian Context

Jesus taught by means of parables, simple stories and analogies drawn from the details of ordinary life. These are two parables he used to describe the "Kingdom of God," which is the heart of his teaching. Therefore this passage suggests two areas of reflection: the spiritual method of teaching by parables, and the meaning of the Kingdom of God in Jesus' teaching.

Earlier Jesus had said to his disciples that he taught publicly by parable but that to them the "secret of the Kingdom has been given." Although he taught openly to everyone, there was a difference in how people responded or understood. He respected each person's different capacity for understanding. But Christian teaching emphasizes that everyone is called equally to holiness and can attain it if they wish to cooperate with the working of Grace.

The Kingdom of God is better translated as the "reign" or "power" of God to capture its dynamic meaning. It is, as John Main said, not a place but an experience. Jesus said (Matthew 11:25) that the Kingdom is revealed not to the learned and clever but to the humble and simple. At the end of his life when he was challenged to save himself from death by using his kingly power, he said he was a king but that his Kingdom was "not of this world."

The Kingdom is revealed through the interaction of the teaching of Jesus with his listeners, and this *uncovering* of truth is the dynamic of the "Word of God."

In the parables about the Kingdom of God, Jesus says that its meaning is paradoxical—like the seed that falls into the ground, it must die if there is to be a harvest. The two parables quoted here also use images of natural growth to describe the way in which the Kingdom is realized. We see it, therefore, to be a lifelong process.

In the first parable, Jesus describes how the Kingdom grows within a person day by day without their being conscious of it in an ordinary way. It leads to a harvest: Jesus said that he came so that "people may have life in all its fullness." The Kingdom is, therefore, the fullness of human life, which means a full participation in the nature of God.

The second parable shows that the fullness of life is not a private, individual experience. It begins in a small way that is within the limits of our individual egotism, but as it grows it transcends these limits to become an experience of boundless openness and generosity.

Although the symbols of king and kingdom suggest earthly power, Jesus emphasizes that the power of God does not employ force or violence but love. Therefore the qualities that characterize the Kingdom, according to the New Testament, are "love, joy, peace, patience, kindness, goodness, gentleness, fidelity, and self-control."

THE TRANSFIGURATION
Luke 9:28–36

About eight days after this conversation he took Peter, John, and James with him and went up into the hills to pray. And while he was praying the appearance of his face changed and his clothes became dazzling white. Suddenly there were two men talking with him; these were Moses and Elijah, who appeared in glory and spoke of his departure, the destiny he was to fulfill in Jerusalem. Meanwhile Peter and his companions had been in a deep sleep; but when they awoke, they saw his glory and the two men who stood beside him. And as these were moving away from Jesus, Peter said to him, "Master, how good it is that we are here! Shall we make three shelters, one for you, one for Moses, and one for Elijah?" But he spoke without knowing what he was saying. The words were still on his lips when there came a cloud which cast a shadow over them; they were afraid as they entered the cloud, and from it came a voice: "This is my Son, my Chosen; listen to him." When the voice had spoken Jesus was seen to be alone. The disciples kept silence and at that time told nobody anything of what they had seen.

The Christian Context

At this point in the narrative of Luke's Gospel, Jesus has just miraculously fed the hungry crowd of five thousand and then given his strong teaching on discipleship: "Anyone who wants to be a follower of mine must renounce self. Whoever wants to save his life must lose it." This prepares us for the verses that follow, in which we find a unique revelation of the hidden inner light in Jesus, a light that shines out in both mind and matter, body and spirit.

This passage is a mysterious one. It has its roots in an actual event that is mentioned elsewhere in the New Testament, but it is also described in a highly symbolic way. One of the main symbols is the conversation with Moses and Elijah during the Transfiguration vision. Moses was the channel for the Law, or Torah, of Judaism, and Elijah was one of the greatest Jewish prophets. Together they represent the twin pillars of the Jewish religion: communication with God through the Torah and the Prophets. Jesus, therefore, is associated with this tradition but is also seen as a culmination of the tradition.

Jesus was, of course, Jewish in culture and religion. Yet his personal experience of God led him to a transcendence of both his separate individuality and his cultural conditioning.

The more interior symbols of the passage suggest the nature of the enlightenment of Jesus. First, in the vision he is described as talking with Moses and Elijah about his "departure" or death and the destiny he will fulfill in Jerusalem: his Crucifixion and Resurrection. This means that the fulfillment of his enlightenment will come through suffering.

The meaning of the cruel death that Jesus underwent is not, however, that we are saved by suffering. Rather, his death on the Cross represents the lengths to which the divine love will go to communicate itself to human beings. Therefore the Cross is really a symbol of love and a means of transformation. Suffering is therefore given a positive or redemptive meaning.

The disciples with Jesus at his Transfiguration were his closest disciples. Yet here, as elsewhere, they show they were not yet able to understand him fully. Full understanding only came to them after the Resurrection when Jesus appeared to them and sent his Spirit into them. His disciples' limited capacity to understand his meaning at that time explains why Jesus told them not to talk about what they had seen.

The deepest symbol in the story is the revelation of God, through the "cloud," that Jesus is his Son, his Chosen One, and that people should listen to him. As this is a mystery beyond the limits of space and time, what happens in and through Jesus both before and after his death can be considered as in some way identical.

The cloud is a biblical symbol of the mystery of God, who always remains unknowable even in self-revelation. This unknowability of God, who can be known only through love, is the essence of all Christian mysticism.

THE MISSION
Luke 9:1–6

He now called the twelve together and gave them power and authority to overcome all the devils and to cure diseases, and sent them to proclaim the Kingdom of God and to heal. "Take nothing for the journey," he told them, "neither stick nor pack, neither bread nor money; nor are you each to have a second coat. When you are admitted to a house, stay there, and go on from there. As for those who will not receive you, when you leave their town shake the dust off your feet as a warning to them." So they set out and traveled from village to village, and everywhere they told the good news and healed the sick.

The Christian Context

The Gospel of Saint Luke was probably written after the destruction of Jerusalem by the Romans in A.D. 70. It is traditionally said that Luke was a doctor and a young disciple of Saint Paul. He is the most literary of the four Gospel writers. The opening of his Gospel says that he did a great deal of research to gain firsthand historical knowledge about Jesus.

This passage occurs in a section that recounts some of the many miracles of Jesus. But Luke's emphasis is specifically on the way Jesus empowers his disciples both before and after his death to carry on his mission and his message to them.

Jesus calls the select group of twelve apostles together and gives them "power and authority." These are spiritual qualities he possesses in his own right and can therefore transmit to others. The power is especially linked to the overcoming of demons and to the healing of sicknesses. But the primary role of this transmission of power is to proclaim the Kingdom of God. The miracles are signs of power and means of communication, but the essential work they represent is to witness the Kingdom of God: the miracles show that the Kingdom is within people and that it is immediately at hand. In the Gospel of Mark, there is a description in which Jesus tells people not to publicize his miracles.

On another occasion Jesus was asked when the Kingdom of Heaven would appear. People thought the Kingdom would be an external event or state. But his reply was, "You cannot observe the coming of the Kingdom because in fact the Kingdom of Heaven is within you."

After the death of Jesus, his Holy Spirit descended upon his disciples and empowered them to preach the full mystery of salvation and the true nature of Jesus. But during his lifetime the message they preached was the coming of the Kingdom.

The link between the preaching of the Kingdom and the healing of sickness is an important Christian theme. The Kingdom is not a private abstraction. Of all the defenses human beings erect against God, the most vulnerable are our places of suffering. Healing, therefore, speaks to the deepest and often most hidden part of us. The Kingdom is realized, or entered, in the context of ordinary human life. Suffering calls forth compassion in Jesus, as it does in us. Of course it is easy to focus only on the physical cure and to neglect the healing of the whole person, which is the total meaning of the Kingdom.

The instructions Jesus gives to his disciples as they leave to preach the good news portray a particular attitude and lifestyle. The attitude is that of complete dependence on God. Their lives must manifest complete detachment from the success or failure of their mission. If their message is rejected, they must "shake the dust off [their] feet" and move on to another place.

The lifestyle of a disciple of Jesus is one of material poverty and of a radical simplicity. In a literal sense this is a description of monastic life, but symbolically it describes the path of any true spiritual seeker or disciple. This also assumes that people specially charged with teaching have a right to be supported by the wider community.

Faith
John 12:44–50

Jesus proclaimed: "To believe in me, is not to believe in me but in him who sent me; to see me, is to see him who sent me. I have come into the world as light, so that no one who has faith in me should remain in darkness. But if anyone hears my words and disregards them, I am not his judge; I have not come to judge the world, but to save the world. There is a judge for anyone who rejects me and does not accept my words; the word I have spoken will be his judge on the last day. I do not speak on my own authority, but the Father who sent me has himself commanded me what to say and how to speak. I know that his commands are eternal life. What the Father has said to me, therefore, that is what I speak."

The Christian Context

The Gospel of John is traditionally said to have been written by the "beloved disciple" of Jesus. It describes Jesus as the *Logos* (Greek for "word" or "wisdom") of God. The life and teaching of Jesus is seen in the light of universal wisdom that gives symbolic meaning to every detail of the life of Jesus. The earliest traditions did not speak of Jesus as God. That was a later development. But Saint John speaks of the intimate relation between Jesus and God. Jesus stood in a unique relation to God as *Son* to *Father.*

This passage summarizes many of the discourses of Jesus in the Gospel of John. In these words we are able to hear the voice of Jesus as well as the thinking of early Christians about Jesus.

Jesus always places his center of consciousness in the Father. So if people believe in him, they really believe in God, not only in Jesus. He says that the Father sent him—this means that Jesus' life was a *mission.* To see Jesus is to see the Father who sent him. The relationship between Jesus and the Father is unbreakable, or *advaitic.*[60]

Jesus describes himself as light coming into the world to dispel darkness. "Faith" in Jesus, therefore, means much more than dogmatic belief. It means a personal relationship with him and so with the reality with which he was in communion. This relationship is itself the process of enlightenment that dispels the darkness of ignorance and fear from the human heart. The relationship of faith is the *hodos* or Way of Christian life. Jesus once said, "The Father and I are one." He also said, "The Father is greater than I." These are two aspects of the relationship of Jesus to his Father, who is also *our* Father.

Over the centuries, Christian thinkers developed the doctrine of the Trinity to describe this relationship that saves, transforms, and completes. The Father is the ground of being, invisible and unknowable; the Son (who became incarnate as Jesus) is loved by the Father; and their mutual love is the Holy Spirit, the third person of the Trinity. God is therefore "three in one." Jesus promised to send the Holy Spirit to the world after he was no longer visible on earth—after his death, Resurrection, and final return to the Father.

In this passage Jesus makes it clear that he does not judge the world. If anyone rejects his truth, this is judgment by itself, because everything Jesus has said contains the Truth of the Father.

Jesus says that the commands of the Father are "eternal life." He also says that he came so that people could enjoy fullness of life. Eternal life does not only mean an unending existence. It means the full development of the human potential for consciousness. The only command Jesus emphasized was to love one another. Full consciousness is therefore the fulfillment of the human capacity to love. Love is the nature of God (the Father loves the

Son and this love is the Holy Spirit). All human beings are called to share in the nature of God, to be made divine by love (as we saw in the first extract from Matthew) in order to learn to love as God loves—unconditionally and universally.

THE RESURRECTION
John 20:10–18

So the disciples went home again; but Mary stood at the tomb weeping. As she wept, she peered into the tomb; and she saw two angels in white sitting there one at the head, and one at the feet, where the body of Jesus had lain. They said to her, "Why are you weeping?" She answered, "They have taken my Lord away, and I do not know where they have laid him." With these words she turned round and saw Jesus standing there, but did not recognize him. Jesus said to her, "Why are you weeping? Who is it you are looking for?" Thinking it was the gardener, she said, "If it is you, sir, who removed him, tell me where you have laid him, and I will take him away." Jesus said, "Mary!" She turned to him and said, "Rabbuni!" (which is Hebrew for "My Master"). Jesus said, "Do not cling to me, for I have not yet ascended to my Father. But go to my brothers, and tell them that I am now ascending to my Father and your Father, my God and your God." Mary of Magdala went to the disciples with her news: "I have seen the Lord!" she said, and gave them his message.

The Christian Context

The Resurrection of Jesus is the basis of Christian faith. None of the Gospels describes the actual moment of the Resurrection. Yet each Gospel describes the appearance of Jesus to his disciples in a bodily form—a subtle or spiritual body—after his death. The story of the life of Jesus in the four canonical Gospels is written backward from the standpoint of this Resurrection experience.

In all the Gospels, Jesus first appears to women after his death. In this passage from Saint John's Gospel, Jesus first appears to Mary Magdalene, a close disciple of Jesus, traditionally identified with the reformed prostitute of an earlier Gospel story. The first encounter with the Risen Jesus creates confusion and misunderstanding and even complete disbelief among the disciples, even though Jesus had predicted his Resurrection "after three days." Three days is a biblical symbol for a complete cycle of time.

Mary Magdalene looks into the empty tomb and sees two "angels." The Greek word *angelos* means "messenger." She does not recognize them as such. But when they ask her why she is weeping, she asks where the body of Jesus has been placed. Then she turns and sees Jesus standing beside her. He also asks her why she is weeping. She thinks he is the gardener and asks him to tell her where he has put the body of Jesus. Jesus then calls her by her name. This opens her mind, and she recognizes Jesus and calls him "Master."

Calling Mary by name echoes an earlier passage in the Gospel of John in which Jesus compared himself with the good shepherd who calls each of his sheep by its individual name. In biblical tradition, a person's name signifies his or her real self. To know the Risen Jesus, it is necessary to know one's True Self.

Jesus tells her not to cling to him because he has not yet ascended to the Father. The old form of relationship to Jesus is over. In the final stage of his life he is to be reabsorbed into his source. The Ascension took place a symbolic forty days after the Resurrection. But Jesus promised to remain with his disciples until the end of time. Today, Christians understand Jesus as being both "there" and "here."

Jesus tells Mary he is going to ascend to his Father and her Father, to his God and her God. This reminds us of the statement Jesus made to his disciples shortly before his death. He said that he saw them not as his servants but as his friends, because he had shared with them all he had learned from his Father. Christians believe, therefore, that in union with the glorified, transfigured humanity of Jesus we are all able to share in his unique relationship to the "Father," to "share in the nature of God."

An ontological change occurred in human nature as a result of the birth, life, death, Resurrection, and Ascension of Jesus. But this is realized in each person as we live out the stages of our life, incorporating his experience in ours.

At a doctrinal and philosophical level of dialogue, the importance of the Resurrection is that it shows the *uniqueness* of Jesus. Uniqueness is not to be confused with exclusivity. His uniqueness does not exclude other revelations of the Truth, but Christian belief would see Jesus as the full self-revelation of God in human form. This also manifests the true nature of humanity, its full self-revelation in the divine formlessness as well as its fullest capacity for life, consciousness, and union with God.

The Resurrection is also important, however, because it shows that the greatest human fear, of death, is based on illusion. Death is not the end of life but the final entry into fullness of life, which is sharing in the being of God.

GLOSSARY OF CHRISTIAN TERMS

Aelred of Rievaulx (1109–67). Saint Aelred of Rievaulx was an English Cistercian abbot and theologian renowned for his Christ-centered insight into love. Strongly influenced by Cicero's *On Friendship* as reflecting the link between human and divine love, he was the author of *Mirror of Charity.* See *Augustine of Hippo; Cicero.*

Angels. Angels are spiritual beings found in most ancient religions who act as intermediaries between the higher realm and the world of humanity. The word derives from the Greek *angelos* for "messenger," although on some occasions in the Bible angels are seen as a direct manifestation of God. In addition, there is the belief that an angel is assigned to every person at birth. There are complex theories concerning the celestial hierarchy of angels, which can also be interpreted as stages or powers within the human soul.

Apophatic. Describes an approach to discourse about God and mystical experience arising from the unknowability, transcendence, and inexpressibility of God and of all experience of God. "By love we can know him, by thought never" (*The Cloud of Unknowing*). See *Catophatic.*

Apostles. The twelve apostles whom Jesus called and who formed his inner group of disciples symbolize the twelve tribes of Israel. The word *apostle* derives from the Greek for "one who is sent."

Aquinas, Thomas (1225–74). Thomas Aquinas was a great Catholic theologian and philosopher whose masterpiece of intellectual architecture, the systematic *Summa Theologica*, exerted decisive influence on Christian thought up to the modern era. This work is conceived in commentaries on Aristotle and the Bible and deals thoroughly with all main areas of Christian practice and belief.

Ascension. Forty days after his Resurrection, Jesus left the world of perceptible form entirely. He was reabsorbed into the suprasensory reality of God in his full human reality of body, mind, and spirit. This is described as his Ascension to the Father in heaven. (See Acts of the Apostles 1:9.)

Augustine of Hippo (354–430). The African-born Saint Augustine of Hippo was one of the greatest of early Christian theologians. He was the author of *City of God* and *Confessions*. Like Saint Aelred of Rievaulx, the English monk, he was influenced by the theme of friendship in Cicero's writings as reflecting on the link between human and divine love. *See Aelred of Rievaulx; Cicero.*

Baptism. Baptism is the Christian rite of initiation by immersion or the pouring of water in the name of the Trinity. It can be performed by anyone and, when necessary, can be effective even without any external actions. Baptism is seen as a symbolic identification of the Christian individual's entire life experience with the life, death, and Resurrection of Jesus; it is thus regarded as the beginning of a new way of life. Originally an adult life-choice, the baptism rite has over time become widely performed at infancy.

Beatitudes. Derived from the Greek *makarios*, which means both "blessed" and "happy," the Beatitudes is a section of the Sermon on the Mount describing the characteristics of the human experience of the Kingdom of God and the qualities of Christian "perfection." *See Gospels; Kingdom of God; New Testament; Scriptures; Sermon on the Mount.*

Benedict of Nursia (died c. 580). All that is known of the life of Saint Benedict is contained in the semi-legendary account in Book Four of the *Dialogues* of Saint Gregory the Great. His humane and balanced personality is perceptible in the legislative details of his *Rule for Monasteries*. *See Rule of Saint Benedict.*

Bernard of Clairvaux (1090–1153). Saint Bernard of Clairvaux led a reform of the monastic life and became one of the most influential individuals of Europe. His writings show a great intellect as well as a mystical insight into the poetry of Scripture.

Bible. The word "Bible" derives from the Greek for "book." The Bible is an amalgam of different books written as history, prophecy, laws, and poetry. The Christian addition to the Biblical corpus is the four Gospels and the Letters of the New Testament. *See Gospels; New Testament; Scriptures.*

Catophatic. An approach to theology and mystical writing that is complementary to the apophatic approach. It is based on what can be said about God, although always by way of analogy. The words used of God have a different meaning from the same words used in human affairs. *See Apophatic.*

Christ. Jesus Christ is really Jesus *the* Christ. The term *Christ* derives from the Greek for "anointed one" and translates the Hebrew *messiah*. It was originally a title but became used as a name being applied to Jesus of Nazareth in the light of his fulfillment, for his disciples, of the Jewish expectation of the Messiah, or Savior, of Israel: a figure universalized in the later Christian concept of the Cosmic Christ. The followers of Jesus were first called "Christians" in Antioch in the first century. *See Incarnation; Jesus; Logos; Son.*

Cicero (143–106 B.C.). The Roman author Cicero wrote the treatise *De Amicitia* (*On Friendship*), a work that summarized classical thought on the topic of friendship and greatly influenced later Christian writers, in particular Saint Aelred of Rievaulx and Saint Augustine. *See Aelred of Rievaulx; Augustine of Hippo.*

Contemplation. According to Thomas Aquinas, contemplation is the "simple enjoyment of the truth." The many schools of Christian spirituality suggest complementary ways into the enjoyment. It can be understood as a movement beyond thought and image toward union and love.

Creator. The basic doctrine of the bringing into being of the Universe through the free will of God the Creator is central to Judeo-Christian belief. God simultaneously sustains and perfects Creation in the same act of Creation because time and space are also "creatures" in which God is present but remains unlimited. Scientific knowledge qualifies the imagery by which this doctrine is expressed (such as the Genesis myth) but need not essentially conflict with it. Human creativity is seen as a participation and reflection in the great act of Creation.

Cross. The Cross symbolizes the death of Jesus by crucifixion, a common method of execution for criminals under the Roman empire. In the light of the Resurrection the tragedy of the Cross was seen as a preparation for the release of the healing, salvific energy of the Spirit. Many metaphors have been used to explain how the Cross worked in this "economy of salvation": redemption, sacrifice, self-offering, obedience to Truth. The idea that it was a punishment exacted vicariously by God on his Son for the sins of Adam is one among other explanations, one that has, however, achieved a false prominence in the historical theology of the Cross over the centuries. The imagery often preferred today is psychological rather than mythological: that is, that the Cross represents the power of projection and the ego's attempt to deny the true Self. However powerfully the Cross allows personal identification, its cosmic significance remains mysterious and should not be considered except in relation to the Resurrection from which it derives its importance. *See Resurrection; Salvation.*

Crucifixion. See Cross.

Desert Fathers. The term is applied to the founders of Christian monasticism who settled first as hermits and later in communities in the Egyptian desert between the fourth and fifth centuries. John Cassian (c. 360–435) introduced their teachings to the West from his monastery in Marseilles. The Conferences of Cassian were recommended by Saint Benedict in his *Rule* for monks as a basic element of their spiritual formation.

Elijah (ninth century B.C.). Elijah was a Hebrew prophet who sustained the worship of Yahweh despite the rise in pagan cults in Israel. He also denounced social injustice and urged interior renewal. Later generations believed that his return would be a prelude to the liberation of Israel. At times, Jesus was identified as the second coming of Elijah.

Eternal life. In Christian doctrine, eternal life is not an endless and tedious passing of time; instead, it is the timeless present that preexists the creation of all dualities, even the dualities of beginning and end.

Eucharist. Literally "thanksgiving," the Eucharist, or Mass, is the Christian adaptation of the Jewish passover as celebrated by Jesus at the Last Supper; it also symbolically exemplifies the vision of the cosmic sacrifice. The Eucharist is celebrated differently in different Christian traditions with a variety of underlying theologies; however, common to all is the basic idea of "remembering" the bond of Christ with all generations. Catholic belief attributes a "real presence" of Christ in the bread and wine as well as in the faith of the participants. Holy Communion is the ritual receiving by the participants of communion with Christ through taking the consecrated bread and wine. *See Last Supper; Resurrection; Risen Body of Jesus; Sacrament.*

Evangelists. The term "evangelist" is generally applied to the authors of the four canonical Gospels. The word derives from the Greek for "good news."

Faith. Faith is understood as a way of seeing what the mind and the physical eye cannot. It is the capacity for transcendent perception in each person.

Father. The Father, the first person of the Trinity, is often described as the unknowable and infinitely transcendent aspect of God, "who dwells in unapproachable light . . . . No one has ever seen or ever can see him," as the First Letter to Timothy expresses it (6:16). The Son is the "image" of the Father; so in the Gospel Jesus can say that he and the Father are One (John 10:30) and that anyone who has truly seen him has seen the Father (John 14:9). The term "Father" reflects the patriarchal nature of the ancient world. Today, feminist theologians and others stress its metaphorical nature. *See God; Holy Spirit; Incarnation; Son; Trinity.*

God. God is a term for the absolute in being, meaning, truth, and life. According to Saint John, God is love. Philosophically, in the formulation of Saint Ambrose, God is greater than anything that can be thought or imagined, and as such is inexpressible and impossible to conceptualize or objectify. The ultimate mysteriousness and unknowability of God is paradoxically affirmed in the fact that, according to Christian mystical teaching, God can be known by love but not by thought. The Christian insight into the personal nature of God is the Trinity: God is a communion of three "persons" (Father, Son, and Spirit) who are co-equal, co-eternal, and infinitely present to each other in unity. Anything that is said about God is inadequate metaphor and, while words and images are unavoidable, they run the risk of being taken literally. According to Saint Thomas Aquinas, the medieval formulator of the most complete Christian theological system, the words we use about God have inherently different meaning from the same words applied to human experience. *See Father; Holy Spirit; Incarnation; Son; Trinity.*

Gospels. The Gospels are the four key canonical books of Matthew, Mark, Luke, and John. Several other "apocryphal gospels" exist, and many others have disappeared. All of the four main Gospels agree on the essentials of the life and teaching of Jesus of Nazareth and describe these in the light of the Resurrection experience. But each Gospel, written for a different kind of audience, shows differences of emphasis and interpretive color from the others. *See Beatitudes; Bible; New Testament; Scriptures; Sermon on the Mount.*

Grace. Grace is the perceptible but supraconceptual energy of divine creativity and love in every atom of Creation and every movement of human consciousness, working in and through nature rather than against it. Grace is the direct assistance toward liberation and salvation given by God to human beings through the means and situations of this life. Theologians since Augustine have struggled with its meaning and its relationship to free will. Catholics in particular see the sacraments as means of receiving Grace, but there is a variety of interpretations on how this occurs and what is required of the person celebrating the sacrament. *See Sacrament.*

Gregory of Nyssa (c. 330–95). Saint Gregory of Nyssa, the brother of Saint Basil and a contemporary of Saint Augustine, was one of the Cappadocian mystical Fathers. With great originality he taught about the Trinity, the Incarnation, and other key

Christian beliefs and related them to the interior life of prayer and the mystical meanings of Scripture.

Gregory the Great (c. 540–604). Saint Gregory the Great was a wealthy Roman who gave his money to the poor and founded several monasteries, one of which he entered. He became Pope in 590 and stabilized the position of the Church in a time of great turmoil. He sent Saint Augustine of Canterbury with other monks to convert the English. He spoke movingly about the difficulties of reconciling the spiritual life with the duties of an administrator and showed a great sympathy for the monastic life, which he encouraged by recommending the *Rule of Saint Benedict* as the preferred guideline in the Western Church. He wrote prolifically, and in his *Dialogues,* he gathered the legendary sources of the life and miracles of Saint Benedict, obviously more valuable for their insight into the Saint's theology and spirituality than as a record of the historical events of Benedict's life. *See Benedict of Nursia; Rule of Saint Benedict.*

Griffiths, Father Bede (1906–93). English-born author of *The Golden String, The Marriage of East and West,* and other works, who, from his Christian ashram in India where he spent the last forty years of his life, was a prophetic advocate of East-West spiritual dialogue. Bede Griffiths last met with the Dalai Lama in Australia in April 1992.

Heaven. Heaven is the abode of God and of all who have been purified. In the biblical world view, it is imagined as above the sky, but its essential meaning is experiential rather than spatial. Human entry into heaven may be conceived of as a gradual process, and the whole of Creation will eventually be subsumed into the Heaven of the Creator at the end of time.

Hell. Hell expresses both the Jewish place of the dead and the Greek place of punishment. The pain of hell in Christian thought is separation from God, symbolized as fire. The Creed states that Christ "descended into Hell," and this is interpreted both as the connection of earlier generations with his Resurrection as well as the ultimate salvation of all souls.

Holy Communion. See Eucharist.

Holy Spirit. The Holy Spirit, or third person of the Trinity, which is the Christian insight into the personal reality of God, was the advocate or counselor that Jesus promised he would send to the world after his death and Resurrection. The Holy Spirit is present in biblical thought from the Creation, where she (the Spirit is often attributed with feminine characteristics) hovered over the waters of the pre-creation Void and manifested at the Baptism of Jesus, empowering him for his public ministry. Saint John describes Jesus breathing the Holy Spirit into his disciples after the Resurrection. The Holy Spirit is also identifiable with the personal spirit of Jesus by virtue of his own identity as the second person of the Trinity. The Spirit proceeds from the Father and the Son and can, therefore, also be understood as the love of God, or the nondual spirit of divine oneness present formlessly in all forms of existence. *See Baptism; Christ; Father; God; Trinity.*

Incarnation. As source, guide, and goal of all that is, God expresses (Him)self in all forms of reality. The Incarnation, in Christian faith, is the physical and psychological assumption of human nature and consciousness by the eternal Son of God, the second person of the Trinity. At a definite point in history, human and divine nature were thus united in a single individual human being. The meaning, purpose, and consequences of this unique event became central to human self-understanding and history's meaning. Early in the reflection on the Incarnation, Christian theology stated that God became Man so that Man might become God. The uniqueness of God's self-revelation in the Incarnation affects the meaning but does not diminish the value of the other ways of experiencing absolute truth or of any religion in which the mystery of God is made known. *See Christ; Jesus; Logos; Son.*

Inverbation. This term describes the process by which the sacred words of Scripture are transformed through deep reading and reflection into a living part of the reader. It requires that the reader is saturated in the Scriptures so that thinking and feeling on their fields of meaning becomes an unconscious process.

Jerusalem. Jerusalem was probably inhabited as early as 3,000 B.C. Its Christian history focuses on the Crucifixion and Resurrection of Jesus there in approximately A.D. 33. It is a city of sacred sites for Muslims, Christians, and Jews and, therefore, a powerful modern symbol of multireligious convergence.

Jesus. In Christian usage *Jesus* implies the approachable and sympathetic human nature of Jesus of Nazareth. *Christ* is the title given him in his Resurrected life and elevates our understanding to his divine nature. According to Christian belief, he was fully human *and* fully divine, not half and half. The balance and integration of the human and divine natures of Jesus are the creative tension in all Christian thought. Theologies and even types of Christian lifestyles express the relative emphasis placed on this balance.

The variety of terms by which Jesus can be described in Christianity derive from the doctrine of his uniting in his one human person the two distinct natures of humanity and of God. He is, therefore, capable of being related to as both Lord and Brother. The terms by which Jesus described himself were simple images. In calling himself Son of Man, he was saying little more than "a person." It is inconceivable that he called himself "God," although he seems to have been immersed in an experience of union with God whom he intimately called his "Father." He refers to himself as a shepherd, a gate, a way, the light, the bread of life, a vine, and so on. At the Last Supper, he said to his disciples, "I call you servants no longer; a servant does not know what his master is about. I have called you friends, because I have revealed to you everything I have learned from my Father" (John 15:15). *See Christ; Father; Incarnation; Last Supper; Logos; Son; Trinity.*

John. Saint John, the fourth evangelist and attributed author of three New Testament Letters and the Apocalypse, belonged to the inner group of Jesus' disciples present with his brothers James and Peter at important moments such as the Transfiguration. Tradition identifies him as the "beloved disciple" who reclined on the bosom of Jesus at the Last Supper. His Gospel is remarkable for its intense symbolic presentation of the life of Jesus, its sense of the power of Jesus, and its portrayal of his human emotions and reactions.

Judgment. From the Greek "crisis." Jesus said he did not come to judge but to save the world. God does not punish; sin contains its own judgment and punishment. When human beings forgive one another, divine life is manifested. *See Penance; Sin.*

Kingdom of God. The Kingdom, or Reign, of God translates the Greek word *basileia.* Its roots lie in the Jewish concept of the power of God in "heaven," which is not always visible on earth. Jesus modified the idea and stressed the inner life that is required in order to "enter the Kingdom." The Kingdom is, therefore, both within us and among us (Luke 17:21). There is also a social and eschatological meaning to the term that relates to its more mystical meanings. In the Kingdom human beings are equal and justice prevails. It is also an encounter with the mortality of human life.

Last Supper. The Last Supper of Jesus with his disciples the day before his death is traditionally associated with the ritual Jewish meal of Passover. It is especially commemorated by Christians on Holy Thursday before Easter. Before his last meal with them, Jesus washed his disciples' feet and enjoined them to friendship rather than hierarchical relationship. This meal is also relived daily or occasionally (according to different Christian traditions) in the Eucharist where the bread and wine acquire the sacramental reality of the physical and spiritual wholeness of the Risen Jesus. *See Apostles; Eucharist; Risen Body of Jesus.*

Lectio divina. This is the monastic practice of a slow, meditative reading of Scripture which nourishes both mind and heart and prepares the reader for deeper stages of prayer. *See Scriptures.*

Logos. Greek for "word" or "reason," *logos* is an ancient Greek philosophical term used by Christians with reference to the second person of the Trinity. The first great usage was by Saint John in his Gospel: "In the beginning was the Word" (John 1:1). He describes the Logos as the eternal creative principle that became incarnate in Jesus of Nazareth. Later Christian thinkers saw the relating of the Logos to the Son as a way of making Christianity compatible with non-Christian belief systems. *See Christ; Incarnation; Son; Trinity; Word of God.*

Love. One English word must serve to describe the love of friendship, the love of desire, and the love of God. *Agape,* divine or selfless love, is what is meant in Saint John's phrase "God is Love."

Luke. Saint Luke was, according to ancient tradition, a physician, a gentile, and a companion of Saint Paul on some of his missionary journeys. His Gospel is the third of the four and may have been written before A.D. 64. Luke claims to have gathered his material from eyewitnesses, but his Gospel also draws heavily on that of Mark as well as on another common source called by scholars "Q." The message of Luke's Gospel emphasizes the universality of the meaning of Jesus and is remarkable for its insistence on the worth of those who are outcast and marginalized. In addition, this Gospel refers to women in the life and ministry of Jesus with unusual respect and frequency.

Mark. Saint Mark was a companion of Saint Paul on his missionary journeys and later was in Rome with Saint Peter, from whom tradition says he took the notes that became his Gospel. The Gospel was probably used by both Matthew and Luke in their writings. Written in Greek it is in literary terms the shortest and least elegant of the Gospels. Forming a continuous narrative on the life of Jesus, it is, however, a favorite text for public readings or performances.

Mary Magdalene. Mary Magdalene, Gospel character and disciple of Jesus embellished in legend, was early on identified popularly with the woman who was a "sinner" and anointed the feet of Jesus (Luke 7:37), and the woman from whom he cast out seven devils (Luke 8:20). She stood with Mary, the mother of Jesus, beside the Cross; later she found the tomb empty and received an appearance of the Risen Jesus and on the same day was the first person to recognize the Risen Jesus.

Matthew. Saint Matthew was one of the twelve apostles; the Gospel bearing his name has been traditionally attributed to him since the second century. As with all scholarly arguments about dates and authorship of the Gospels, however, nothing is certain. In Matthew 10:3, he is described as a tax collector ("publican"). The Gospel of Matthew, previously regarded as the first of the Gospels to be written, accentuates the relationship of the teaching of Jesus to the Jewish Law, which it "fulfills," and emphasizes the primacy of Peter among the twelve apostles.

Meister Eckhart (1260–1327). Meister Eckhart was a German Dominican famous for his preaching on mystical insights; he died during his trial for heresy. He taught the "Oneness" of God, in the Platonic tradition, but related it boldly to the Christian Trinity. According to Eckhart, God "reproduces" himself through the second person of the Trinity and in each human individual.

Merton, Thomas (1915–68). Trappist monk, poet, and author, Merton's best-selling autobiography, *The Seven Storey Mountain* (1948), established him as a contemplative voice relevant to the modern world. His personal evolution led him into dialogue with the East as well as to a strong stand against the Vietnam War. He retired to a hermitage on the Gethsemani monastery grounds in Kentucky where he wrote on prayer, peace, and social justice. He died during a meeting of Asian contemplatives in Bangkok.

Moses. Moses was the great Lawgiver of Israel. Born in Egypt during the period of Israelite enslavement, he received a divine mission to lead his people to the Promised Land. He saw the Promised Land from a distance after wandering for forty years in the desert, but he died in Moab before entering it. Tradition claims that Moses wrote the Pentateuch (the five mythical and legislative books of the Bible). In Christian thought Moses symbolizes the Law that first covenanted humanity and God. Moses is also seen as a prophetic foreshadowing of Christ, who led humanity from the slavery of sin to the Promised Land of the Kingdom of God. *See Kingdom of God; Ten Commandments.*

New Testament. The Gospels and the Letters of the New Testament form the two main elements of the primary Christian Scriptures. The Gospels are accounts of the life and teaching of Jesus in the light of the post-Resurrection community experience of the Risen Jesus. The Letters of Saint Paul, Saint John, Saint Peter, Saint James, and the letter to the Hebrews deliver primary Christian theology in the form of letters of exhortation or correction to early churches in places such as Corinth, Rome, and Ephesus. *See Bible; Gospels.*

Nicholas of Cusa (1401–64). German cardinal and philosopher. His major work *De Doctora Ignorantia* expounded the ideas associated with his thought: that truth, which is absolutely simple, is unknowable to human intellect except through "unknowing," and that truth, therefore, leads beyond reason. In God all contradictions meet: neither one nor two but three, infinitely small and great, here and everywhere.

Origen (c. 185–254). Origen was a disciple of the great Clement of Alexandria. Despite the political troubles in which he was embroiled, he wrote prolifically on biblical criticism and spiritual matters such as prayer. In defining the triple meaning-levels of Scripture (literal, moral, and allegorical), he provided a key to later generations of Christians whose reading of the Bible was itself often a mystical encounter. Philosophically he could be daring and asserted that in the end all creatures, including even the devil, would be saved by the love of God.

Original Sin. Original Sin has never been described better or in a more universal myth than in the story of the Fall of Adam and Eve (see Genesis 2). It is no longer credible as it was in the past to understand this account as a historical event. Yet, like all myth, it helps explain the existing state of affairs. Human inhumanity, lack of freedom, and failure to realize potential are symptoms of this "fault" in human nature for which no *one* is to be blamed. The myth has been explained as illustrating personal psychological development (the emergence from the undifferentiated state of infancy into adulthood). In a more social sense the consequences of an "original sin," such as child abuse or racial hatred, explain generational interdependence. In the context of the biblical story of Creation and redemption the idea of Original Sin is a fundamentally hopeful diagnosis of human weakness and sickness. *See Judgment; Penance; Sin.*

Paul. Saint Paul, originally Saul of Tarsus, underwent a conversion to Christ on the road to Damascus while persecuting the early Christian sect in Judaism. Having only encountered the Risen Christ, not the historical Jesus, Paul became the "apostle to the gentiles," traveling widely around the Mediterranean world until his martyrdom in Rome some time around A.D. 65. He is arguably the most powerful single personality in the history of Christianity. Through his Letters (collected in the New Testament), he laid the foundations on which Christian theology was to be built. Central to his vision of Christ is the doctrine of the Indwelling Spirit as well as the Cosmic Christ and a radical freedom in the Spirit from all external religious or internal psychological restraints.

Saint Paul's Letter to the Ephesians was written while he was in prison. It is characterized by Paul's insight into the mystical and cosmic meaning of Christ as well as by practical instructions for the life of the early Christian community.

Penance. Penance is the purifying discipline of self-knowledge by which one's faults are acknowledged, retribution made to those who have been harmed, and the resolution made to forever avoid those faults and the egotism that engenders them. *See Judgment; Sin.*

Peter. Saint Peter is the chief of the apostles of Christ, named by Jesus as the "rock" on which he would build his church. The word *rock* plays on the double meaning of the name Peter in Greek. Nevertheless, Peter is portrayed as denying and abandoning Christ at the time of Christ's arrest and trial, a fault for which he later bitterly repented. After the Ascension, Peter took the leadership of the apostles and spoke as their representative. He was executed in the anti-Christian persecutions of the Emperor Nero in Rome in A.D. 64. There is archaeological support for the belief that Saint Peter's Basilica in Rome is built over his tomb.

Pharisees. The Pharisees were one of a number of Jewish groups active in Israel at the time of Jesus. The term derives from the Hebrew for "separated ones." They were expert at legalistic interpretations of the Law that allowed compromise without the loss of righteousness. Jesus confronted them and earned their enmity. Nothing is heard of the sect again in Judaism after the Fall of Jerusalem in A.D. 70.

Pope John Paul II. Polish-born, His Holiness Pope John Paul II was Bishop of Rome (the defining role of the Pope since Saint Peter, the first Pope) from 1979 to 2005. His papacy was characterized by an impassioned emphasis on social justice as well as on traditional Catholic moral, dogmatic, and hierarchical values.

Praktike. A Greek term in Christian mystical theology used by the Desert Fathers to describe the practical work and discipline necessary to follow the path of self-transcendence and discipleship. It is an essential prerequisite for teaching the spiritual life.

Presence. The Hebrew word for the abiding glory of God, *shekhinah*, suggests the all-embracing presence that is perceptible in all forms of human experience and encounters.

Redemption. Liberation by love from the egotistical power of sin and isolation. *See Penance; Sin.*

Resurrection. The Resurrection is the principle of regeneration through death and as such is exemplified in the cycles of nature as well as in the Easter cycle of the death and rising of Jesus. Specifically, the Resurrection is the total raising of Jesus to boundless life on the third day after his Crucifixion. It is a fundamental of Christian faith as well as the core of the earliest preaching of the Gospel of Jesus, although the individual Gospel writers differ in the details of their accounts. The way of experiencing the person of the Risen Jesus is "no longer after the manner of the flesh" but is instead realized in the Spirit. The Resurrection is the core experience of Christian life and faith because it anticipates the destiny of each human being to be transformed in totality of being to enjoy the fullness of being in the life of divinity. *See Cross; Eternal life; Risen Body of Jesus.*

Risen Body of Jesus. The Risen Body of Jesus is not, according to Saint Paul, the old physical body of Jesus but is instead a "spiritual body." Thus it is free of all material and mental constraint, and changed, not abandoned, after death. While existing in its own right, the new or glorified bodily form of Jesus can be seen operating and manifesting itself in other dimensions: for example, as the presence of Christ in the Eucharist under the form of bread and wine; as one with his disciples, thus allowing us to speak of the Church as the Body of Christ; and also as coterminous with the material universe for which Creation of the second person of the Trinity, incarnate in Jesus, was the means. *See Christ; Holy Spirit; Resurrection; Son; Trinity.*

Rule of Saint Benedict. Written by Saint Benedict of Nursia (died c. 580), the *Rule of Saint Benedict* for monks became for several centuries the most influential document on the Christian life apart from the Bible. Its sane, balanced, and moderate organization of life integrates the needs of body, mind, and spirit, balancing individual and social factors and emphasizing love as the creative and cohering power of personal and institutional relationships. It continues to inspire men and women in all walks of life today. *See Benedict of Nursia.*

Sacrament. Generally, an outward sign of the grace inherent in nature; specifically, one of the seven principal rituals, many of which correspond to major rites of passage, by which Christians affirm the sacredness of life. *See Grace.*

Salvation. In Christian understanding human nature, wounded and incomplete, is healed (*salved*) and fulfilled by its union with the human nature of Jesus and is empowered by that union to enter fully into the divine life. Thus the wound of separation is healed by the power of unifying love. *See Christ; Jesus; Love.*

Satan. Satan is the embodiment and personification of evil in Judeo-Christian thought and mythology. In the myth of the Fall, the serpent is interpreted as the Devil, and in the philosophical treatment of suffering in the biblical Book of Job, the character also appears explicitly. Until modern times much theological speculation was given to the nature of the sin that caused Lucifer's fall from the highest of the angelic orders. Contemporary interpretation favors less externalization and projection of evil out of the realm of human responsibility, although this approach does not deny the possibility of autonomous forces within the psyche. *See Original Sin; Redemption; Salvation; Sin.*

Scriptures. All religions distinguish between primary scriptures (such as revelation or the founder's teachings) and secondary writings that are commentary on these. Christian primary scriptures are collected in the New Testament but are also seen as a fulfillment and conclusion to the Jewish Bible or Old Testament. For many centuries commentaries on the Scriptures, such as those by the "Fathers of the Church" in the first six centuries of Christianity, formed the essential means of Christian theological and mystical discourse. *See Beatitudes; Bible; Gospels; New Testament; Sermon on the Mount.*

Sermon on the Mount. This is the spiritual teaching on the Kingdom of God and the life appropriate to realizing, or entering, it. Jesus gave this Sermon early in his public ministry, and it is recorded with slight variants by three of the Gospels. Saint Luke situates the Sermon on a plain rather than a mountaintop. The Sermon outlines the Christian ethic based on the Kingdom experience and includes the Beatitudes and the Lord's Prayer. One should especially refer to the Gospel of Matthew, chapters 5–7. *See Beatitudes; Gospels; Kingdom of God; New Testament; Scriptures.*

Sin. Literally, in the Greek, "to miss the mark," sin is that which alienates human consciousness from the truth. A result of illusion and selfishness, sin contains its own punishment (God does not punish), but it has both personal and social origins. A consideration of the concept of sin raises the question of free will, as in the case of addictions, and challenges moral theologians today to develop a new language to discuss sin as what all people experience but understand so diversely. In the light of modern psychology, theologians today, more than in the past, are beginning to recognize the role of the unconscious in sin. *See Judgment; Original Sin; Penance; Redemption; Salvation.*

Son. Son denotes the relation of the second person to the first person of the Trinity, in that the Son issues forth eternally from the Father, or ground of being. Identified in Greek thought with the universal Logos, the Son can be regarded as comparable to the *purusha* of Indian theology. The Son is the principle of Creation and the means of all knowledge of the Truth, who, in time, incarnated in the material world as Jesus. *See Christ; Father; God; Holy Spirit; Incarnation; Jesus; Logos; Trinity.*

Ten Commandments. According to Exodus 20:1–17 and Deuteronomy 5:6–21, the Ten Commandments, or the Decalogue, were revealed to Moses on Mount Sinai. Some scholars date them to the nomadic or settled communities of Israel in the seventh century B.C., but serious weight is also given to their more ancient origin. The Ten Commandments constitute the core of biblical ethical systems; they address both the relationship of humans to God (honoring God and rejecting idolatry) and the relationships between human beings (sexual and economic justice). *See Moses.*

Tools of good works. In chapter four of his *Rule,* Saint Benedict lists seventy-two "tools," or "instruments," of good works, ranging from "not to love much talking" to "praying for one's enemies in the love of Christ." He calls them the "tools of the spiritual craft" to be used unceasingly day and night, and the monastery is the workshop in which these tasks are performed. As a practical and simple means of achieving consistency between ideal and practice in daily life, Benedict's tools of good works may be compared with the Buddhist concept of *skillful means. See Benedict of Nursia; Rule of Saint Benedict.*

Transfiguration. The Transfiguration is the event described as a historical occurrence in the three synoptic Gospels (Matthew, Mark, and Luke). In the presence of three of his closest disciples, Jesus was physically illumined and glorified in their sight and appeared with Moses and Elijah. It was on this occasion that Jesus warned his disciples of the coming ordeal of his death. The event is remembered each year on August 6, as a major feast day of the Catholic Church. *See Moses.*

Trinity. The Trinity expresses the Christian perception of the nature of God not as an isolated monad but as a communion of love lived in the mystery of three *persons* (Father, Son, and Holy Spirit) who share one nature and in whom all existence "lives and moves and has its being." *See Christ; Father; God; Holy Spirit; Incarnation; Jesus; Logos; Son.*

Virgin Mary. Mary, the mother of Jesus, acquired a high degree of attention from the followers of Jesus from Gospel times. From the fifth century, the doctrine of her perpetual virginity highlighted the unique identity of Jesus. Her title as "Mother of God" and the later doctrine of her bodily Assumption and her sinlessness illustrates the theological and symbolic value she has acquired, especially in the Catholic and Orthodox Churches. Devotion to Mary has often needed to be restrained by the

Catholic Church, but her importance takes on new aspects with each generation. See "The Othercentredness of Mary" in John Main, *Community of Love* (Continuum, 1999). *See Jesus.*

The Way. The Way (Greek *hodos*) expresses the meaning of Jesus as a vehicle or bridge between humanity and God. It also describes the way of life that this belief entails. The early Christians were known as followers of the Way and their early communities as the "New Way."

Word of God. The Word of God is a central biblical concept describing the self-communication of God that always occurs through the life-giving, revitalizing, healing, and creative "Logos." In Christian belief Jesus is the human embodiment of this Word-action of God. *See Bible; Lectio divina; Logos; Scriptures.*

THE BUDDHIST CONTEXT

by Thupten Jinpa

T HE GOOD HEART SEMINAR was a deeply inspiring experience for me. I can still evoke the atmosphere of serenity fused with warmth that was so potent throughout the conference. Looking back, it seems that I went through the entire event as if being led by an invisible spirit. My most powerful memory still remains the clarity of mind and the sense of togetherness that I felt with the participants at the Seminar. And to feel that I was personally involved in all this, in my humble capacity as the Dalai Lama's interpreter, certainly added to the depth of my own experience. Perhaps the spontaneous warmth that was established between the Dalai Lama and Father Laurence Freeman, the two key participants at this Buddhist-Christian conversation, set the tone for the entire event. Perhaps it was the solemnness of the occasion.

The historic nature of this dialogue cannot be exaggerated. For the first time in history, the head of a major non-Christian religion was publicly teaching and commenting on the sacred Christian Gospels. To hear the words of the four Gospels spoken by the Dalai Lama was a truly moving experience. As we experienced the juxtaposition of a voice and tone so familiar with the words and imagery of a non-Tibetan scripture, it was as if a totally new scripture was being taught to the congregation. This was truly a spiritual moment, and many people felt this at a deep level. In moments of such profound spirituality, each and every one of us is capable of transcending our ordinary perceptions of separateness. Thoughts of all "isms" are eclipsed when we succeed in going beyond the bounds of rational, cognitive limits. Whether one calls this transcendence, religious experience, or spiritual awakening is secondary. What is important is that all sacred teachings of the world's major religions are capable of leading us to such religious depth.

It is these thoughts that come to mind as I sit down to write a brief overview of Buddhism for this beautifully presented volume of *The Good*

Heart. I hope to provide a broad survey of the Buddhist path so the Dalai Lama's comments can be appreciated within a richer, fuller context by the reader new to Buddhism. In one sense there is no real need of such an introduction, for the title of the book itself captures the entire essence of the Buddhist message. When asked to summarize the essence of the Buddhist teachings, His Holiness the Dalai Lama always has a simple answer: "Help others if you can; but if you cannot, at least refrain from harming others." This, of course, is the central teaching of the Buddha. Needless to say, at this level there is no real difference between the teachings of the Buddha and those of Jesus Christ. Both teach a path to salvation through compassionate service to others; both expound a way of transcending the narrow confines of self-centered existence; and both acknowledge the presence of a seed of spiritual awakening within us all. Yet, in another sense, there *is* a need for an appreciation of the distinctness of each path. If nothing else the differences of language, imageries, and underlying cultural and historical conditions demand a recognition of their separate identity. We must not let diversity alienate us from the common core, nor must we allow similarities to obliterate the distinct lines. It is a genuine appreciation of this dual aspect that makes the Dalai Lama's approach to the teachings of Christian Gospels so remarkable. Let us now try to identify the lines that define the Dalai Lama's own spiritual world, the world of Tibetan Buddhism, so that the forms that emerge from his comments can come into sharper relief.

The Buddha and His Teachings

The Dalai Lama's religion and spirituality are firmly rooted in the ancient teachings of the Buddha and their more than 2,500 years of historical evolution. Buddhist philosophical training forms the core of his intellectual development and continues to constitute the basis of his worldview. An emphasis on a combination of learning and reflection is characteristic of a Buddhist orientation to life and exerts a powerful influence on His Holiness's general attitudes toward existence. So, what is Buddhism? Of course, we could simply state the obvious: Buddhism is the religion of the Buddha. It is, however, important that by doing so we do not give the false notion that there is a homogeneous tradition called "Buddhism" with a unitary system of beliefs and practice. Like any major spiritual tradition of the world, Buddhism has over time evolved into many different lineages—all of which share the same banner of "the teaching of the Buddha." All of these schools trace their evolution to the teachings of Gautama Buddha, who is also known as Buddha Shakyamuni, the so-called historical Buddha who lived sometime around the sixth century B.C.

It is extremely difficult to determine which of the many scriptures in the various Buddhist canons were genuinely spoken by the Buddha. (There are more than 100 large volumes attributed to the Buddha in the Tibetan canon.) Nevertheless, it is still possible to discern certain key ideas that lie at the heart of the Buddha's spiritual message. The Buddha taught a path to freedom from suffering that involves a deep understanding of the nature of existence. He saw the condition of existence in terms of a perpetual cycle of dissatisfaction and believed that the key to ending this cycle lies in an insight into its true nature. For the Buddha, an understanding of the dynamics of cause, conditions, and effects is critical to an individual's spiritual quest. Nothing comes into being without a cause, and when all the conditions are created, there is nothing that can prevent the consequence. According to the Buddha, the principal cause of our own perpetual cycle of suffering is our deeply ingrained clinging to the sense of a permanent "self." This grasping gives rise to a host of defilements—especially attachment, hatred, and ignorance—creating the basis for a confused psychological and emotional life. Attachment toward those whom we perceive to be close to this "true me" and aversion toward those whom we think threaten the well-being of this "self" become the mode of our interaction with fellow beings. This, in turn, leads to deeds that are detrimental to both self and others. The true path to freedom lies in the development of insight into the absence of such a permanent "self."

Therefore, unlike all other religious teachers of his time, the Buddha taught the path of "no-self" (anātman), whereby the notion of a fixed personal essence or self is seen to be the root of all suffering. The philosophical arguments used to demonstrate the impossibility of any such fixed self or immutable essence are often quite detailed and intricate, but many such arguments focus on the state of flux that a causal existence necessitates. In short, anything that has arisen from causes is necessarily impermanent, in part because such a thing cannot exist before its production. Inasmuch as we too have arisen from causes, we must also be impermanent. Hence, as impermanent beings, we cannot have any fixed, unchanging essence or self, despite our unwarranted belief to the contrary.

The principles sketched above appear in the Four Axioms, a traditional formula that is said to summarize Buddhist thought: (1) all conditioned things are transient, (2) that which is defiled by negative mental states necessarily produces suffering, (3) all things are empty of any fixed essence or self, and (4) nirvana is true peace.

These same principles underlie the Four Noble Truths, another traditional formula that guides Buddhist practice: (1) suffering exists, (2) there is an origin of suffering, (3) there is a cessation of suffering, and (4) there exists a path leading to that cessation. The first of these Truths, the fact of suffering, relates to the notion of impermanence, for much of our suffering stems from the presumption that the world and our lives should somehow offer some fixed, static point of reference, even though all of our experiences point to the inevitability of change. The second Truth, the origin of suffering, is connected to negative mental states or "defilements," for such states are what prompt one to live in a way that produces suffering. The cessation of suffering, the third Truth, is itself nirvana, a state that is "peace" precisely because all suffering has been eliminated. Finally, the fourth Truth, that there is a path that leads to nirvana, is closely related to the principle of selflessness, for much of Buddhist practice focuses on the realization of selflessness, since this realization allows one to eliminate the negative mental states that cause suffering.

Although the Four Axioms and the Four Noble Truths provide a concise summary of Buddhist thought and practice, one crucial element must also be mentioned: great compassion. From the earliest days of Buddhism, love and compassion figured prominently in Buddhist practice, but compassion takes on particular significance in the practice of the *Mahayana* (the "Great Vehicle"). Whereas all Buddhists espouse the doctrines cited above, these doctrines leave open the question of the final goal of one's practice; that is, to what extent does one seek to end the suffering of others as well as one's own? For Mahayanists, such as His Holiness the Dalai Lama, the goal of practice is not simply to end one's own suffering and obtain personal happiness but to end the suffering of all beings and ensure their lasting happiness. Since only a fully enlightened person can hope to accomplish such a goal, a Mahayanist seeks to attain the full awakening (*bodhi*) of buddhahood. In their most concise form, the Mahayanist's practices consist of the six perfections, which are oriented toward one's own personal development, and the four means, which are oriented toward developing the minds of others.

The six perfections are generosity, morality, patience, joyous effort, concentration, and wisdom; the four means are giving what is urgently needed, always using gentle speech, giving ethical guidance to others, and demonstrating these principles through the example of one's own life. These two sets of practices, the six perfections and the four means, together form what is known as the *bodhisattva ideal*, a topic to which I shall now turn.

The Bodhisattva Ideal

Arguably the key religious concept that emerges through the Mahayana movement within Buddhism is the bodhisattva ideal. A bodhisattva, literally meaning "one with a heroic aspiration toward enlightenment," is an altruistic being with tremendous courage. Bodhisattvas are those individuals who, though capable of personal liberation, choose to take upon their shoulders the task of freeing others from suffering. The compassion of such a being is boundless and transcends all considerations of division. The bodhisattva is a friend, a servant, and a spiritual kin to all beings regardless of personal acquaintance. The depth of a bodhisattva's heartfelt compassion is expressed through various media, including the visual arts. In Tibetan culture, perhaps the most famous depiction of this infinite compassion can be found in the legend of Thousand-Armed *Chenrezig*, the Bodhisattva of Compassion. In this legend, we see that Chenrezig's compassionate concern for all beings was so intense, he found that unless he had a thousand arms and a thousand eyes, he could not adequately fulfill the wishes of the infinite sentient beings. It was the force of his single-pointed aspiration that one day gave him those thousand arms and thousand eyes. To this day, this image remains a potent religious symbol to the followers of Mahayana Buddhism.

A bodhisattva's compassion for others should not be perceived purely in terms of emotion. It is not a feeling rooted in attachment, nor is it based on any self-regarding considerations such as thinking that being compassionate is good for one's health or spiritual well-being. It is a feeling arising spontaneously from a perception of others' suffering and the simple recognition that others are sentient beings just like oneself. In other words, there is a sense of connectedness and deep empathy with others yet with a degree of freedom from attachment. There is neither attachment nor detachment. Of course, such compassion arises only through deliberate cultivation. It is here that insight plays a crucial role in the Buddhist path. Insight is the skillful navigator that steers the course of the compassionate ship. According to the Mahayana scriptures, a bodhisattva shuns personal enlightenment because of his or her compassion, and through this insight, he or she transcends the world of fluctuating existence. In other words, the bodhisattva steers a middle course between the solitary peace of nonexistence and the perpetual flux of becoming.

The first stage of the bodhisattva's path is what is known as "generating the heroic motive." This is a bodhisattva's solemn pledge to seek full enlightenment in order to free others from suffering. This pledge must arise from deeply felt compassion toward all sentient beings and from an unshakable conviction in the nobility of dedicating one's existence to benefiting others. A bodhisattva's conviction must be such that he or she is prepared to spend infinite lifetimes, if necessary, in order to fulfill the wishes of even a single being. The following prayer—which is, incidentally, one of the verses most quoted by the Dalai Lama—captures this spirit succinctly:

> As long as space abides,
> and as long as sentient beings remain,
> may I too abide
> and dispel the suffering of beings.

Once this heroic motive is generated, a bodhisattva's task then becomes the practice of the six perfections and the four means. He or she must make these practices the primary purpose of his or her life. For such a person, religious practice cannot be just another aspect of life; instead, it must be life itself. It becomes life's sole pursuit. There are many Mahayana classics that outline the way of life of the bodhisattva. Of these, perhaps the most well-known and certainly the most influential is Shantideva's *A Guide to the Bodhisattva's Way of Life*.[61] Shantideva was a seventh-century Indian Buddhist poet who is still highly venerated as a saint in the Mahayana Buddhist world. His work became the standard scripture on the study and practice of the bodhisattva ideal in Tibet. Anyone who has attended a discourse by the present Dalai Lama may have observed the overwhelming influence this book exerts on his thoughts and deeds. The reader of this volume will also notice the liberty and spontaneity with which the Dalai Lama refers to this celebrated Mahayana text.

The Role of Insight

Earlier we observed that according to Buddhism the development of insight is the key to liberation. For a Buddhist, the religious life is a life in pursuit of perfect enlightenment. Since our unenlightened state is understood to be rooted in a fundamental misapprehension of the nature of our own self and reality, understanding their true nature is thus critical to the process of enlightenment. However, this is not to say that knowledge alone is adequate. An understanding of "the way things are" must be integrated into one's personal life. In other words, we must comprehend it in such depth as to affect the very core of our being. This integrated knowledge is called "wisdom" and arises only out of a genuinely tranquil mind. In Buddhist parlance, this is known as the "union of tranquil mind and penetrative insight." At the beginning of the Dalai Lama's comments in *The Good Heart*, these two aspects of the Buddhist contemplative path are called "analytic meditation" and "absorptive meditation." The latter fuses the mind with the chosen object, while the former probes its deeper nature. For a genuine practitioner, these two must be complete within a single cognitive act.

As regards the exact nature of an understanding of "the way things are," there evolved within Buddhism four main philosophical schools in ancient India. The *Vaibhāṣika* school, while denying the existence of a permanent, unchanging "self," accepts the existence of indivisible units of reality called dharmas. The *Sautrāntika* school rejects this but conceives reality in terms of objective, indivisible atoms and units of time. The *Cittamātra* school refutes any objective basis to the material world and argues that the only thing that is ultimately real is the mind. And the *Madhyamaka* school perceives all of these as mere postulates and rejects them on the ground that upholding any of these views represents the reification of something that does not exist in reality. According to this school, the true nature of all things and events is emptiness—that is, all things and events lack intrinsic existence or identity. This emptiness is the truth, the ultimate reality, and the final status of things and events. It is insight into this profound voidness that opens the door to liberation and spiritual freedom. The Tibetan Buddhist tradition maintains that the Madhyamaka school represents the apex of Buddhist philosophical thinking and comes closest to the noble silence of the Buddha. One of the greatest paradoxes in Buddhism is the relationship between its thoroughgoing emphasis on a rational approach and the fundamentally silent nature of its ultimate spiritual vision. The Madhyamaka teachings on emptiness go a long way toward resolving this. The most noted personalities who represent this lineage of thought are Nagarjuna (the second-century founder of the Madhyamaka school), Aryadeva (Nagarjuna's principal student), Chandrakirti (the sixth-century founder of the *Prāsaṅgika* school, a subdivision of the Madhyamaka), and Shantideva (the author of *A Guide to the Bodhisattva's Way of Life*).

The Buddhism of Tibet

Buddhism came to Tibet around the seventh century A.D. and soon became the dominant religion and philosophy of its people. Over the centuries since its introduction, it evolved into four major schools: *Nyingma, Kagyu, Sakya,* and *Gelug*.[62] The difference between these schools has more to do with their chronology and the lineages of their teachers than with their actual doctrinal positions. All four traditions adhere to Mahayana Buddhism; all maintain that the Madhyamaka represents the highest standpoint in Buddhist philosophical discourse. Most importantly, all four schools accept the preeminence of *Vajrayana* Buddhism as the ultimate spiritual path to enlightenment. Vajrayana, which literally means the "adamantine vehicle," could be best described as the esoteric tradition of Buddhism. Characteristics of this path include, among other things, an emphasis on non-duality as a fundamental perspective, recognition of emotions such as attachment as a means on the path to enlightenment, and the use of rich psychological symbolism as a key element of meditative absorption.

The Nyingma, literally meaning "old translation school," is the earliest Tibetan Buddhist school and traces its origin to the teachings of the Indian masters Padmasambhava and Shantarakshita who came to Tibet during the eighth century A.D. The remaining three schools are collectively called the "new translation schools." (The reference to "old" and "new" pertains to the periods of translation of the Buddhist canon into Tibetan.) The Kagyu school was founded by the eleventh-century Tibetan translator Marpa Lotsawa (1012–97), who in turn was following in the lineage of the Indian master Naropa (1016–1100). The Sakya school was founded in the eleventh century by Khon Könchok Gyalpo, who studied under the Tibetan translator Drokmi Lotsawa (992–1072). Finally, the Gelug school emerged as an independent school following Tsongkhapa's (1357–1419) radical reform of Buddhism in Tibet. Tsongkhapa drew tremendous inspiration from the reforming spirit of the *Kadam* movement begun by the great Indian missionary to Tibet Atisha (982–1054) and his chief Tibetan disciple, Dromtönpa. Because of this influence, the Gelug also became known as the New Kadam school. From the fourteenth century onward, this new, reformed school became the dominant tradition in Tibet, Mongolia, and many other Central Asian Buddhist countries. Traditionally both the Dalai Lama and the Panchen Lama, the two highest spiritual leaders of Tibet, come from this reformed school.

Tsongkhapa's Gelug school can be roughly described as a genuine synthesis. It maintains the earliest schools' emphasis on strict adherence to an ethical discipline as the foundation of a true spiritual life. Because of Tsongkhapa's profound admiration of the Kadam teachings, this new school adopts in its practical aspects of the path a category of instructions collectively known as *lo jong*, "mind training" or "thought transformation." A key characteristic of these teachings is advice on how to turn even the most adverse circumstances into conditions favorable to the enhancement of compassion and altruism. In its philosophical orientation, the Gelug embraces fully the Madhyamaka teachings on the doctrine of emptiness. In addition, there is an acknowledgment of the importance of critical analysis as an integral part of one's path to enlightenment. Yet, despite its emphasis on a rational approach, the Gelug tradition perceives the Vajrayana teachings as articulating the final vision of the attainment of perfect buddhahood. Such an integrated approach, of course, demands a deep appreciation of multiple perspectives, each appropriate to and valid within its own context and framework. It is this multilayered aspect of Tibetan Buddhism that makes it both profound and complex at the same time. So, just as we learned that there is no justification for conceiving of something called *the* Buddhist position, it is also meaningless to speak of *the* Tibetan Buddhist view. Therefore, when reading the Dalai Lama's comments on the Gospels, it is important to bear in mind the multiplicity of perspectives and the rich spiritual resources from which he is drawing his insights. A serious reading of scriptures always demands the use of sophisticated hermeneutic skills. It is only when approached in such a way that the profundity of the scripture can be fully appreciated.

Before closing, a few words on the general attitudes in Buddhism toward other religions is in order. Like any other major religion, Buddhism perceives its path to be universal in that it addresses the fundamental problems of human existence. In this sense, it does not see its message and normative doctrines as being limited to any specific historical or cultural context. Yet, right from an early stage of the evolution of the Mahayana, Buddhism has accepted the existence of other paths that may be better suited to the spiritual temperament of individuals. There is an acknowledgment of diversity at the most fundamental level of spiritual orientation. As one of the Mahayana classics puts it, "There exist diverse inclinations, diverse interests, and diverse spiritual paths." This, I think, is the basis for the Dalai Lama's often stated "supermarket of religions." According to Buddhism, all these spiritual paths are valid in themselves for they answer the fundamental yearning of millions of individuals. The validity of a spiritual teaching should not be judged on the basis of its claim to metaphysical truth. Rather the criterion must relate to its efficacy in providing spiritual salvation, or freedom. The long history of both Buddhism and Christianity testifies to this efficacy. Given this, a genuine conversation between these two profound religious traditions can lead not only to the enrichment of each other's teachings, but can also deepen the world's appreciation of the spiritual dimension of human life. The famous religious historian Paul Tillich said that from the meeting of Christianity and Buddhism would come a spiritual revolution. Perhaps he was right.

GLOSSARY OF BUDDHIST TERMS

Unless otherwise noted, all transliterations are in Sanskrit.

Anātman. No-self or no-soul. That doctrine of the Buddha that contradicts the notion of a pure, eternal, subtle self, or *ātman*. The doctrine serves to eliminate attachment to or grasping onto a self, which grasping constitutes the fundamental ignorance binding sentient beings to the suffering of conditioned existence. *See Emptiness; No-self.*

Aryadeva (Āryadeva). The principal disciple of Nagarjuna. *See Nagarjuna.*

Ātman. In Sanskrit, self or soul. *See No-self.*

Bhikṣu (Pali: bhikkhu). A fully ordained monk in the Buddhist monastic tradition. In the Tibetan monastic tradition, a fully ordained monk holds 253 vows; a novice monk, 36 vows.

Bhikṣuṇī. A fully ordained nun in the Buddhist monastic tradition. Although the ordination lineage for fully ordained nuns in the Tibetan tradition was lost several centuries ago, the lineage for full ordination for nuns still exists in Chinese Buddhism. Like novice monks, a novice nun in the Tibetan tradition holds 36 vows. A fully ordained nun holds 364 vows.

Bodhisattva. A key religious concept in Mahayana Buddhism. A bodhisattva, having developed unbiased compassion for all, is a person who is on the way to perfect buddhahood. Thus, he or she has dedicated his or her life to the well-being of others, having vowed to lead all sentient beings to complete and perfect enlightenment. *See Bodhisattva ideals; Buddhahood.*

Bodhisattva ideals. The bodhisattva ideals include the *six paramitas*, or *perfections*, for one's own personal development, and the *four means* aimed at developing others. The six perfections are (1) generosity, (2) morality, (3) patience, (4) enthusiastic effort, (5) concentration, and (6) wisdom. The four means are (1) giving what is urgently needed, (2) always using gentle speech, (3) giving ethical guidance to others, and (4) showing these principles through one's own example. A bodhisattva, after having generated the heroic intention to seek perfect enlightenment for the benefit of all, pledges to engage in these practices.

Brahman. A key metaphysical concept in some non-Buddhist philosophical schools of ancient India. Roughly speaking, brahman is understood as the absolute, the ground of being, the primal source of all existence. In this context, the phenomenal world is an illusion which exists only insofar as our perceptions of separate, individual egos (*ātman*) remain. This illusion comes to an end when one cognizes the true nature of *brahman. See No-self.*

Buddha. Literally, "awakened one." A person who has attained enlightenment, that is, liberation from all faults and the perfection of all qualities, and who is thus fully capable of benefiting others. *See Buddhahood.*

Buddha-nature. See Tathāgata-garbha.

Buddha Shakyamuni. See Buddhahood; Shakyamuni.

Buddhadāsa Bhikkhu (1906–93). Ajahn Buddhadāsa was one of the most revered and, at the same time, controversial Buddhist teachers of Thailand. His inspiring teachings and practical advice encouraged both lay and monastic Buddhists to become actively engaged in socially beneficial works. Since his death in 1993, his numerous disciples of many different nationalities continue his wide-ranging work to help humanity.

Buddhahood. The state of full enlightenment in which all physical and mental faults and stains have been purified and eliminated, and all abilities and virtues have been attained and perfected. Generally speaking, "buddha" is a generic term applicable to anyone who has attained perfect enlightenment. It is, therefore, important to understand the difference between the historical Buddha—Buddha Shakyamuni—and a buddha as someone who is fully enlightened. *See Enlightenment; Three Kāyas.*

Causality. The principle of causality figures prominently in Buddhist thought and practice. From the perspective of practice, the Buddhist path is explicitly causal, for it presumes that the relief of suffering is achieved through the elimination of its causes. The immediate cause of suffering is unwholesome *karma*, the negative imprints left on the mind when one engages in negative physical, verbal, or mental actions. Such imprints later "ripen" in experiences of unpleasant states of mind—

that is, one suffers. The more distant causes of suffering are the attitudes and mental habits that induce one to engage in negative actions; foremost of these is ignorance, the habitual misapprehension of relative and changing reality as fixed and absolute. From a more philosophical perspective, causality is the most obvious mode of interdependence, and causal interdependence is frequently used to show that, since all things are necessarily interdependent, all things are necessarily devoid of any fixed, intrinsic essence. *See Four Noble Truths; Interdependence; Karma.*

Chandrakirti (Candrakīrti). One of the main philosophers of the Prāsaṅgika subschool of the Madhyamaka.

Chenrezig. Chenrezig is the Tibetan name of Avalokiteśvara, the Bodhisattva of Compassion who embodies the great compassion of all the buddhas. Tibetans believe that Chenrezig is the patron deity of Tibet and that all the successive Dalai Lamas are human manifestations of this deity.

Compassion. See Karuṇā.

Conditioned existence. See Samsara.

Deer Park Sermon. The first sermon given by the historical Buddha, Śākyamuni. After attaining buddhahood while meditating beneath a *pipal* tree in what is now the town of Bodhgaya in north India, Śākyamuni Buddha made his way to the town of Sarnath on the outskirts of Varanasi. There he encountered the five ascetics with whom he had once practiced extremely rigorous austerities. Upon catching sight of the Buddha, these five companions resolved to ignore him, for it was clear that he had abandoned his vows of extreme asceticism. When the Buddha drew near, however, they were overwhelmed by the joy and understanding that he radiated, and they implored him to teach them what he had realized. Śākyamuni Buddha proceeded to give his first formal teaching in which he encouraged his former companions to avoid the extremes of carnality and asceticism. Pointing out that these paths would only lead to more suffering, the Buddha explained the "middle way" that avoids all such extremes. His sermon focused on the Four Noble Truths, for they summarize the Buddha's realizations and point out how one can put an end to suffering. *See Four Noble Truths.*

Dhammapada. Known in its Sanskrit version as the Dharmapada, this collection of sayings from the Buddha is certainly one of the most well-known of all Buddhist scriptures. It contains 423 verses and outlines the key ideas of the Buddhist understanding of the human condition. A lucid English translation of this text exists in the Penguin Classics series entitled *The Dhammapada* (Penguin, 1973).

Dharma (Pali: Dhamma). Derived from the etymological root meaning "to hold," Dharma denotes the teachings of the Buddha, the "truth" or the "way," and the practice of those teachings: in this context, the Dharma is that which holds us back from suffering and its causes. The Tibetan equivalent *chos* literally means "change" or "transformation" and refers to both the process of spiritual transformation and the transformed result. There are many other additional connotations of the term. For example, a classical text lists ten such meanings: perceptible phenomenon, path, nirvana, object of consciousness, merits, life, scriptures, material object, regulation, and doctrinal tradition. *See Three Jewels.*

Dharmakāya. Truth Body of a buddha. *See Three Kāyas.*

Duḥkha (Pali: dukkha). Often translated as suffering, *duḥkha* denotes the fundamental unsatisfactoriness and transitoriness of existence and is the first Noble Truth. *See Four Noble Truths.*

Dzogchen. Literally meaning "great perfection," the teachings of Dzogchen belong to the body of the Vajrayana and emphasize the realization of primordial awareness as the means to attain enlightenment.

Eightfold path. The fourth Noble Truth, True Path, has eight aspects: (1) right understanding, (2) right thought, (3) right speech, (4) right action, (5) right livelihood, (6) right effort, (7) right mindfulness, and (8) right concentration. Together, these eight aspects form the core of a genuine spiritual path.

Emptiness. A key philosophical concept of Mahayana Buddhism, the doctrine of emptiness, or *śūnyatā*, traces its origin to the *Perfection of Wisdom Sutras* of the Mahayana Buddhist canon. Emptiness refers to the absence of inherent existence in persons or things. One must always remember that emptiness is not an ontological state, for emptiness itself is also empty of inherent existence. It was Nagarjuna who first developed the doctrine in its fullest expression in his famous *Mūlamadhyamaka.* *See Anātman; Nagarjuna; No-self.*

Enlightenment. This English word is used within the Buddhist context to convey the state of complete spiritual awakening of an individual. The Tibetan equivalent *jang chup* literally means "one who has purified obscurations and is perfectly realized." A fully enlightened person is called a buddha. *See Buddhahood; Three Kāyas.*

Five aggregates. According to Buddhist philosophical thought, all physical and mental phenomena are classified under the heading of five aggregates, or *skandhas.* These five aggregates (sometimes called psychophysical constituents) are form, feeling, perception, volition, and consciousness. Together, they form the basis of an individual's sense of "self" and personal identity.

Four factors of goodness. These four are (1) spiritual liberation, (2) worldly prosperity, (3) Dharma practice, and (4) wealth. The first two are resultant in nature, whereas the second two are causal. The first two demonstrate two distinct kinds of happiness: the first, supermundane and the second, mundane. Because of their different natures, their achievement also requires different means. Thus, the practice of Dharma is that which leads to liberation, while wealth results in worldly prosperity.

Four Noble Truths. The Four Noble Truths are (1) suffering (*duḥkha*) exists; (2) the origin of suffering is attachment; (3) there is a cessation of suffering; and (4) there exists a path leading to that cessation. All Buddhist traditions agree that these four principles lie at the heart of Buddha's spiritual message. There are, within this formula of the Four Truths, two sets grouped according to cause and effect. The first is associated with conditioned cyclic existence: Truth of Origin (the cause) and Truth of Suffering (the effect). The second set is related to liberation from conditioned existence: True Path (the cause, or means, to liberation) and True Cessation (the effect, the state of liberation itself). In brief, the teaching on the Four Noble Truths outlines the Buddhist understanding of the nature of samsara and nirvana. *See Nirvana; Samsara.*

Gelug. The reformed school of Tibetan Buddhism founded by the great Tsongkhapa (1357–1419). Although he has studied the teachings of all four schools of Tibetan Buddhism, the Dalai Lama was principally educated in this school.

Geshe. The Tibetan term *geshe* literally means "spiritual friend." Currently, this title is generally conferred in Gelug tradition on those who have successfully completed many years of monastic education and have thus attained a high degree of doctrinal learning.

Guru. The Sanskrit *guru* (Tibetan: *lama*) denotes a spiritual mentor and teacher who possesses the spiritual qualifications as described in the scriptures. The minimum qualities a guru must possess are compassion toward the student, inner discipline, a degree of serenity, and more knowledge on the subject that is being taught than is possessed by the student.

Hinayana (Hīnayāna). Literally "lesser vehicle," the term *Hinayana* is primarily used by Mahayana practitioners to distinguish those who practice Buddhism in order to attain their own individual liberation from those who, with a Mahayana

motivation, engage in spiritual practice to attain enlightenment in order to liber-
ate *all* sentient beings from suffering. This division is largely regarded by current
Buddhist scholars as artificial, and is usually considered somewhat pejorative, especially by practitioners of the southern schools of Buddhism (the teaching traditions found in Sri Lanka, Thailand, Burma, Cambodia, Indonesia, and Vietnam),
to whom the term is usually applied. *See Theravadan tradition.*

Impermanence (anityatā). Along with *suffering* and *absence of self-identity,* impermanence is a fundamental characteristic of existence according to Buddhism.
Impermanence is understood to embrace both the transient nature of things that
we experience and also the momentary nature of subtle change that takes place at
a profound level. According to Buddhism, nothing endures through time, and the
process of change is dynamic and never-ending.

Interdependence (Sanskrit: pratītyasamutpāda). Often cited as the central principle
of Buddhist philosophy, the doctrine of interdependence maintains that anything
that is real necessarily exists in dependence on something else. Interdependence
is closely linked with emptiness, for all things are causally interdependent if and
only if all things are necessarily empty of any nondependent essence or intrinsic
nature. Three progressively more subtle forms of interdependence are frequently
cited: (1) causal interdependence, whereby any object (such as a tree) is necessarily
a product of causes and conditions (such as a seed, soil, sunlight, and so forth); (2)
part/whole interdependence, whereby any object (for example, a car) necessarily
depends on a collection of parts or characteristics (tires, axles, engine, and so on);
and (3) cognitive, or reciprocal, interdependence, whereby any object can be said to
exist only insofar as some consciousness identifies it as "x" in opposition to "non-x."
See Causality; Emptiness.

Jataka Tales. These tales recount the past lives of Buddha Śākyamuni. They illustrate how the Buddha dedicated himself to the bodhisattva's way of life through the
various skillful ways in which he worked for the well-being of other sentient beings
in his previous lives. In the Tibetan Buddhist canon is an anthology of these tales
composed by Āryasura, entitled the *Jātakamālā.*

Kagyu. Literally, "oral lineage." One of the four principal schools of Tibetan Buddhism, founded by Marpa Lotsawa in the eleventh century.

Kangyur. The Tibetan Buddhist canon, which contains more than 100 large volumes of discourses and texts attributed to the Buddha. *Kangyur* literally means "the
translated sacred words," and all works in the collection were almost exclusively

translated from original Sanskrit sources. The compilation was by the fourteenth-century Tibetan encyclopedist Bu-tön Rinchen Drub.

Karma. The Sanskrit term *karma* refers to an important metaphysical concept related to action and its consequences. This doctrine is common to all religious philosophies of India. The concept embraces both the acts themselves and the psychological imprints and tendencies created within the mind by such actions. In its general usage, *karma* refers to the entire process of causal action and the resultant effects. *See Causality.*

Karuṇā. Although translated as "compassion," *karuṇā* should not be mistaken for pity or for what may be called mercy. In its etymology, there is a sense of engaging in another's pain or suffering. *Karuṇā* literally means "the stopping of bliss" and refers to a state of compassionate empathy with another's pain to such an extent that it becomes impossible to experience pleasure.

Lam-rim. Literally meaning "stages of the path," *lam-rim* refers to the graded step-by-step presentation of the Buddha's teachings and practices. This presentation of the teachings was developed in order to suit the differing mental levels of spiritual practitioners on the path to enlightenment. The *lam-rim* tradition began in the eleventh century with Atisha, the great Indian missionary to Tibet, and his short text, *Lamp on the Path to Enlightenment.*

Liberation. See Nirvana.

Lo jong. See Thought transformation.

Mahayana Buddhism (Mahāyāna). Literally meaning "the great vehicle," the Mahayana is one of the two main traditions that emerged within Buddhism in ancient India, the other being Hinayana. Generally associated with the northern Buddhist traditions of Tibet, China, Japan, and Korea, a key characteristic of the Mahayana is its insistence on an altruistic and compassionate sense of universal responsibility for the welfare of all beings as a necessary prerequisite for attaining full enlightenment. *See Hinayana.*

Maitreya. Maitreya, whose name means "loving one," is the coming buddha and the embodiment of the loving-kindness of all the buddhas. There is also a Bodhisattva Maitreya as well as a historical person by the same name who is the author of several important Mahayana texts.

Mandala (maṇḍala). In general usage, the term *mandala* refers to a cosmic symbol that characteristically displays certain concentric circles and symmetries. Mandalas are also used as contemplative visual tools in many Buddhist meditations that involve the art of visualization. In this latter context, mandalas invariably represent the purified states of the meditator's own mind.

Manjushri (Mañjuśrī). Manjushri is the Bodhisattva of Knowledge and Wisdom and is the embodiment of the insight of all the buddhas. He is traditionally depicted wielding the sword of wisdom with his right arm while in the left he holds the stem of a lotus flower on which rests the *Perfection of Wisdom Sutra.*

Mental scattering. A level of mental excitement that obstructs the calm of a meditative state. Mental scattering arises when the mind is distracted by external objects. It is a form of attraction, or attachment, to objects and has the destabilizing effect of causing the loss of any concentration one may have achieved. *See Tranquil abiding of the mind.*

Mental sinking. Along with mental scattering, mental sinking is one of the principal obstacles to the practice of meditative stabilization. It is a mental factor that underlies such obstructive states as sleepiness, torpor, and lethargy. Its main manifestation is a feeling of being down and weary where you experience a low level of energy and alertness. Buddhist meditation manuals describe mental sinking as a slightly subtler form of mental scattering. *See Tranquil abiding of the mind.*

Method. In Mahayana Buddhism, *method* refers specifically to all the aspects of the path that are associated with the enhancement and development of compassion and the altruistic actions of the bodhisattva. This is contrasted with the *wisdom* aspect of the path that directly relates to the development of insight into emptiness. Of the six perfections, the first five belong to the method aspect and the last to the wisdom aspect. A genuine spiritual path, according to a Mahayana perspective, must embrace a perfect union of method and wisdom. Such a union is sometimes also called the "union of wisdom and compassion." *See Bodhisattva ideals; Two truths; Wisdom.*

Metta (maitri). If compassion is the will to share in the suffering of others, *metta,* or loving-kindness, is the genuine aspiration that wishes others to be happy. As with *karuṇā,* or compassion, *metta* is truly altruistic and other-regarding and arises from a deep feeling of empathy with others.

Milarepa (1040–1123). As Tibet's revered poet-saint, Milarepa's struggles with life, his single-pointed devotion to his teacher Marpa Lotsawa, and finally, his lifelong pursuit as a wandering meditator have been a source of great spiritual inspiration to generations of Tibetan people. His songs of spiritual experience can be read in English in Garma C. C. Chang, *The Hundred Thousand Songs of Milarepa* (Boulder: Shambhala, 1977) and in *Drinking the Mountain Stream* (Boston: Wisdom Publications, 1995).

Nagarjuna (Nāgārjuna). Nagarjuna is perhaps the second most important historical person in Mahayana Buddhism after the Buddha and can be viewed as the founder of the Mahayana. His religious and philosophical writings remain today as the highest authority on many issues of philosophical concern within Buddhist thought. His key work is the *Mūlamadhyamaka*, which is the basis for all subsequent writings on the Buddhist philosophy of emptiness. English translations of this text can be found in Frederick Streng's *Emptiness: A Study in Religious Meaning* (Nashville: Abingdon Press, 1967); Kenneth Inada's *Nagarjuna: A Translation of His Mūlamadhyamaka-karika* (Tokyo: Hokuseido Press, 1970); and Jay Garfield's *Fundamentals of the Middle Way* (Oxford: Oxford University Press, 1995).

Nirmāṇakāya. Emanation Body of a buddha. *See Three Kāyas.*

Nirvana (Nirvāṇa; Pali: Nibbāna). Literally meaning "passed beyond pain and sorrow," *nirvana* refers to a total freedom from suffering and its underlying origins. Such freedom can be attained only when all emotional and mental afflictions have ceased their process. Therefore, *nirvana* is sometimes also known *nirodha*, true cessation, or *mokṣa*, release.

No-self (anātman). The doctrine of no-self, or selflessness, sometimes also translated as "no-soul," is a key philosophical concept of Buddhism. In brief, it relates to the Buddha's insight that the state of unenlightened conditioned existence is rooted in a false belief in the existence of a permanent, enduring "self." It is an insight into the absence of such a self that opens the door to liberation from the suffering of conditioned existence. Within Buddhism, different schools have differing understandings of this key teaching of the Buddha. *See Anātman; Emptiness.*

Nyingma. The oldest school of Tibetan Buddhism, founded in the eighth century by Padmasambhava.

Pali Canon. This is the Buddhist canon of the *Tipiṭaka*, the "three baskets," and is the set of Buddha's discourses accepted by the Theravadan tradition. Most of the scriptures from the Pali Canon have been translated into English and published by the Pali Text Society.

Parinirvāṇa. The Buddha's final nirvana at the moment of his death at Kushinagar in northern India.

Prāṇa. A Sanskrit term that literally means "wind" or "breath," in Buddhist tantra *prāṇa* refers to the various types of subtle energy that animate the mind/body complex. These "winds," or psychophysical energies, thought to travel through channels in the body, are an integral part of all physical and mental functions. The most subtle form of wind is identical with the most subtle form of mind itself, and a major focus of tantric practice is the attempt to gain mastery over this most subtle wind so as to transform the mind at its most subtle level. According to tantric theory, a practitioner who has gained control over the winds at both their coarse and subtle levels can manipulate them to produce various effects, some of which can be called emanations.

Prāsaṅgika-Madhyamaka. A sub-school of the Madhyamaka that evolved on the basis of Buddhapalita's reading of Nagarjuna's works. The tenets of this school constitute the dominant philosophy of all four traditions of Tibetan Buddhism. *See Nagarjuna.*

Pure land. In Mahayana Buddhism, a purified environment created by the strength of compassion and wisdom of a buddha or bodhisattva where sentient beings may aspire to be born in order to complete the path to enlightenment in more propitious circumstances. *Pure land sects* refers to the Buddhist schools of practice (primarily found in China and Japan) that emphasize almost exclusively practices aimed at rebirth in a pure land.

Rinpoche. Literally meaning "precious one," this title is used when addressing or speaking of reincarnate lamas, lamas of high spiritual realizations, and abbots of monasteries. *See Tulku.*

Sādhu. A traditional Indian mendicant.

Sakya. One of the four principal schools of Tibetan Buddhism, named after the geographical region of Tibet where the founding teachers resided in the eleventh century.

Samādhi. Meditative stabilization. The ability to single-pointedly concentrate the mind on a designated object without distraction, a state preliminary to the actual cultivation of tranquil abiding, or *śamatha. See Tranquil abiding of the mind; Vipaśyanā.*

Sambhogakāya. Body of Perfect Resource of a buddha. *See Three Kāyas.*

Samsara (saṃsāra). The cycle of conditioned existence in which all sentient beings perpetually revolve without choice due to the force of their karma and delusions. Samsara is the state of unenlightened existence. True Cessation, the third Noble Truth, refers to the cessation of conditioned existence, or samsara, which is the state of liberation, or nirvana. *See Four Noble Truths; Nirvana.*

Sangha (Saṅgha). The term *Sangha* refers alternatively to the community of practitioners of the Buddhist path; the community of ordained monks and nuns; or one who has attained the direct realization of the wisdom of emptiness of all phenomena. *See Three Jewels.*

Selflessness. See No-self.

Shakyamuni (Śākyamuni; 563–483 B.C.). Fourth of the one thousand founding buddhas of this present world age. Born a prince of the Shakya clan in north India, he taught the sutra and tantra paths to liberation and full enlightenment, and was the founder of what came to be known as Buddhism. Shakyamuni means "Sage of the Sakya clan." *See Buddhahood; Sutra; Tantra.*

Shantideva (Śāntideva). A seventh-century Indian Buddhist sage and philosopher, Shantideva, whose name means "peaceful god," composed one of the most beloved of Mahayana texts, the *Bodhicaryāvatāra,* or *A Guide to the Bodhisattva's Way of Life.* The Dalai Lama often teaches and frequently quotes from this well-known text, which provides the practitioner with detailed instructions on the practice of the bodhisattva path of altruism. Shantideva is also well known for his clear philosophical arguments propounding the Prāsaṅgika view of emptiness. He also composed the *Compendium of Practices (Śikṣāsamuccaya).*

For an English translation of the Tibetan version of the *Bodhicaryāvatāra,* see Stephen Batchelor's *A Guide to the Bodhisattva's Way of Life* (Dharamsala, India: Library of Tibetan Works and Archives, 1979). There also exists a translation from the Sanskrit sources in the Oxford World Classic series entitled *The Bodhicaryāvatāra* (Oxford: Oxford University Press, 1996).

Śamatha. See Tranquil abiding of the mind.

Śūnyatā. See Emptiness.

Suffering (duḥkha; Pali: dukkha). In the Buddhist context, "suffering" denotes both the physical sensations of pain and, more importantly, the psychological and emotional afflictions. It also embraces the wider underlying feelings of perpetual boredom and dissatisfaction that are so characteristic of many mundane experiences. Therefore, the scriptures speak of three types or levels of suffering: (1) the suffering of suffering, referring to what we ordinarily regard as a painful experience; (2) the suffering of change, that is, all experiences that we conventionally consider to be pleasurable but which are not immutably so; and (3) the suffering of conditioned existence. The third category refers to the basic state of dissatisfaction, propensity to suffering, and susceptibility to delusion that underlies an unenlightened existence. *See Duḥkha; Four Noble Truths; Samsara.*

Sutra. The Sanskrit term *sūtra (Pali: sutta)* denotes any scripture that is attributed to the historical Buddha Shakyamuni. Consequently, it is used as a suffix to the title of works that the traditions accept as representing the true words of the Buddha, as in *The Heart of Wisdom Sutra*. In the context of a second sense of the term, *sutra* is contrasted with *tantra* and denotes the general, non-esoteric Mahayana teachings and the associated system of practices. *See Tantra.*

Tantra. Literally meaning "continuum," *tantra* refers to the set of esoteric teachings and practices of Buddhism. In this context, the path of *tantra* is contrasted with the path of *sutra*, which relates to the mainstream exoteric Mahayana path. *See Sutra; Vajrayana Buddhism.*

Tara (Tārā). One of the most important female deities in Mahayana Buddhist iconography, Tara, usually depicted in green color, represents the perfect energy and activity of all the buddhas. The legend of Tara is a source of profound inspiration to millions of women in the Mahayana Buddhist world through its portrayal of the spiritual power and potential of women. According to this legend, Tara vowed to retain her female form throughout her spiritual journey and, as there are so few female buddhas, to attain perfect enlightenment in that same form.

Tathāgata. Literally meaning "thus gone," Tathāgata is an epithet for an enlightened being in general, and Buddha Shakyamuni in particular.

Tathāgata-garbha. Literally meaning "the essence of thus gone," *tathāgata-garbha* refers to the presence of the seed of buddhahood, or buddha-nature, within all sentient beings. According to Mahayana Buddhism there exists within each of us a natural potency that makes it possible for us to eliminate all delusions and attain perfect enlightenment. *See Buddhahood; Enlightenment.*

Tengyur. In contrast to the *Kangyur*, the *Tengyur* contains all the translations of commentarial treatises written by Indian Buddhist masters. In this collection there are more than 200 volumes, which cover all subjects of Buddhist religious and philosophical studies as well as medicine and astrology.

Theravadan tradition. The form of southern Buddhism flourishing in Sri Lanka, Thailand, Burma, Cambodia, Indonesia, and Vietnam. *See Hinayana; Mahayana.*

Thought transformation. Thought transformation, translated from the Tibetan term *lo jong*, refers to a category of teachings and practices aimed exclusively at enhancing one's compassion and altruistic intention. One of the main characteristics of this teaching is the extensive practical instructions given on how to turn even the most adverse situations into conditions favorable to one's spiritual practice. *Lo jong* is associated with the *Kadam* movement, which took place in Tibet around the eleventh century A.D.

Three Jewels (triratna). The Three Jewels of refuge in Buddhism are the Buddha, Dharma (the doctrine), and Sangha (the spiritual community). Together they are considered to be objects worthy of refuge for a true seeker of spiritual liberation. Among these three, the actual refuge is the Dharma, for it is only through one's experience of the truth that liberation can take place. Buddha is the enlightened teacher who shows the path through his or her expertise and experience, while the Sangha, or spiritual community, provides the precious companionship of friends on the journey. These three are called "jewels" because they are considered to be rare and precious. *See Buddhahood; Dharma; Sangha.*

Three Kāyas. The doctrine of the three *kāyas* presents the Mahayana understanding of the nature of perfect enlightenment, or buddhahood. The Sanskrit term *kāya* translates as "body" or "embodiment." The *dharmakāya*, or "Truth Body," is the ultimate expanse that is the final reality of a buddha's enlightenment. It is the inexpressible sphere from which spontaneously arise all the noble deeds of an enlightened being, or buddha. The *sambhogakāya*, or "Body of Perfect Resource," is the actual form of the enlightened mind that remains in the perfected realms of existence. This subtle embodiment of enlightened beings can only be perceived by bodhisattvas at high levels of spiritual evolution. Therefore, in order to benefit ordinary sentient beings like ourselves, the buddhas have to assume physical embodiments that resemble our own existence. In other words, they have to emanate forms that suit our temperament. Such an emanation is called a *nirmāṇakāya*, or "Emanation Body."

It is quite obvious how a parallel could be drawn between the doctrine of the three *kāyas* and the Christian doctrine of the Trinity. The *dharmakāya* resembles the Father, the *sambhogakāya*, the Holy Spirit, and the *nirmāṇakāya*, the Son. The parallel becomes all the more striking when one examines the functions and the nature of the relationship between the three *kāyas*.

In Vajrayana Buddhism the concept of the three *kāyas* has a wider application. Each of the three *kāyas* is correlated with the purification of the respective states of death, intermediate state, and rebirth; thus the doctrine of the three *kāyas* also encompasses a fundamental perspective concerning all phenomena. *See Buddhahood; Enlightenment.*

Tranquil abiding of the mind (śamatha). A meditatively cultivated state of mind characterized by the absence of distraction by external objects and a stabilized focus on a chosen object. It possesses the qualities of "tranquility," which is the calming of distractions, and "abiding," which is the attainment of a high level of single-pointedness of the mind. Tranquil abiding is often conjoined with *vipaśyanā* in discussion of meditation in Buddhist literature. *See Samādhi; Vipaśyanā.*

Triratna. See Three Jewels.

Tulku. *Tulku* literally means "emanation body." A tulku is a reincarnate lama: that is, one who has been formally recognized as the reincarnation of his or her predecessor. *See Rinpoche.*

Two truths. The doctrine of the two truths—ultimate truth and relative, or conventional, truth—is perhaps the most important philosophical concept in Buddhism. This doctrine outlines a way of understanding the complex relationship between the phenomenal world of perpetual change and flux and the underlying reality of unchanging emptiness. *Ultimate truth* is the empty nature of all phenomena; it is the total absence of intrinsic reality and identity of all things and events. According to Mahayana Buddhism, this is the final truth, the realization of which is the key to liberation from suffering. In contrast, all that we experience in our ordinary state, such as birth and death, pain and pleasure, and so forth, takes place within the relative world. These things and events are real only as *conventional,* or *relative, truths.* *See Emptiness; Method; Wisdom.*

Vajrayana Buddhism (vajrayāna). Literally, the "diamond vehicle" or "adamantine vehicle," the Vajrayana is the esoteric aspect of Buddhism. *See Tantra.*

Vinaya Sutra. This is the authoritative scripture taught by the Buddha outlining the precepts and ethical codes of monks and nuns. The text also deals with many issues of monastic administration and procedures for conflict resolution. It is customary for the abbot of a monastery to read from this text once every fortnight when the members of the community gather for their regular confessional ceremonies.

Vipaśyanā. Literally meaning "special seeing," *vipaśyanā* refers to a profound, penetrative insight that is gained through a combination of subtle analysis and single-pointed concentration. *Vipaśyanā* and *śamatha,* or tranquil abiding of the mind, form the culmination of the union of absorptive meditation and analytic meditation. *See Samādhi; Tranquil abiding of the mind.*

Wisdom (Prajñā). The two complementary aspects of the Buddhist path are *wisdom* and *method.* These are likened to the two wings of a bird, without both of which a bird is unable to fly. Similarly, without both wisdom and method, a spiritual practitioner cannot attain the goal of enlightenment. The *wisdom* aspect of the path directly relates to the development of insight into emptiness. The Sanskrit *prajñā*—often translated as simply "wisdom," although "insight" is perhaps a more appropriate translation—is traditionally defined as "the discriminative awareness of the essence, distinctions, and particular or general characteristics of any object within one's perceptual range, at the conclusion of which all doubts are removed." This is not a passive state of knowledge nor is it store-like in nature. On the contrary, wisdom is an active cognitive process. In the Mahayana context *prajñā* mostly refers to one's deep insight into the empty nature of things and events. *See Emptiness; Method; Two truths.*

NOTES

1. The John Main Seminar is an annual event in honor of the founder of the World Community for Christian Meditation. More information about John Main, the WCCM, and the John Main Seminar can be found at the back of this book.

2. Charles Taylor is a Canadian philosopher and author of *Sources of the Self.* Jean Vanier is the founder of L'Arche, an international Christian-inspired community centered on the care of the mentally handicapped.

3. Christianity is composed of a number of communities, each of which expresses a different emphasis of interpretation of the essentials of a common faith. Roman Catholicism and the Eastern Orthodox churches represent a more sacramental, hierarchical, and mystical tradition, whereas some branches of Anglicanism and the Reformed churches stress the importance of Scripture, preaching, and social action. Catholic monastic and religious orders have flourished, for example, while Protestant churches have stressed the vocation to holiness of all the people. The long history of contradiction and competition between these traditions is today greatly modified by a new ecumenical spirit of mutual respect and sharing of viewpoints.

4. Referred to here are three of the major Catholic religious orders: The Benedictine Order, which originated in the *Rule of Saint Benedict* (c. 480–550), is characterized by local monastic autonomy, a common life in preparation for that of the hermitage, regular daily prayer in community, and a balanced contemplative-active orientation. The Franciscan Order gave institutional expression to Francis of Assisi's (1181–1226) charismatic poverty and love of nature, and his itinerant preaching and emphasis on the humanity of Christ. The Jesuit Order or Society of Jesus was established by the Spanish mystic Ignatius of Loyola (1491–1556) as a kind of spiritual army in the Catholic Church with special obedience to the Pope and an emphasis on the conversion of the most influential people in society, a priority that has more recently been modified by the "option for the poor."

5. On many occasions, such as arrivals, departures, special events, and so forth,

Tibetan people present each other with long, white silk scarves called *katags* as a sign of welcome, generosity, and respect for the recipient.

6. Eileen O'Hea, an American Sister of Saint Joseph who is a therapist and spiritual director; John Todd, a British author and John Main's publisher; Isabelle Glover, a British Sanskrit scholar and teacher; William Johnston, an Irish-born Jesuit author who has taught and studied in Japan since 1951.

7. On his first and last visit to Asia, Thomas Merton, the American Trappist monk, had a number of conversations with the Dalai Lama on which both later commented warmly. Merton's comments can be read in *The Asian Journal of Thomas Merton* and his collected *Letters*.

8. John Henry Newman (1801–90) was a convert to Roman Catholicism at the age of forty-five from the Church of England while a don at Oxford University. A prolific author (see especially *Apologia Pro Vita Mea*, 1864, and *A Grammar of Assent*, 1870), he stressed the difference between real and notional assent and analyzed the role of conscience. He was made a Cardinal in 1879. His brilliant intellect, literary grace, and deep interiority have been increasingly recognized in recent times.

9. *Spiritual Friendship*. Washington: Cistercian Publications, 1974, chapter 3, verse 62.

10. Ibid., chapter 1, verse 9.

11. Gospel of John 15: 15.

12. Thich Nhat Hanh, a Vietnamese Buddhist monk living in France as an exile since his involvement in the peace movement during the Vietnam War, is renowned for teaching the path of ordinary, daily mindfulness. His book *Living Buddha, Living Christ* stresses many of the similarities between Christian and Buddhist spiritual practice, while the Pope's book, published shortly before, tends to highlight the important differences of belief between the traditions.

13. Opus Dei is a traditionalist Roman Catholic organization often criticized by fellow Catholics for its failure to live the spirit of the Church's manifesto of openness and renewal promulgated in the Second Vatican Council (1962–65). The Reverend Ian Paisley is an outspoken leader of the extreme Protestant community in Northern Ireland.

14. Luke 11: 9–10.

15. Saint Irenaeus (c. 130–200) was the first great Catholic theologian. He was Bishop of Lyons, but he wrote in Greek. In his debate with Gnosticism he

developed his idea of "recapitulation," which sees human evolution as summarized in the human Incarnation of Jesus.

16. God is inclusive in the sense that nothing existent or nonexistent can be outside God. All is in God and God is in all. According to Saint Paul, "God is all in all." The non-duality of God means that while God cannot be identified with anything, nothing can be said to be separate from God. God is, therefore, the ground of all Being: the "I am that I am" of the initial biblical revelation to Moses.

17. *Rule of Saint Benedict*, chapter 4.

18. Here "post-imperial guilt" refers to the collective feeling of shame experienced by modern people when studying the historical abuses of power by earlier generations in their community. Such guilt needs to be modified by a recognition of the power of conditioning.

19. This phrase is used by many evangelical Christians to summarize their relationship to Christ and the need as they see it for all to embrace this relationship in order to be saved. The long history of Christian intolerance on this matter is, however, approaching its end. The Catholic Church, for example, now officially teaches that "salvation" extends to those who are not Christians. This may not come as a surprise to non-Christians, but in fact, it opens a new era of interreligious dialogue.

20. In this phrase from his Letter to the Colossians (2:9) Saint Paul suggests the totality of the Divine Reality or "Godhead" is present in the humanity of Jesus.

21. Lao Tsu (c. 570–490 B.C.) is a founder of Taoism and the author of the most translated of all Chinese works, the *Tao Te Ching*. His teaching is that the *tao*, or *way*, can best be realized by relinquishing categories and values and coming instead to a direct perception of reality.

22. The first Christian thinkers inherited the Jewish biblical belief in a single personal God who worked in history for the good of the world. They also found themselves face to face with the philosophical and mythological speculation of the Greeks, the predominant belief system of the time, with its emphasis on abstraction, in contrast to Jewish realism, and a pantheon of divinities, in contrast to the single Deity of the Judeo-Christian view.

23. Heraclitus (c. 540–475 B.C.) was a founder of Greek philosophy and metaphysics. He emphasized the transitoriness of all things, even the most apparently stable (a person cannot step into the same river twice), and in ethics he attacked superstition and stressed the importance of the individual

surrendering to the greater harmony. His only certainly attributable work is "On Nature," but there are several fascinating collections of fragments of his thought.

24. The point here is that uniqueness does not necessarily mean exclusivity. At one level of our individuality uniqueness divides us from all others, although it does not necessarily make us "better" than others. However, at a deeper level, a higher realization of truth, individuality is a state in which we are unique but indivisible from all others. Christian uniqueness can therefore be interpreted as divisive at one level but integrative at another.

25. Francis Xavier (1506–52) preached Christian faith widely and with numerical success most notably in India and Japan. Born into a rich Spanish family, he became one of the first Jesuits.

26. *Vedanta* (*Vedānta*) is the most successful of six schools of ancient Indian speculative philosophy. Its greatest exponent, Shankara (c. 788–850), advocated the way of knowledge, formulated a system of non-dualism (*advaita*), and founded a monastic order. This system asserts that only *brahman* is real and that unreality is dispelled through meditation and enlightenment. *See note 60.*

27. Matteo Ricci (1552–1610) was a Jesuit missionary in China who won the respect of his hosts by means of his culture and scientific knowledge. He dressed and thought in the style of a Chinese philosopher, but in Rome his approach was regarded as controversial and earned him official disapproval. The question of "inculturation" is still a major issue in Christian life outside Western influence.

28. The *Bhagavad Gita* ("Song of God") is one of the most influential and best loved of Indian sacred texts. It forms a part of one of the great works of Sanskrit literature, the *Mahābhārata*, and deals with the essential themes of karma, non-attachment, and *bhakti*, or devotion to God, through the medium of a dialogue between Krishna and Arjuna on the field of battle.

29. These key terms in the Christian vocabulary can easily be misunderstood by a spirituality that becomes too obsessed with a sense of sin at the expense of an understanding of the divine likeness of human beings. To see them in the following combinations can refresh their meaning considerably: poverty as non-possessiveness in spiritual as well as material terms; repentance as the embracing of the shadow side of the psyche; loss of self as the transcendence of the ego; being in Christ as the union of our consciousness with his; simplicity as the state of undivided consciousness; Spirit as the highest form of

communication; mystery as that which lies beyond mental understanding but is experienced as the strongest reality.

30. This story is recounted in the *Cūḷamālunkyasutta*, or *Shorter Discourse to Mālunkyaputta*, found in the *Majjhima Nikāya*, or *Middle Length Discourses of the Buddha* (Wisdom, 1995).

31. Luke 10:21.

32. 2 Corinthians 10:3.

33. Naturally, this does not mean that Buddhism is theistic, even "unconsciously" so. *God* is a term encompassing many meanings and the speaker and context will define its meaning on each occasion. The Buddha, however, did not describe *nirvana* as a purely subjective experience: "There is an unborn, not become, not made, uncompounded and were it not for this unborn . . . no escape could be shown for what is born, has become, is made, compounded" (*Udāna* 18). Christian and Buddhist interpretations of this statement will differ but there are many points of convergence. For a study of this, see *Mysticism: Buddhist and Christian, Encounters with Jan Van Ruusbroec, Paul Mommaers, and Jan Van Bragt*, New York: Crossroads, 1995, from which this quote is taken.

34. *The Cloud of Unknowing* is a fourteenth-century anonymous English mystical treatise written in the apophatic tradition of Christian prayer. See William Johnston's translation, (Image Books, Doubleday, 1973).

35. Sermon XCIX.

36. Nicholas of Cusa. *The Vision of God*, chapter 12.

37. "Breaking of the Word" refers to the reading of Scripture and the deepening of insight into its many levels of meaning.

38. Saint Paul says that the letter kills while the spirit gives life. His meaning is that a literal interpretation of Scripture or of religious regulations stifles the spirit. The true meaning of religious language or behavior must be interpreted by the heart, not by the literal (fundamentalist) mind.

39. The Book of Joshua in the Jewish Bible ("the Old Testament") describes the journeys of the Israelites after the death of Moses. The story of Rahab describes how she hid the Israelite spies in the city before it fell and in return saved her family from the sword (Joshua 2:1).

40. Commentary on Romans, chapter 7, verse 1.

41. See entry on faith in the Glossary of Christian Terms.

42. Ramana Maharshi (1879–1950) underwent an experience of death at the age of sixteen from which he emerged in full consciousness of the Self. He lived and taught mostly in silence from an ashram that grew up around him at the foot of the sacred mountain Arunachala in southern India. The authenticity of his witness appealed to Carl Jung, S. Radhakrishnan, Arthur Osborne, and a stream of visitors from around the world that today still visits the ashram where his *darshan* rests. In his teaching he resolutely recalled people to their true Self by means of the simple practice of "self-enquiry": who am I?

43. In Christian terms, all consciousness derives from the Being of God and participates in the divine life. According to Saint John, "God is Light and there is no darkness in God." Light is a favorite symbol in Christian imagery, both for Christ (the "Light of the World") and for those human beings who reflect or radiate the divine consciousness ("you are the light of the world").

44. The eleventh-century Benedictine monastery of Montserrat near Barcelona is a place of pilgrimage. Saint Ignatius of Loyola, founder of the Jesuits, relinquished his military career there after his conversion. Legends also locate the Castle of the Holy Grail on this same site. The Dalai Lama visited this monastery during a European teaching tour in September–October 1982.

45. In October 1986 His Holiness Pope John Paul II invited religious leaders from around the world to join in Assisi to pray for peace. All major leaders, including His Holiness the Dalai Lama, were present. It proved to be a memorable event, and similar gatherings have occurred several times since then, in Rome, in Poland, and in Asia.

46. Lourdes has been a major pilgrimage center in southern France since the apparitions there in 1858 of the Blessed Virgin Mary to the fourteen-year-old peasant girl Bernadette Soubirous. It has become a place of both physical and mental healing.

47. Translation of this prayer by John Dunne.

48. Light is an important symbol in Christian worship. A light burns continuously in the presence of the Blessed Sacrament in Catholic churches, and candles on the altar at the Eucharist symbolize the presence of Christ as the "light of the world."

49. The Sanskrit title is *Śikṣāsamuccaya*.

50. It is clear from his *Treatise on First Principles* and his theory of the soul that Origen in the third century thought that reincarnation, which he studied in

Greek and Gnostic thought as *metempsychosis*, was worthy of serious debate. Less clear, however, are his own views on it, which were raised in his commentary on the gospel text that is often cited as proving the prevalence of such beliefs at the time of Jesus (Matthew 11:14).

51. The term *self-grasping* here refers to the innate psychological propensity to "grasp" or hold onto an illusory self, or ego. This propensity is the fundamental ignorance taught by the Buddha as the primary source of beings' continual suffering in conditioned existence.

52. As the unitary source of all diversity and duality in the world, God is not restrictable to male or female gender while at the same time remaining in some real sense personal. However, the patriarchal roots of Christianity have led to the attribution of maleness to God. This was reinforced by the human maleness of Jesus and his being seen as the "Son" of the "Father." With two of the persons of the Trinity imagined as male, the third, the Holy Spirit, has traditionally been sensed as the feminine side of God. Today, however, feminist theologians are emphasizing the possibility of a feminine perception of the Godhead as well as the wide range of imagery in the biblical tradition available for describing God. See, for example, *She Who Is*, by Elizabeth Johnson.

53. "The Eight Verses of Thought Transformation" by Geshe Langri Thangpa. This short text belongs to the teachings on *lo jong*, or thought transformation, and was composed during the period of Buddhist history when the Kadam school was flourishing in Tibet. The translation is based on a rendering by Lama Thubten Zopa Rinpoche.

54. The most famous biblical image of the rainbow occurs in the story of the Flood (Genesis 6:5–9) that God brought upon the earth to destroy all things because of human wickedness. Only Noah and representatives of all species were saved in the Ark. Parallel Flood stories occur in Mesopotamian mythology. The rainbow after the waters subsided was the sign of a covenant between God and humanity that God would not punish the world in this way again. Clouds are biblical symbols of the present mystery of God, as, for example, the cloud that settled on Mount Horeb while Moses was in conversation with God, or the cloud that led the Israelites through the desert.

55. For more about this famous lake and the role it played in finding the young boy who would become His Holiness the Dalai Lama, see *Freedom in Exile: The Autobiography of the Dalai Lama* (HarperCollins, 1990), p. 11, and p. 141 of Vicki Mackenzie's *Reincarnation: The Boy Lama* (Wisdom Publications, 1996).

56. Saint Paul says that "the mystery is this: Christ within you." The interiority of the personal presence of Christ is central to Christian faith, but it is complementary rather than contradictory to the belief in the cosmic proportion of Christ's presence.

57. Translated by Jeffrey Hopkins and Lati Rimpoche in *The Buddhism of Tibet* (George Allen & Unwin, 1975).

58. Our understanding of goodness need not be restricted to moral terms. For example, we speak of a "good" pair of shoes meaning shoes that are well made and in sound condition. The Hebrew concept of goodness contains both this and the moral sense of being in harmony with the Spirit of God, which is unfailingly benevolent and healing. Thus Jesus tells us to be "perfect as your Heavenly Father is perfect." Perfection here is the perfection of love, not of mere law-keeping.

59. *Advaitic* literally means *not-two* and refers to the Hindu doctrine of nonduality. God and the world, for example, are not one, but nor are they two. *See note 26.*

60. For an English translation of the Tibetan version of this text, see Stephen Batchelor's *A Guide to the Bodhisattva's Way of Life* (Library of Tibetan Works and Archives, Dharamsala, 1979). There also exists a translation from the Sanskrit sources in the Oxford World's Classic series entitled *The Bodhicaryāvatāra* (Oxford University Press, 1996).

61. A brief historical introduction to all these four schools of Tibetan Buddhism from the heads of these traditions can be found in Graham Coleman (ed.), *A Handbook of Tibetan Culture* (Rider, 1993).

INDEX

BIOGRAPHIES

Tenzin Gyatso, the Fourteenth Dalai Lama

HIS HOLINESS THE DALAI LAMA, TENZIN GYATSO, , was born on 6 July 1935 in the province of Amdo in northeastern Tibet. His family was were poor peasants, and of his fifteen brothers and sisters only six would survive: two girls and four boys. When he was two years old, he was recognized as the fourteenth in the line of Dalai Lamas, the previous Dalai Lama having died in 1933. The title Dalai Lama means "ocean of wisdom," and holders of that title are considered to be the manifestations of the Bodhisattva of Compassion, Chenrezig. With his family, the young Dalai Lama moved to Lhasa, where he underwent extensive spiritual and religious formation. He was officially enthroned on 22 February 1940. In 1959 the Fourteenth Dalai Lama took his final exam in Lhasa, during the annual Prayer Festival of *Mönlam*, and passed with honors, being awarded the highest level geshe degree, roughly equivalent to a doctorate degree in Buddhist philosophy.

Tenzin Gyatso was the first Dalai Lama to come into full contact with modern technology, and he retains a keen interest in science. One of his hobbies is fixing radios.

Before the 1950s, Tibet was governed as a religious state, and the Dalai Lama exercised both spiritual and secular power there. But on 7 October 1950 the Chinese army invaded Tibet's sovereign borders, and the imminent danger to his own life forced the Dalai Lama to flee Tibet and take refuge in India where the Indian government accorded him the right to settle in Dharamsala, Himachal Pradesh. Many thousands of Tibetans have followed him into exile. In 2012, he relinquished political authority in his exile government and turned it over to democratically elected representatives.

The Dalai Lama has consistently declared that he will pursue a policy of nonviolence. Any solution based on the use of force, he believes, can by its nature only be temporary. "Outer disarmament comes from inner disarmament. The only guarantee of peace lies within ourselves." His uncompromising commitment to peace was accorded global recognition when in 1989 he was awarded the Nobel Prize for Peace. In 2006, he received the United States Congressional Gold Medal.

The Dalai Lama talks of human nature in a simple and moving way. His mastery of the full depth and intricacy of Buddhist thought has been so fully absorbed that he not only teaches but is felt to embody the Dharma. Buddhism, for him, is neither a dogma nor a religion but a way to live in peace, joy, and wisdom. He emphasizes universal responsibility and the interdependence of all individuals and nations in the realization of the essential goodness of human nature. For many years the Dalai Lama has traveled extensively and tirelessly as a teacher of peace and a dispenser of wisdom and joy.

At the 1994 John Main Seminar, the Dalai Lama commented for the first time on the Christian Gospels and entered into a dialogue on their meaning with Christians. This is in line with his long advocacy and practice of interfaith dialogue, a vision he shared and practiced many times during meetings with Pope John Paul II. He sees that the peaceful respect and reverence between religions that this world era demands must emerge from a sharing not only of thought but, even more profoundly, of contemplative experience. Thus, three times each day, the Dalai Lama meditated in silence with the participants of the Seminar.

Father Laurence Freeman, OSB

LAURENCE FREEMAN is a Benedictine monk and the director of the World Community for Christian Meditation. Before entering monastic life he studied English at Oxford University and had experience with the United Nations, in banking and journalism. He travels widely as an international speaker and retreat leader. He is the author of many articles and books including *The Selfless Self, Jesus: The Teacher Within*, and *First Sight: The Experience of Faith*. Since the Good Heart Seminar Fr Laurence has conducted dialogues and peace initiatives such as the historic "Way of Peace" with the Dalai Lama and is active in inter-religious dialogue with leaders of other faiths. He is the director of *Meditatio*, the outreach of the community to the wider world and the institutions of medicine, business, and education.

Robert Kiely

ROBERT KIELY is the Donald P. and Katherine B. Loker Emeritus Professor of English and American Literature and was master of Adams House at Harvard University 1973–1999. He has taught courses in nineteenth- and twentieth-century fiction, the English Bible, the literature of Christian reflection, and the pre-novel. He is now teaching on beauty and Christianity and the rhetoric of belief. His research focuses on narrative and narrative theory. His books include *Robert Louis Stevenson and the Fiction of Adventure* (1964), *The Romantic Novel in England* (1972), *Beyond Egotism: The Fiction of James Joyce, Virginia Woolf, and D. H. Lawrence* (1980), and *Reverse Tradition: Postmodern Fictions and the Nineteenth Century Novel* (1993). Robert Kiely is a Benedictine Oblate of the World Community for Christian Meditation.

Geshe Thupten Jinpa

GESHE THUPTEN JINPA has been the Dalai Lama's principal translator since 1985. During that time he has also earned advanced degrees with high honors at Ganden Monastic University, India, and at Cambridge University, England. He has translated and edited many books by the Dalai Lama, including *The World of Tibetan Buddhism*, *Essence of the Heart Sutra*, *The Middle Way*, and *Practicing Wisdom*. He is currently the president and the editor-in-chief of the Institute of Tibetan Classics, a nonprofit educational organization dedicated to translating key Tibetan classics into contemporary languages.

The Participants

Maureen Allan was born in 1923. She served in the Women's Royal Naval Service in Colombo, Mombasa, and in London during World War II; was the Flag Lieutenant to the Head of British Admiralty Delegation; and was Combined Chief of Staff in Washington, DC. She was greatly involved in volunteer work with her husband's, Lord Allan of Kilmahew's, London Parliamentary constituency. Since 1955 she has been farming in Froyle, Hampshire, where she is an active member of the local Anglican Church. She has practiced meditation and studied Advaita, or the philosophy of nondualism, as a member of the Study Society for over thirty years.

Ajahn Amaro (Jeremy Horner) was born in Kent, England, in 1956. He studied psychology and physiology at Bedford College, University of London. Upon completing his degree, he visited northeast Thailand, where he stayed at a Thai monastery. He became an *anagarika* (lay renunciant), and then a *samanera* (novice monk) four months later, in 1978. The following year he received *upasampada* (full ordination) from Ajahn Chah. Venerable Amaro remained in Thailand for two years. When he returned to England, he joined Ajahn Sumedho at the newly established Chithurst Monastery.

In 1983 Ajahn Sumedho asked him to take up residence at Harnham Vihara. Venerable Amaro requested, and was given permission, to make his way there on foot. In 1984 he wrote a book about the 830-mile walk entitled *Tudong: The Long Road North*.

Isabelle Glover teaches Sanskrit and Pali at two centers in London, as well as through a Distance Learning Course that she pioneered. She has studied Vedanta and its relevance for Christians for forty years. Isabelle Glover has led retreats on the themes of "Indian scriptures as spiritual reading for Christians" and "gentle Sanskrit for Yoga teachers." She meditates and is a Benedictine Oblate. She loves music and gardening.

Peter Ng is founder partner of Avanda Investment Management and was previously Chief Investment Officer at Government of Singapore Investment Corporation. He is the National Coordinator for WCCM in Singapore.

Eileen O'Hea (1936–2005) was a sister of St Joseph of Brentwood, New York, a psychotherapist, and a spiritual director. She served as a member of the Guiding Board of WCCM and was an inspirational force in the setting up of the "School of Meditation." She traveled widely giving retreats and workshops and led the 1990 John Main Seminar. Her works include *In Wisdom's Kitchen* and *Silent Wisdom, Hidden Light*. Her collected poems were published as *Manifesting in Form*.

JOHN MAIN

JOHN MAIN was born in London in 1926 into an Irish family. He studied law, learned Chinese, and then served in the British Foreign Service in Malaya. There he was introduced to meditation by an Indian monk. At this time silent, nonconceptual prayer was rare and unfamiliar for most Christians. The long-standing Christian contemplative tradition had been forgotten and had been replaced largely with "mental prayer" and ritual. After his service in the East, John Main returned to Europe where he continued his meditation practice and became a Professor of International Law at Trinity College, Dublin.

John Main became a Benedictine monk in 1958 in London and was advised to stop meditating as the practice was not deemed part of the Christian tradition of prayer. But in 1969 he rediscovered a Christian tradition of meditation, or "pure prayer" as it was called. This early form of meditation was taught in the fourth century by John Cassian, who transmitted the teachings of the Desert Fathers, the first Christian monks, to Saint Benedict and the Western church.

Having returned to his practice of meditation, John Main then dedicated the rest of his life to teaching this lost tradition of Christian prayer to laypeople. He believed it was important for the world to restore a spiritual practice of depth to people's ordinary lives. He recommended two periods of meditation, each morning and evening, which could also be integrated with other forms of prayer.

In 1980 Father John welcomed His Holiness the Dalai Lama to an Interfaith event at the Cathedral in Montreal. Father John had been invited here by the Archbishop of Montreal to establish in the heart of the city a Benedictine community that would be dedicated to the practice and teaching of Christian meditation. When His Holiness visited the Community, he had a private meeting with Father John. And during this meeting they shared their view on the importance of cooperation between spiritual traditions in order to bring wisdom and peace to the modern world.

John Main died in 1982. His work is continued today by a growing worldwide network of Christian Meditation groups. The World Community for Christian Meditation now has an International Center in London and organizes the John Main Seminar each year.

The John Main Seminar—1984 to 2015

2015　David Tracey: "Spirituality and Religion in a Secular Age"

2014　Daniel Madigan, S.J.: "Muslims and Christians: Listeners for the World"

2013　Joseph Wong, OSB Cam: "Desert Wisdom and Oriental Spirituality: Inner Silence"

2012　Leonardo Boff, Friar Betto: "Spirituality and Environment"

2011　Timothy Radcliffe, OP: "Alive in Christ"

2010　James Alison: "The Shape of God's Affection"

2009　Robert Kennedy, SJ: "When God Disappears"

2008　Cardinal Walter Kasper: "Unity: Local and Global"

2007　a panel of speakers: "Still Present: Life and Legacy of John Main"

2006　Margaret Rizza: "The Fire of Silence Through Music and Mystics"

2005　Richard Rohr, OFM: "A Lever and a Place to Stand"

2004　Joan Chittister, OSB: "Heart of Flesh: Feminist Spirituality for All"

2003　speakers panel on Bede Griffiths, OSB

2002　Bishop Kallistos Ware: "The Kingdom of the Heart"

2001　Archbishop Rowan Williams: "Spirit in the Desert"

2000　The Dalai Lama and previous JMS Presenters: "The Way of Peace"

1999　Huston Smith: "Return to the Light"

1998　Thomas Keating: "Heart of the World"

1997　Mary McAleese: "Reconciled Being"

1996　Raimon Panikkar: "The Silence of Life"

1995　Laurence Freeman: "On Jesus"

1994　The Dalai Lama: "The Good Heart"

1993　William Johnston: "The New Christian Mysticism"

1992　Jean Vanier: "From Brokenness to Wholeness"

1991　Bede Griffiths: "Christian Meditation: The Evolving Tradition"

1990　Eileen O'Hea: "Spirit and Psyche"

1989　Balfour Mount: "On Wholeness"

1988　Charles Taylor: "Christian Identity and Modernity"

1987　Derek Smith: "On Reading"

1986　John Todd: "The New Church"

1985　Robert Kiely: "The Search for God in Modern Literature"

1984　Isabelle Glover: "Indian Scriptures as Christian Reading"

THE WORLD COMMUNITY FOR
CHRISTIAN MEDITATION

JOHN MAIN founded the first Christian Meditation Centre in London in 1975. The World Community for Christian Meditation (WCCM) took form in 1991 after the seed planted then had begun to grow into a far-flung contemplative family. It now continues John Main's vision of restoring the contemplation dimension to the common life of the Church and to engage in dialogue in the common ground shared with the secular world and other religions.

The present director of the Community is Laurence Freeman, a student of John Main and a Benedictine monk of the Olivetan Congregation. The International Centre of the World Community is based in London with centers in many other parts of the world. The Community is a "monastery without walls," with both developed national organizations and emerging communities in over a hundred countries. A major building block of all this is the growing number of small, weekly meditation groups that meet in homes, parishes, offices, hospitals, prisons, and colleges. They form an ecumenical Christian community of diverse gifts and traditions.

Annually the John Main Seminar and The Way of Peace events bring meditators together in dialogue with other traditions and global movements. The Community also sponsors retreats, schools for the training of teachers of meditation, seminars, lectures, and other programs. It contributes to interfaith dialogue particularly, in recent years, with Buddhists and Muslims. A quarterly spiritual letter with news of the Community is mailed and also available online. Weekly readings are available by email and a growing number of online resources are being developed to help the spiritual journey with the help of the latest technology. This enables new initiatives such as teaching of meditation to children, networking young adult spirituality, and the contemplative dimension of the life of priests. Medio Media is the publishing arm of the Community, producing a wide range of books and audio-visual titles to support the practice of meditation.

Meditatio is the outreach program of the World Community initiated to mark its twentieth anniversary. Coordinated from the Meditatio Centre in London, a program of seminars brings a spiritual approach to key social issues of our time such as education, mental health, peace and justice, business, and care for those in recovery and the dying. Meditatio is developing the use of technology in the work of spiritual renewal. It will also help with the formation of a younger generation of meditators who will serve later as leaders of the community.

MEDIO MEDIA

Medio Media is the publishing arm of the World Community for Christian Meditation. It is committed to the dissemination of the teaching of meditation in the Christian tradition and in particular to the work of John Main. It is also committed to furthering the growing dialogue among meditators and seekers from all traditions based on the deeper experience of silence shared among all religions.

mediomedia.com

France: meditationchretienne.org
Germany: wccm.de
Hong Kong: wccm.hk
Indonesia: meditasikristiani.com
Ireland: christianmeditation.ie
Italy: meditazionecristiana.org
Latvia: jesus.lv
Malaysia: wccmmalaysia.org
Mexico: meditacioncristiana.net
Netherlands: wccm.nl
New Zealand: christianmeditationnz.org.nz
Norway: wccm.no
Poland: wccm.pl
Portugal: meditacaocrista.com
Singapore: wccmsingapore.org
South Africa: wccm.org.za
Spain: wccm.es
Spain Catalonia: meditaciocristiana.cat
Ukraine: wccm.org.ua
United Kingdom: christianmeditation.org.uk
United States: wccm-usa.org
Venezuela: meditadores.blogspot.com

Mind in Comfort and Ease
The Vision of Enlightenment in the Great Perfection
Foreword by Sogyal Rinpoche

MindScience
An East–West Dialogue
With Herbert Benson, Robert Thurman, Howard Gardner,
and Daniel Goleman

Opening the Eye of New Awareness
Translated and introduced by Donald S. Lopez, Jr.

Practicing Wisdom
The Perfection of Shantideva's Bodhisattva Way
With Thupten Jinpa

Sleeping, Dreaming, and Dying
An Exploration of Consciousness
Edited and narrated by Francisco Varela

The Wheel of Life
Buddhist Perspectives on Cause and Effect
Translated by Jeffrey Hopkins
Foreword by Richard Gere

The World of Tibetan Buddhism
An Overview of Its Philosophy and Practice
Translated, edited, and annotated by Thupten Jinpa
Foreword by Richard Gere

About Wisdom Publications

Wisdom Publications is the leading publisher of classic and contemporary Buddhist books and practical works on mindfulness. To learn more about us or to explore our other books, please visit our website at wisdomexperience .org or contact us at the address below.

Wisdom Publications
199 Elm Street
Somerville, MA 02144 USA

We are a 501(c)(3) organization, and donations in support of our mission are tax deductible.

Wisdom Publications is affiliated with the Foundation for the Preservation of the Mahayana Tradition (FPMT).